Making Miniature Country Houses

Sharon Pierce & Herb Surman

Sterling Publishing Co., Inc.   New York

DEDICATION

This book is lovingly dedicated
to the memory of Herb Surman,
our husband, father, "papa,"
and friend.

THANK YOU

To Gloria, Herb's wife, who took over building
the projects where Herb left off, and to whom
we can offer thanks for all the finishing touches
and the painting of each "little house."

To Randy, who willingly gave of his time to key
this manuscript into the word processor.

S.P.

Love and deep appreciation to Sharon Pierce,
whose dedication has brought the publication
of this book to fruition.

G.S.

Edited by Rodman Neumann

Library of Congress Cataloging-in-Publication Data

Pierce, Sharon.
    Making miniature country houses / by Sharon Pierce &
Herb Surman.
        p.   cm.
    ISBN 0-8069-6984-9
    1. Miniature craft.   2. Woodwork.   3. Architectural
models.
    I. Surman, Herb.   II. Title.
    TT178.P54   1990
    728'.37'0228—dc20   89-48857
                                                         CIP

Copyright © 1990 by Sharon Pierce and Herb Surman
Published by Sterling Publishing Co., Inc.
387 Park Avenue South, New York, N.Y. 10016
Distributed in Canada by Sterling Publishing
% Canadian Manda Group, P.O. Box 920, Station U
Toronto, Ontario, Canada M8Z 5P9
Distributed in Great Britain and Europe by Cassel PLC
Artillery House, Artillery Row, London SWIP IRT, England
Distributed in Australia by Capricorn Ltd.
P.O. Box 665, Lane Cove, NSW 2066
Manufactured in the United States of America
All rights reserved
Library of Congress Catalog Card No.: 89-48857
Sterling ISBN 0-8069-6984-9   Paper

CONTENTS

Color section follows page 64.

❖ Preface ❖

This book is filled with plans for making delightful little houses, churches, and an outstanding 1900s barn. I am happy to share with you the designs of a very special and talented man, Herb Surman.

Unfortunately for all of us, Herb passed away before he could complete all of the houses we had originally planned, which makes this book an even greater treasure for the many wonderful miniature buildings it does contain.

The houses in this book make outstanding display pieces that will give visual emphasis to any area of the home or office. And, if you are so inclined, they can be distinctive gifts that will likely become cherished heirlooms.

An option that can be exercised with virtually any of the projects is to leave the back open. The house with no back wall could then be used as a working dollhouse to furnish and add wonderful things, such as fireplaces with mantels, stairways, attics, etc.

These houses can be put to further use in their original calling as toy houses for play. A modern adaptation could be for use with model railroads or motorized miniature car tracks.

These miniature houses make a dramatic effect for any holiday, and especially at Christmastime with little lights placed inside and the houses set amid greenery and berries. They can also be incorporated into a table centerpiece.

Another idea is to make your miniature house into a birdhouse! Simply trim the windows and doors without cutting them out, only cutting an entrance hole for the birds and maybe adding a perch. Then mount the base on a support pole.

You have many options available when you are constructing any of the projects in this book. And, although precise step-by-step instructions are provided, you will easily be able to add or delete items such as trim, porches, shutters, etc. to your own satisfaction, making each construction into your own design. Your choice of color alone can change any project dramatically.

Before you begin any of these projects, I urge that you take time to read over the chapters on General Instructions and on Materials and Equipment. These pages include basic information, hints, and tips that are applicable for every project as well as general principles that are not always stated for individual projects.

Although I sincerely wish that Herb had lived to share more of his talents with us, I know you will thoroughly delight in the making of these wonderful "little houses that Herb built"!

—Sharon Pierce

History of Early Buildings and ❖ Houses ❖

In the earliest of times, man lived in caves and trees, and anywhere he could find shelter. As man learned to make simple tools, he also learned to form small blocks from clay that could be dried in the sun.

Around 3100 B.C. the Egyptians were making flat-topped homes of sun-baked mudbrick. About 2600 years later the Assyrians among others started firing and glazing the bricks, making a harder, stronger brick.

All over the world, different types of houses were built reflecting the climate as well as the natural materials available and the dangers that were imminent. These structures were fashioned from grasses, wood, mud, clay bricks, and stone.

As time passed, man improved his shelter by incorporating fireplaces, windows that opened, elaborate stairways, porches, and eventually indoor plumbing.

Early European colonists to reach North America built log cabins of timber. After the settlements were started, however, many of the colonists built homes resembling the ones that they remembered from England or Holland. To make a warmer house, because of the more rigorous winters than they had experienced in England, the New Englanders built a great central chimney and plank floors, and they devised a blanket of overlapping clapboards, or sometimes shingles, to keep out the cold winds.

In the South, high ceilings helped keep rooms cooler in summer, and many porches were built to help shade the interior of the house.

Styles of houses and buildings have varied widely. Many designs can be traced to particular geographic regions and periods of time.

Colonial-style houses date back to the American colonial period of the 1600s and 1700s. Georgian and Victorian houses developed from styles that originated in Great Britain during the 1700s and 1800s.

The ranch house, which became one of the most popular styles in the United States during the mid-1900s, developed from early homes in the West and Southwest. The ranch-style houses are one level structures often with extensive porches.

Over the centuries, many of these styles have been built as miniature houses by a parent, an itinerant craftsman or, perhaps, the local cabinetmaker—primarily to serve the purposes of play, as toy buildings.

Little buildings are also constructed by architects to be used as models for structures that may eventually be built.

Whatever the style or styles of house you choose to build from this book, you can be sure that you are helping to preserve a little piece of history.

❖ Designing a Miniature House ❖

You don't have to figure out everything at once to begin designing the little house you want to build. But you may already have a general idea in mind. Certainly you will want to consider what styles appeal to you.

As you work through the choices that need to be made, you will find that the design takes shape and becomes clearer with each option you consider.

Once you have decided on the style of house you would like to make, the next thing is to determine the size. Should it be six inches tall, ten inches, twelve inches? Considering where the house might be displayed can help you decide the appropriate scale.

If you intend to make the house as a gift, think carefully about whether the person you will be presenting it to has ample space for the size you have in mind—better too small than too large.

Next you will want to decide how simple or complex the design of your house will be. Of course, if you are designing your first little house, a simple design would be the wisest choice to start with. Even if you have chosen a Victorian style, you can still make the design a simple one.

Make several different sketches to help you decide on porches, dormers, chimneys, shutters, etc. (You can look at general magazines, architectural or home-design magazines, and books for ideas.) Sketch your design with and without siding. You certainly don't need professional-looking sketches, just basic freehand sketches will be fine. Also, you will probably want to sketch your house design with a few different roof angles.

While you are deciding on the main features, be sure to consider the number of windows and placement of the doors and windows.

Now you are ready to work out the exact dimensions of each wall, window, and door. You can also decide on the measurements of any chimneys, dormers, and the like at this time, or you may prefer to wait until the house is "under construction."

When choosing a color scheme, perhaps the very first consideration is whether you would like the house to look new or old, as achieving this look is dependent on the manner in which you paint it. For an old look choose muted color and possibly incorporate some "crackling" (page 11).

When selecting the color or multiple colors, first prepare a basic sketch. Then, using colored pencils, try a couple of different color combinations until you reach the most pleasing one.

Basically, remember that a series of choices needs to be made before you start construction. The following summary can serve as a reminder as you prepare your design and get ready to build.

Style and Size

Roof Style—Roof Angles

High peak
Flat
Slant

Surfaces

Stucco (paint mixed with sand)
Brick (paint to give effect)
Siding
  painted
  stained
Painted
Painted and aged (old crackled look)

Roofing Material

Tin
Wood
Shingles
Slate (painted wood roof or shingles)

Color

Single color
Multiple colors
  color combination

❖ General Instructions ❖

The first step in making any project is to gather the needed materials and to make sure that you have the proper equipment. Also, it is always a good idea to read through the entire directions before you start building the project. These general instructions present steps in construction shared by most, if not all, of the projects.

Once you are ready to begin construction, the next step is to transfer the measurements of the main pieces of the building onto a board of the correct thickness. It is important to use the same *actual measured thickness* as in the materials list, otherwise most of the other dimensions will have to be altered.

If you have access to a carpenter's square, or framing square, you will find that it is an excellent time-saver when you are drawing walls that must be square. When possible, to ensure the greatest strength for each piece and ultimately for your structure, draw patterns onto the wood so that the longer dimension of the pattern aligns with the lengthwise grain of the wood.

Once you've done the layout on the wood, you're ready to start by cutting out the larger pieces, such as the house walls and subroof. Then cut out window and door openings in those pieces. Now is the time to sand each piece. Also remember to sand all the other pieces as soon as they are cut (Illus. 1).

For most houses the rectangular-shaped walls, usually the front and back, butt against the peaked walls (otherwise you will have to sand or plane the short wall to match the roof angle of the peaked wall). Spread a thin bead of glue on the inside face along the margins, or "side" edges, of the front and back sections. Glue these to the side sections, checking to make sure all of the corners are square. With a tack hammer, carefully tap in several brads along each corner.

A delightful option that you can keep in mind as you begin any project is to leave the back wall off for an "open" house. The open

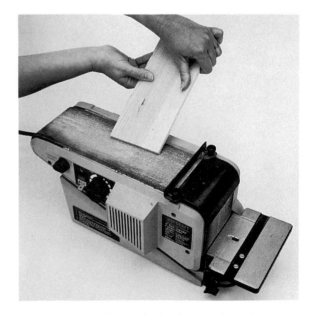

Illus. 1. Sand each piece, by hand or machine, after it is cut to size.

house can be furnished, and a second floor with stairs can be added.

To add the floor, or base, set the house construction on a piece of ¼″ wood, then pencil around the inside perimeter. Cut out the piece carefully just along the outside of the pencil line. Glue and then nail the floor to the house.

Cut a roof ridge to support the roof. This can be cut with the grain from a ¾″ × ¾″ strip to match the inside dimension between roof peaks. Glue and then nail the ridge between both peaks.

Make the window, door, and corner trim from ½″ wood. You will need strips that are cut to ⅛″ thickness. You can cut these with a radial-arm or table saw using a rip fence. You can also use a band saw with a guide, or for any of these saws you can make a simple guide by clamping a block of wood ⅛″ from the blade (Illus. 2). Using the band saw will waste less wood since the blade is thinner.

After the strips are cut, then cut them to fit, first the horizontal window and door trim pieces. Glue these into place flat against the cutout edge, making the inward edge of the trim flush with the inside wall of the house.

Then cut the vertical pieces, attaching them in the same manner (Illus. 3).

Corner trim should be cut to match the height of the rectangular-shaped wall.

Siding can be considered optional whether called for or not. If it is not added when called

Illus. 3. Gluing window trim in place.

Illus. 2. Cutting siding strips with the radial-arm saw.

for, however, cut the window, door, and corner trim from ⅜″-wide wood so it will not protrude more than a slight amount.

To make siding, cut long strips ⅛″ × ¾″ from ¾″ wood. Then cut the pieces to fit between the corner trim pieces for each wall. Work on one wall at a time, and start by gluing a piece flush with the bottom of the house. Attach each successive strip above the previous one with an even overlap of ⅛″. Notch the strip to fit around window and door trim as needed (Illus. 4).

Illus. 4. Attaching siding.

You can choose to make the roof from various materials, such as tin, copper, ⅛″ pine, pine or cedar shingles, using ⅛″ luan plywood for a subroof.

If you choose to use tin or copper, simply use a pair of metal cutters to cut a piece of the metal approximately 1½″ wider and 1½″ longer than the total roof measurement. Then bend the metal in half, usually with the crease parallel to the long dimension.

Predrill holes, using a drill press, if available, where the roof will be nailed to the house. Tack in place using brads.

For a pine roof, cut from ⅛″ pine two roof pieces that are slightly larger than the roof area obtained by measuring outside walls. Apply glue and nail the pieces in place. Then cut a ⅛″ × ⅛″ square strip to fit in the space between the pieces along the roofline, and glue this piece into place.

To make a shingled roof, first cut two pieces of ⅛″ luan plywood to match the measurement of the roof area on each side (outside dimensions). Glue and nail these subroof sections in place. Then, just as for the siding, cut ⅛″ × ¾″ strips from ¾″ wood. From these, cut 1″ pieces for shingles. You can also make authentic-looking shingles by cutting ¾″ × 1″ pieces from cedar shakes.

Start at the bottom of the roofline, and work one row at a time. The first row of shingles is glued along the bottom of the subroof, but with each shingle extending over the edge by about ⅛″. As you add each successive row of shingles, overlap the previous row again by about ⅛″, staggering each row.

To make a flatter, stronger roof, use a strip of wood to clamp each new row as soon as it has been glued in place (Illus. 5). Give ample time for the row to dry, and then go on to start the next row.

Some of the house projects have extra touches, such as chimneys or porches, that can also be included as options for any of the

Illus. 5. Clamping shingles.

other houses. You will find directions for these options throughout the various projects. Use these options to encourage your creativity as you make each project design your own.

The choice of color for the structure is really a simple matter of individual preference, with perhaps some traditional or historical considerations. The colors given for each project or shown in the color photographs are only suggestions to help stimulate your own creative choices.

Inside walls should be painted or stained prior to the addition of the subroof. And often pieces such as chimneys or trim should be painted before they are actually glued in place.

The paints described throughout the book are acrylic folk art paints. These are available in either cans or plastic bottles. This type of paint is more fluid than tube paints and does not need to be watered down. For each particular project the colors suggested are muted colors.

If you would like an aged, peeling-paint sort of look for the clapboard siding, or even just for the shutters and trim or porch railings, you can achieve a very satisfying old "crackled" look using hide glue (Illus. 6). This is available in craft and hardware stores.

First brush the desired area with a thin layer of hide glue. Let this dry for about four hours.

Illus. 6. Wood on the left has been painted, wood on the right has been "crackled."

Then mix the acrylic paint with gesso (a form of base paint in use since at least the sixteenth century) in the proportion of two tablespoons gesso to one tablespoon of paint.

If you use more gesso proportionally, then the cracks will be smaller. Try some different test proportions to get the right amount of crackling for the look you want.

❖ Materials and Equipment ❖

This is a summary of the various materials and tools you will need to make the little houses and buildings in this book. The specific materials, with dimensions and quantities, and the necessary tools, with any accessories, are both listed at the start of each particular project.

MATERIALS

Wood

The basic construction for most of the miniature structures requires ¼″ wood. This, or any other, thickness of wood can be obtained by arranging to purchase ¾″ stock wood, then having it planed to the desired thickness by the lumber yard.

A very light and thin wood material, ⅛″ luan plywood, is used in the construction of subroofs and, in particular, the Barn roof.

The measurements given for the projects refer to the *actual measured thickness* of the wood; you should be aware that if you ask for a ¾″ board you will most likely be given something with an actual thickness of about ⅝″, and similarly a ½″ board will be more like ⅜″, and a 1″ board will be closer to ¾″. So be sure always to specify *actual measured thickness* or to know what standard lumber term it is that you will give you the thickness you actually need.

In only a few instances a board is identified by words, not numerals, as a two-by-four, a four-by-four, or a two-by ten. These names are not true thicknesses but are rough lumber dimensions before the board was planed.

Another option that you may want to consider is using plywood for the large ¼″ pieces. This might be a desirable material for this use, since ends won't show, the plywood won't split as easily, and it is usually economical.

Wooden Dowels

These round wooden sticks are used in various sizes for porch railings and as faux beams for the Mission Church. Larger diameter dowels also are used as logs for the Log Cabin.

Tin and Copper

Thin sheets of either tin or copper metal can be used for roofing. In this book, tin is used for the Farmhouse and Cottage, and copper is used for the roof of the turret for the Victorian house. Use tin snips or other metal cutters for proper cutting (Illus. 7).

Cedar Shakes

Cedar shingles that are used in roofing and sometimes siding for full-scale construction can be cut into ¾″ × 1″ pieces for the little houses. The thickness of the miniature shingles will vary, but it is precisely this variance that helps give your construction an authentic look. Precut miniature shingles can be purchased at many hobby and craft shops and stores selling materials for making dollhouses and miniatures.

Decorative Trim

Premade strips of decorative trim, ¹⁄₁₆″ to ⅛″ thick are generally available also at hobby and craft stores, especially those carrying dollhouse materials and other miniature accessories. Trim is used, in particular, for the Victorian House and the House with Picket Fence, and it can be used in place of cutting thin strips, as required, for house, door, window trim, and cross pieces.

Brass Bells

Available at most craft shops, these bells come in a variety of shapes and sizes. The size required for both churches is about ¾″ to 1″.

Illus. 7. Cutting tin with tin snips.

Sandpaper

Most sanding, whether by hand or by machine, requires medium-grade paper. However, final sanding should always be done by hand, with a fine-grade sandpaper.

Brads

These are very thin, finishing-type nails that work well when used in ¼″ wood (Illus. 8). They are available in various gauges and lengths.

Illus. 8. Use brads, plus glue, to join the walls.

Paint

The paints recommended for each project are acrylic folk art paints, which are available in cans or in plastic, upright containers. These paints are more fluid than tube paints and don't need to be watered down. Most colors are available already mixed to the sort of muted shades that are suggested for many of the constructions.

Stain

Stain is required to get the rustic weathered-log look for the Log Cabin and is suggested as an option for finishing the inside of the houses. It may also be used when a crackled effect is being used. In which case, you will want to be sure to stain the area first, let it dry, and then proceed with the glue and paint mixture (see page 11).

Gesso

This is a thick, base-coat paint, rather like a primer coat that artists use. Gesso can be purchased wherever artists' paints are sold. It is used to achieve an old crackled look as mentioned in the General Instructions.

Brushes

Use artist-quality brushes in ¼″, ½″, and 1″ sizes.

Wood Glue

Yellow wood glue, sometimes called carpenter's glue, or woodworking glue, should be used for all the steps where glue is required to bond pieces. Hold or clamp the glued sections together briefly if they are not going to be nailed immediately.

Hide Glue

This opaque glue is available at hardware and craft stores. Hide glue is sometimes referred to as traditional cabinetmaker's glue. It is used in these projects specifically to achieve the old crackled look. Allow the glue to dry completely before you paint over it.

Solder

When you are using tin to make a roof, it is necessary to solder the joints (Illus. 9). The same is also true for copper.

Emery Cloth

Use a fine emery cloth to sand any joints and surrounding areas that are to be soldered. This slight abrasion will make sure the surface is ready for soldering.

Hinges

Small, ¼″ hinges are required for the Barn and the House with Picket Fence. Use a jeweler's screwdriver to attach these tiny hinges.

EQUIPMENT

Goggles

Always wear some type of eye protection when you are cutting, sanding, or drilling.

Dust Mask

Wear a dust mask when you are sanding to avoid breathing in any fine particles. The same goes for sawing.

Illus. 9. Soldering the joint of a tin roof.

Tabletop Scroll Saw

A scroll saw, like a jigsaw, has a vibrating blade that moves up and down in a vertical position. It is extremely useful for small, intricate cuts and is needed to cut out the window openings for the houses (Illus. 10).

Band Saw

A band saw has a thin continuous blade that moves in one cutting direction (Illus. 11). It can make intricate cuts or saw through a four-by-four. Use a ⅛" blade for intricate work and a ¼" blade for straight cuts. This is a very versatile saw that can be used for all the cutting described in the book except for the window openings, which require the scroll saw.

Radial-Arm Saw and Table Saw

Both of these saws use flat, circular blades available with various kinds of cutting teeth. While not able to do intricate cuts, these saws are good for precise "straight" cuts such as the basic cutting of wall or subroof pieces.

Sander

Use either a sanding disk or a small stationary belt sander as shown in Illus. 1. It is best to use medium-grade sandpaper with any of these machines.

Drill

Any portable hand drill is suitable. A variety of drill bits are necessary for the various projects and are identified as they are required.

Drill Press

This stationary drilling machine can be very helpful when you need it for achieving straight and accurate holes.

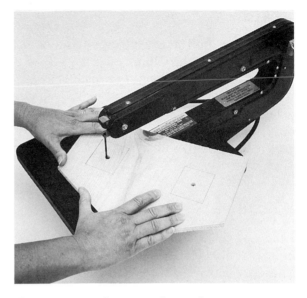

Illus. 10. *Cut windows out with a scroll saw.*

Illus. 11. *A band saw is useful for both straight and curved cuts.*

Hammer

Any small hammer or tack hammer will suffice for the projects in the book.

Jeweler's Screwdriver

Use this tiny screwdriver to fasten the hinges for the Barn and the House with Picket Fence.

Miniature Houses and Buildings

Whether you build one house or an entire village, these little houses will be cherished for decades to come. Not only can they be used as fine accent pieces or built as dollhouses or birdhouses, but also they can be incorporated into any holiday centerpiece, changing accessories just as you would with the home you live in.

They are especially attractive when used around New Year's and at Christmastime, along a mantel or under a tree. And a special charm is created when they are lit with miniature lights inside or out.

And they may be further put to use in their original calling as toy houses for play. Nowadays you might find little houses adorning a model railroad or a motorized miniature car track as much as the mantel or the middle of the holiday table. But certainly their value as gifts for display and as old-fashioned dollhouses will probably remain the greatest. These traditional uses endure.

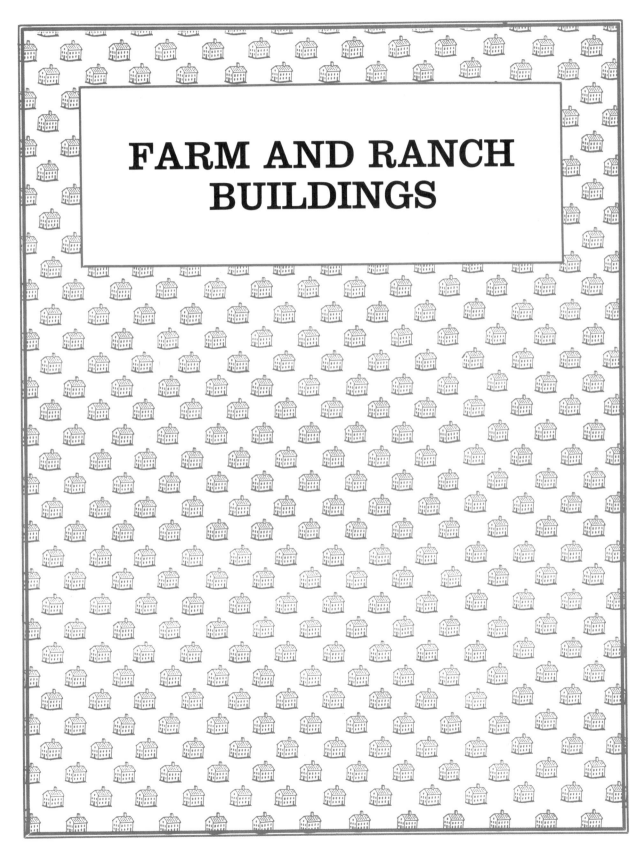

FARM AND RANCH BUILDINGS

❖ Farmhouse ❖

This fundamental but pleasingly handsome little house is distinguished with its two chimneys. It can be made with or without shutters. The tin roof, made to resemble an old crimped, tin roof, may be painted with a green- or rust-colored wash for variety (Illus. 12). You also have the option of building the Farmhouse with a shingle roof.

MATERIALS

Pine or plywood, ¼″ thick, 5′
Pine, ½″ thick, 8″ × 24″ (cut 12 pieces ⅛″ × ½″ × 24″ for shutters, and window and peak trim)
Pine, ¾″ thick, 10″ × 16″ (cut 24 pieces ¾″ × ⅛″ × 16″ for siding)
Pine, ¾″ thick, 1½″ × 5″ (chimney)
Pine, ¾″ thick, 1″ × 8″ (roof support)
Tin, 10″ × 10″
Wire, 18 gauge, 10′
Brads, ¾″, No. 18, one box
Wood glue
Hide Glue
Gesso
Sandpaper
Stain, medium color
Acrylic paint: porcelain white, old ivy green (suggested)

TOOLS

Tabletop scroll saw
Band saw
Table saw
Tack hammer
Block plane (optional)
Drill
Drill bit, ½″
Paint brushes
Solder

Illus. 12. Farmhouse

Soldering iron
Tin snips
Pliers

INSTRUCTIONS

Basic Cutting

Using the dimensions given in Illus. 13, 14, and 15, cut the ¼″ wood for the front, back, two sides, and the porch.

For the shutters, window, and peak trim, use a table saw to cut the ½″ wood into twelve strips, ⅛″ × ½″ × 24″. Also cut four strips, ¼″ × ½″ × 7″, for the corner trim.

Then cut the ¾″ wood into twenty-four strips, ¾″ × ⅛″ × 16″. This will be used for the siding.

Windows

Draw the windows and door in place on all the main house sections: front, back, sides, etc. Then, using a ½″ drill bit, drill a hole into the middle of each area to be cut out for windows. The door can be simply straight-cut, of course.

Disconnect the blade of the tabletop scroll saw, and slide the blade through one of the holes just drilled. Reattach the blade, and then carefully cut out the window. Repeat this procedure for each required opening.

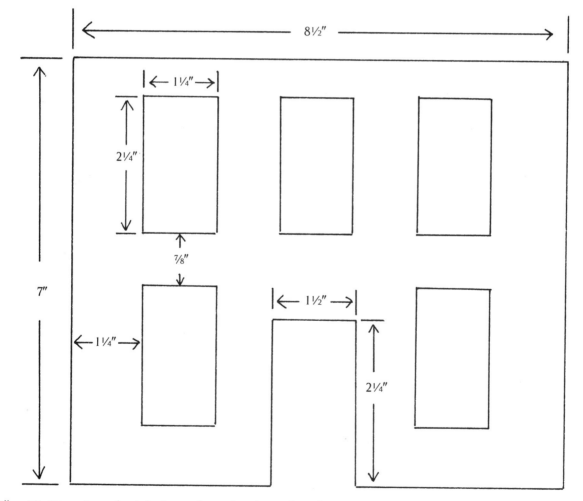

Illus. 13. Dimensions—front, back same but replace door with window.

House Assembly

Spread a thin bead of glue on the side edges of both side sections. Glue the house together so that the sides are inset into the front and back (Illus. 16). Then nail the joints together using several brads for each corner.

Once the glue has set, place the house on the remaining piece of ¼" wood, leaving an adequate length of scrapwood to cut the roof caps if you plan to build a shingle roof rather than the tin roof. Pencil along the inside perimeter of the house, and then cut out this section for the house base, or floor. Cut this

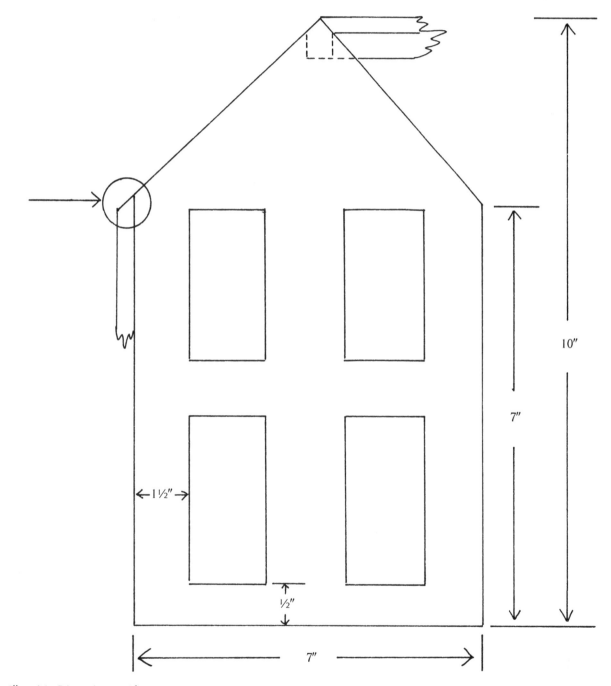

10"

7"

←1½"→

½"

7"

Illus. 14. Dimensions—side

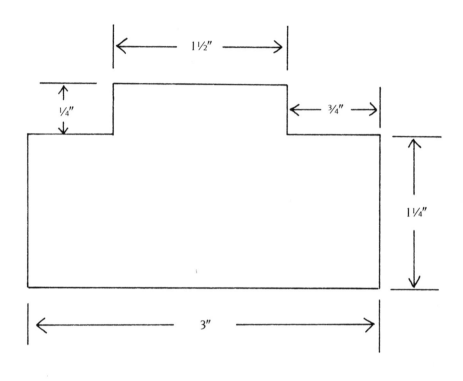

Illus. 15. Dimensions—porch

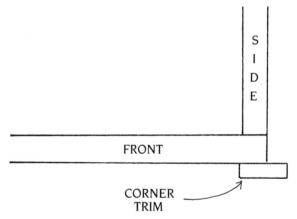

Illus. 16. Corner joint

carefully just to the outside of the pencil mark to ensure a good fit. Glue and nail this piece in place.

Stain, paint, or perhaps wallpaper the inside of the house at this point before you construct the roof.

Roof Support

Cut a roof support from ¾″ wood. The finished support should measure ¾″ × 1″ × 8″, but carefully measure the inside distance of the roof peaks between the side sections before cutting.

Using either a band saw or a block plane, trim along the top edges of the support to match the slope of the roof. Glue and nail the support into place.

Corner Trim

Attach the 7″ lengths of corner trim as shown in Illus. 16. The trim should protrude beyond the side by ¼″. Glue and nail the four pieces in place.

Window Frames

Cut, to fit, four pieces for each window frame from the ⅛″ × ½″ × 24″ strips. When you are gluing the frames, be sure the inside edges of the pieces are flush with the inside walls. Glue only.

Siding

Starting from the bottom, measure and cut, to fit, pieces of siding from the previously cut twenty-four strips. As you work upwards, overlap each row by ⅛". Glue each one into place as you go.

Shutters and Peak Trim

Using the ½" × ⅛" strips, cut two shutters per window, to match the length of the windows. Also cut four pieces of peak trim to fit along the roof line.

For the tin roof the trim fits up against the tin under the overhang, whereas for the shingle roof the pieces are flush with the edge of the shingles and is topped by the roof cap as shown in Illus. 17. In either case mitre-cut the edges to be joined at the peak. Outline the door with this same trim, giving a rounded arch to the top edge of the door lintel piece.

Paint the shutters and trim before attaching them to the house.

Painting

To achieve an old crackled look, first apply hide glue with a brush to the entire house. Let this dry about 4 hours before painting. Mix acrylic paint with gesso (2 tablespoons gesso to 1 tablespoon paint). The more gesso you use the smaller the cracks will be.

For the siding an off-white color was used; for the trim a pale, grey-green was chosen. Since the selection of a color combination for paints and the choice of finishing technique are a matter of preference, you may find a great deal of satisfaction in using your own creativity here.

When the paint has dried thoroughly, glue the shutters and door trim in place, and then glue and nail the peak trim.

Roof

If you prefer to make the shingle roof, then follow the instructions for the Ranch House for the subroof and shingles (pages 38 and 40) adjusting for the Farmhouse dimensions.

To make the tin roof, use tin snips to cut a 10" × 10" piece of tin for the roof. Bend this piece in half to match the slope of the roof, then cut nine 11" pieces of wire.

Illus. 17. Peak trim

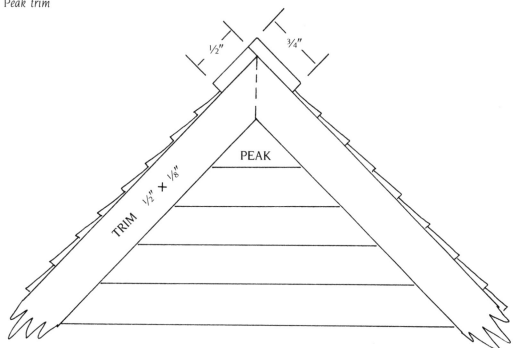

Bend each piece of wire in half, once again matching the roof angle. Evenly space the wires on the roof, then bend the ends under the roof edge using pliers. Solder the wires at the roof edges only. Tack roof into place (Illus. 18).

Chimney

Cut two chimneys from the ¾" wood to measure ¾" × 1½" × 1¾" (Illus. 19). Cut a "V" into the 1½" side to correspond with the angle of the roof. Glue the two chimneys in place on the roof cap, if you chose to make the shingled roof with the roof cap, or directly on the tin roof.

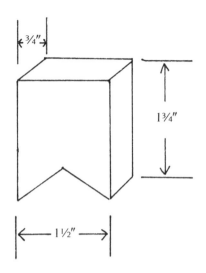

Illus. 19. Chimney dimensions

Illus. 18. Tacking on roof.

❖ 1900s Barn ❖

This reproduction of an antique toy barn features a hay loft, silos, and grooved doors that really open—a prized heirloom to be passed from generation to generation in your family (Illus. 20).

Pine, ¾″ × ¾″, 10′ length (ridge and braces)
Wood blocks, 1″ thick, 2½″ square, two (silo top)
      ¾″ thick, 1¼″ square, two (vents)

Illus. 20. Barn

MATERIALS

Pine, ³⁄₁₆″ thick, 4″ × 24″ (cut 14 strips ³⁄₁₆″ × 24″)
Pine, ¼″ thick, 12″ wide, 8 board feet (barn doors, etc.)
Pine, ½″ thick, 4″ × 28″ (silos)
Luan plywood, ⅛″ thick, 2′ × 2′ (roofing)

¾″ thick, ¾″ square, two (vents)
Wood dowel, ¼″ diameter, 8″ length
Hinges, ¼″, 6 sets
Brads, ¾″, No. 17, 1 box
Wood glue
Wood putty (nonshrinking)
Acrylic paint: white, red, blue-grey (suggested)

TOOLS

Tabletop scroll saw
Band saw
Table saw
Tack hammer
Drill
Circle-cutting bit, 2½"
Drill bit, ½"
Disk sander
Drill press
Carriage bolt and nut
Wood rasp
Brushes

INSTRUCTIONS

Basic Cutting

From the ¼" pine, cut the barn walls and base: front, 5½" × 22"; back, 5½" × 22"; two sides, 10" × 11"; and base, 9½" × 22".

Note that the sanding should be done prior to attaching any of the pieces throughout the project.

Doors and Windows

Draw the doors and windows on the barn wall pieces using the dimensions given in Illus. 21,

22, and 23. Cut out the doors, and then, using a ½" drill bit, drill a hole into the middle of the area where each window will be cut out.

Then, disconnect the blade of the tabletop scroll saw, and slide the blade through one of the holes. Reattach the blade, and then carefully cut out the window. Repeat this procedure for all of the remaining windows.

Basic Structure

First glue and nail the front and back sections to the base (Illus. 24), making sure the front, end door is to the left side. Then glue and nail the sides to the base; the door on the right side should be towards the back, the door on the left side towards the front.

Roof Ridges and Braces

The 1900s Barn has a gambrel roof, with a lower steeper slope and an upper flatter section on each of the two sides, that is particularly characteristic of the United States.

From the ¾" × ¾" wood, cut three roof ridges 22" long and two cross beams 9½" long. Glue and nail both of the cross beams into place. They are positioned 8" from each end, and flush with the top edge of the front and back wall sections.

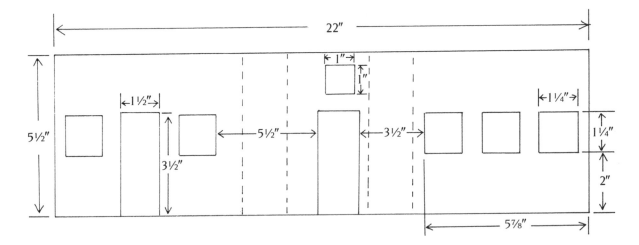

Illus. 21. Dimensions

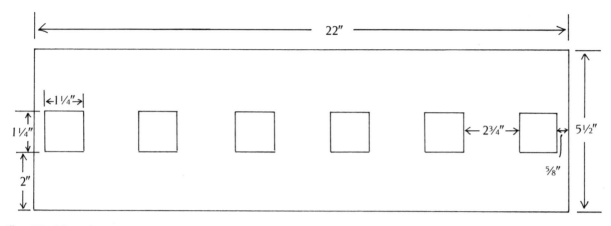

Illus. 22. Dimensions

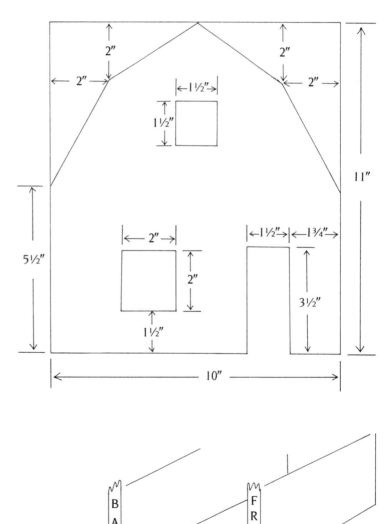

Illus. 23. Dimensions

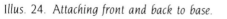

Illus. 24. Attaching front and back to base.

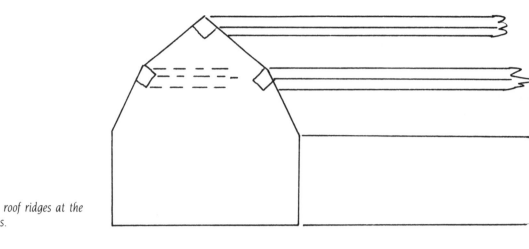

Illus. 25. Nail roof ridges at the peaks.

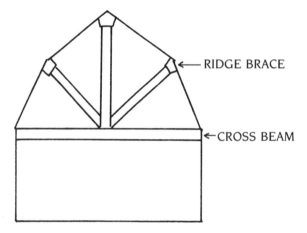

Illus. 26. Side view, cross beam, ridge braces

Glue and then nail the three roof ridges for the gambrel roof into place at each roof peak as shown in Illus. 25.

Measure and cut, to fit, two sets of ridge braces and glue into place as shown in Illus. 26. There are one perpendicular and two angled braces, providing a support for each cross beam.

Roof

From ⅛" luan plywood, cut two 4½" × 24" pieces and two 4" × 24" pieces.

Glue and nail into place the 4½" pieces first, starting at the lower roof peaks. Attach the 4" pieces in the same manner, making sure they meet at the top roof peak. The edges of the lower roof will overlap the walls, and the edges

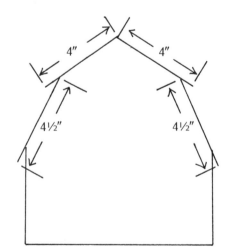

Illus. 27. Barn roof

of the upper roof will overlap the lower roof sections (Illus. 27). Fill in the top seam with wood putty as needed.

Dormers

To make the three dormers, first cut three triangular window sections from ¼" pine to the dimensions shown in Illus. 28. Drill a ½" hole into the section to be removed for the window. Using the scroll saw, cut out all of the window sections.

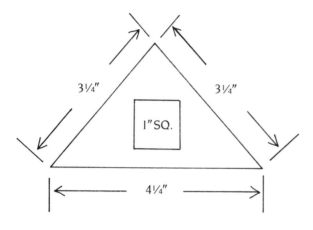

Illus. 28. Dimensions—dormers

From ⅛" luan plywood, cut six roof sections to the dimensions shown in Illus. 29.

Sand or cut the bottom edges of the three triangular ¼" pieces to match the slope of the roof sections. Glue the dormers together, and then glue one to the middle of the front lower roof section (just under the overlap). The remaining two should be glued equidistant between the middle dormer and the ends of the roof section.

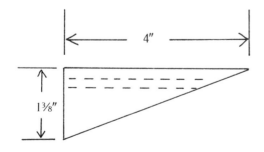

Illus. 29. Roof section

Door and Window Frames

From the ³⁄₁₆" strips cut, to fit, frames to go around all of the doors and windows. Then glue them into place, flush with the opening.

Cut a horizontal cross pane for each window. Then cut two vertical panes, and glue the pieces to form a cross. Insert the assemblies and glue them into the window openings.

Use two 22" strips and two 10⅜" strips for barn trim. Glue the trim ¼" above the top of the windows.

Measure the door openings, and cut both the small and large doors from ¼" pine. Groove the doors by using a carving tool or jackknife to give a planked look (Illus. 30).

Nail a medium-sized brad into each door to serve as a door knob. The brad should protrude about ⅛". Attach each door with two of the tiny hinges.

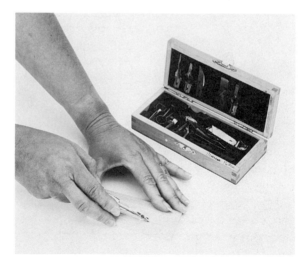

Illus. 30. Groove doors with a carving tool.

Vents

From ¾" wood, cut four blocks: two 1¼" square for the base of each vent, and two ¾" square to be moulded for the tops. Also cut two 1½" squares from ¼" wood.

Cut a "V", corresponding to the rooftop, into the 1¼" square blocks. Glue a 1½" square piece onto each of the base pieces, and then glue the ¾" squares on top.

Let the glue dry thoroughly, and then drill a hole into the middle of the top using a ³⁄₁₆″ bit. Using a sanding wheel, sand the tops into a rounded pyramid shape.

Cut four 1¼″ lengths of ³⁄₁₆″ dowel. Shape these into "lightning rods" using a jackknife or carving tool. Glue a rod into the top of each vent to finish off the entire assembly (Illus. 31). Then glue these vents onto the roof. The remaining two lightning rods are for the silos.

Silos

To make the silos, first cut six 2″ circles from ½″ wood. Then from ⅛″ wood, cut twenty-four strips ½″ × 11″ for the vertical siding of the silos.

Glue and nail the siding to the circles, placing three circles equidistant as shown in Illus. 32. Make sure the siding is flush with top and bottom.

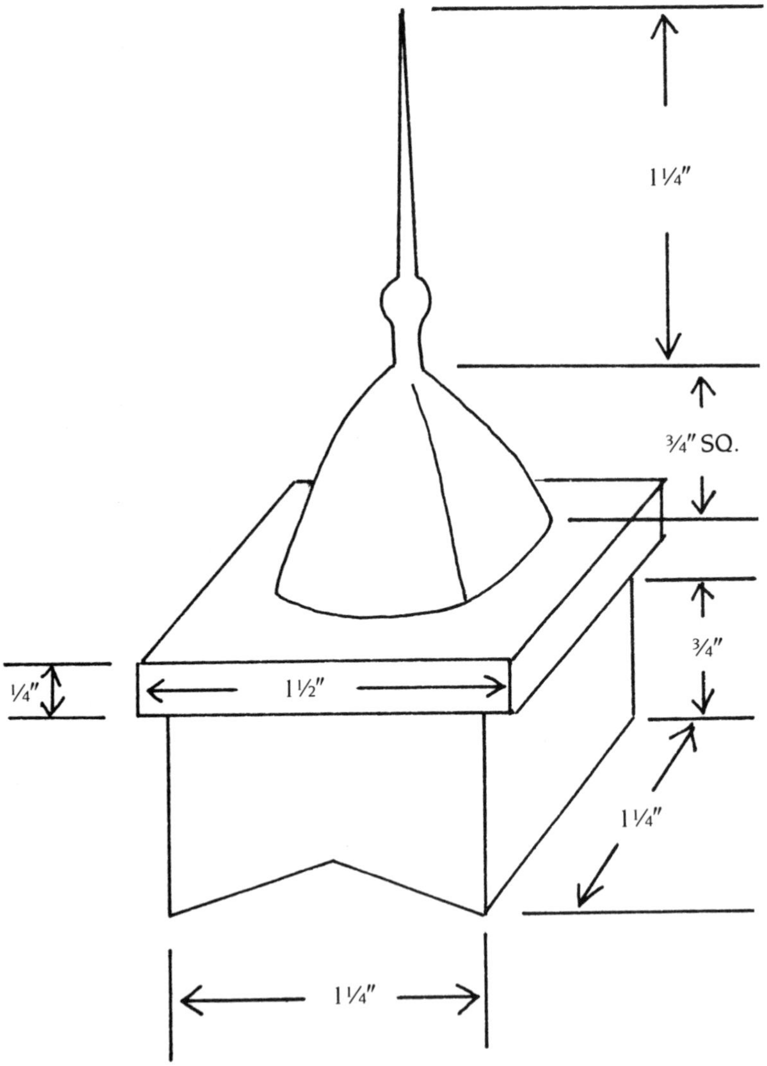

Illus. 31. Vent

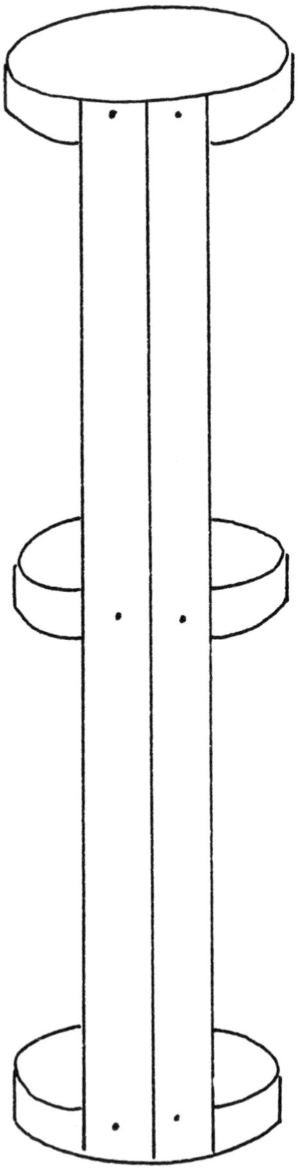

Illus. 32. Nail siding to wood circles to make the silos.

For the top of each silo, cut two 2½″ circles from 1″ wood, using a circle-cutting bit/device on your drill. Make a hole in the middle of both circular pieces to fit the shaft of a carriage bolt.

Insert the carriage bolt into this hole in one of these circular pieces. Fasten the bolt tightly with a nut, and then insert the end of the bolt into the drill press.

With the drill turning the piece at high speed, shape the circle into a dome by using a wood rasp and sandpaper (Illus. 33). Glue the dome to the top of the silo. Use the drill to expand the hole to ³⁄₁₆″ in the top of each dome, then attach the lightning rods.

Painting

Use white acrylic paint for the barn sides, front and back (above the trim), the silos, roof vents, and all trim and doors.

Paint below the trim line with a dark red. When this is completely dry, paint thin white lines to create the look of brick wall.

Paint the gambrel roof a blue-grey color.

Illus. 33. Making the dome for the silo.

❖ Ranch ❖

This little one-storey ranch house features a wraparound porch on three sides and a hip roof (Illus. 34). Some of the charming details you can add on your own are a corner porch swing, a mounted flag pole on the front porch column, and even miniature flower pots to decorate the windows.

Wood, 1/2" thick, 8" × 14"
Wood, 3/4" thick, 8" × 24"
Wood two-by-four, 2½" length (chimney)
Wood dowel, 1/8" diameter, 36" length, three
Luan plywood, 1/8" thick, 2' × 4'
Cedar shakes (to cover roof area)
Wood glue

Illus. 34. Ranch

MATERIALS

Wood, 1/4" thick, 10" × 6'
Wood, 3/8" square, 6'

Hide glue
Sandpaper
Brads, 3/4", No. 18, one box
Acrylic paint: off-white, slate blue, brick red

TOOLS

Table saw or radial-arm saw
Tabletop scroll saw
Drill with ½″ and ⅛″ bits
Tack hammer
Paint brushes

INSTRUCTIONS

Basic Cutting

From ¼″ wood, cut the base, front, back, and two sides to the dimensions given in Illus. 35, 36, and 37. Also cut 6′ of ⅛″ strips; these can be cut as four 18″ lengths. You will use these later to make the porch railings.

For trim and shutters use ½″ wood, and cut ten ⅛″ × 14″ strips.

Windows and Doors

Consult Illus. 35, 36, and 37 for the placement and measurement of the windows and doors. Draw these in place; then, using the ½″ bit, drill a hole through the middle of each drawn window.

Use the tabletop scroll saw to cut out the windows. First detach the blade, and insert it into one of the holes; then reattach the blade.

Make preliminary cuts to the corners, backing up to the middle after each cut, for ease in cutting out the windows (Illus. 38). Repeat this procedure for each window, and then cut out the doors.

House Assembly and Trim

Glue and nail the sides to the front and back sections. Then from the ⅛″ × ½″ × 14″ strips cut, to fit, trim for all of the windows and doors. Glue the trim pieces in place so that their inside edges are flush with the inside walls.

From these same strips, cut four 5″ pieces for corner trim. Glue these to the sides so that they protrude to the front (or back) about ¼″.

There will be a space above the corner trim to the top of the wall since the walls are 5½″ high; however, this will serve as a stop guide for finishing the siding. This is important because the space is needed for anchoring the rafters to the top of the walls.

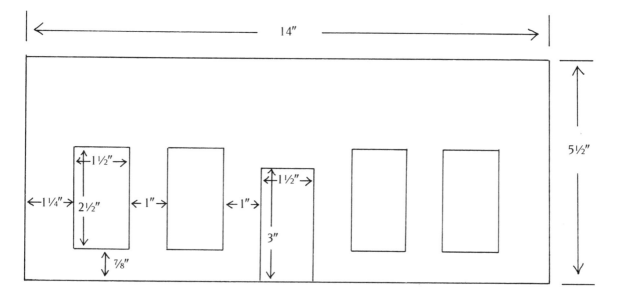

Illus. 35. Dimensions—front

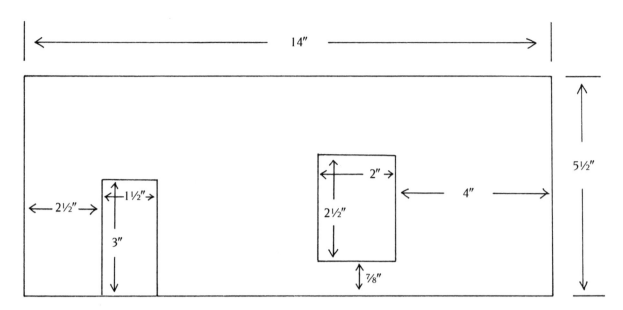

Illus. 36. Dimensions—back

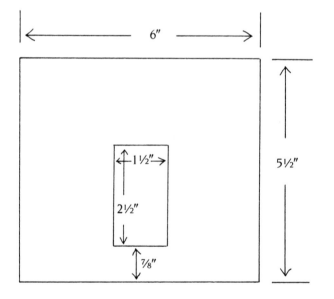

Illus. 37. Dimensions—side

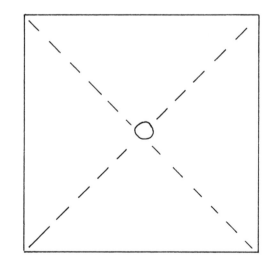

Illus. 38. Make cuts to the corners of the windows.

Roof Rafters

Using ¾″ wood again, cut strips ¼″ × ¾″ for the following roof supports: one top (main), 8¼″; two sides, 5″; four corners, 6″; three front, 5½″; and three back, 5½″.

Each support, with the exception of the main piece, will need to have one end cut at an angle, to fit flush with the main piece. These will also have to be notched to fit the top of the walls (Illus. 39).

Starting approximately one inch from the end of the 5″ side supports, cut out a notch to fit the shape of the wall. Position these supports at such an angle so that there is a 8¼″ space between them to attach the main support piece as indicated in Illus. 39.

Glue and nail the side roof supports to the top of the side walls at the midpoint, equidis-

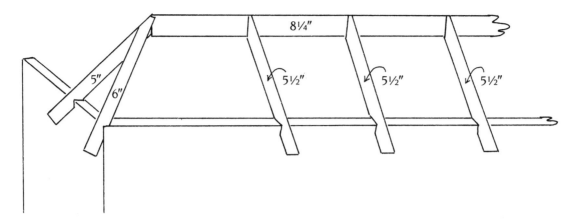

Illus. 39. *Roof ridge—rafters*

tant from each corner. Then glue the main support in place. Attach the front and back supports in the same manner, spacing them equally along the main piece.

Notch and angle the 6″ corner pieces, and glue and nail them to the corners.

Siding and Shutters

To make the siding, cut twenty-two 14″ strips ⅛″ × ¾″ using the ¾″ thick wood. Cut each piece to fit as you progress from the bottom to the top. Glue the first piece in place flush with the bottom, working on one side at a time.

As you work upwards, overlap each row ⅛″ and glue in place, but remember to stop ½″ from the top. Using these same strips, cut two shutters for each window to match the length of the window. Glue the shutters in place.

Now you are ready to stain or paint the inside of the house and the base. Then glue and nail the house to the base. The house should be positioned on the base with the back of the house and back of the base flush, and with the sides of the house equidistant from the side edges of the base.

Porch Supports, Rafters, and Railings

From a length of ⅜″ × ⅜″ wood, cut six 4″ posts. Glue these in place, one at each corner (⅛″ from base edges) and two in front of the

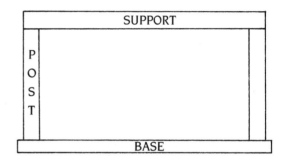

Illus. 40. *Nail supports on top of the porch posts.*

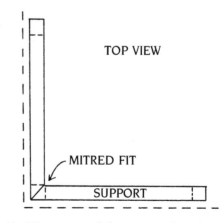

Illus. 41. *Mitre corners of the supports where they meet.*

door (2¼″ apart). Also cut the porch roof supports from this ⅜″ × ⅜″ piece: one, 19⅜″ (front) and two, 9⅜″ (sides).

Glue and nail the supports on top of the posts (Illus. 40). Mitre the corners where the supports join and rest on a post (Illus. 41).

Using ½″ wood, cut ¼″ × ½″ strips for the porch rafters. You will need: three front, 4″; four side, 3½″; two corner, 5¼″.

Notch and angle these in the same manner as the roof rafters. Position these rafters next to the existing roof rafters, then glue and nail them into place (Illus. 42).

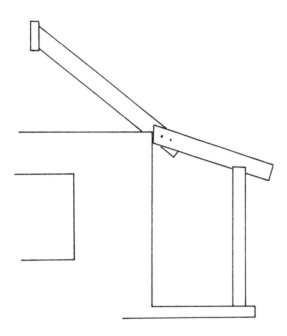

Illus. 42. Side view, connecting porch rafters to roof rafters.

To make the upper and lower railings, cut four 18″ strips ⅛″ × ¼″ from ¼″ wood. Place two strips together and tack a brad into each end to hold them securely.

With a ⅛″ bit, drill a hole at each ½″ interval. Repeat this procedure for the other set of strips. Cut a 7⅝″ and a 8½″ piece from each strip.

Now cut sixty-four 1¼″ pieces from the ⅛″ dowels. Separate the railings, and then glue and insert the 1¼″ dowel pieces to make the porch railings.

Set the porch railings aside until the outside of the house has been painted.

Subroof

The Ranch House has a hip roof, which has sloping ends and sloping sides. Connected to this is a porch roof that extends over the porch.

For the subroof, cut, from ⅛″ plywood, a front, back, and two sides for the hip roof, and also cut a front and two sides for the porch roof. Follow the dimensions given in Illus. 43, 44, 45, 46, and 47. Glue and then nail the front section and the back section in place for the main subroof.

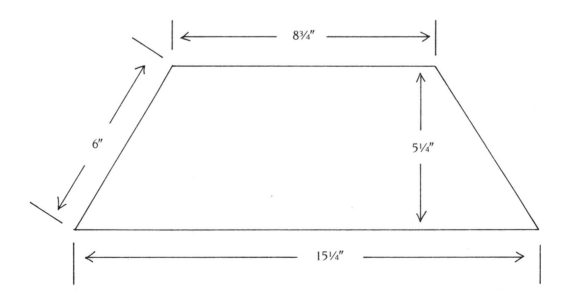

Illus. 43. Subroof—front

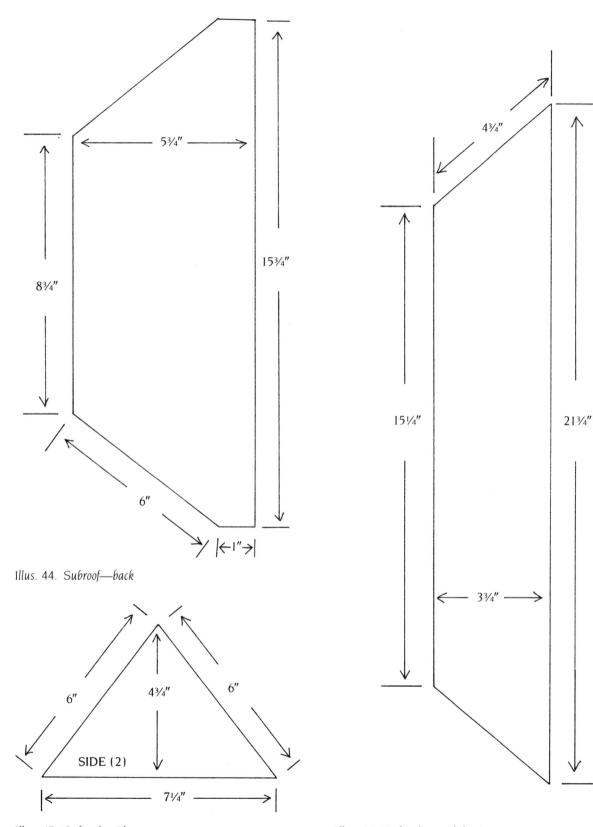

Illus. 44. Subroof—back

5¾″

15¾″

8¾″

6″

|←1″→|

Illus. 45. Subroof—side

6″

4¾″

6″

SIDE (2)

7¼″

4¾″

15¼″

21¾″

3¾″

Illus. 46. Subroof—porch front

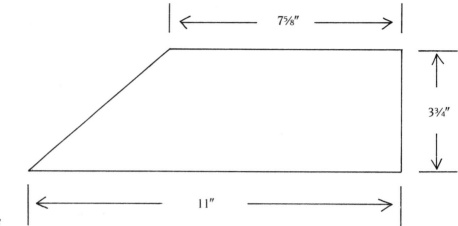

Illus. 47. Subroof—porch side

Be sure to check the dimensions of your structure to see if any slight corrections are needed for the side subroof dimensions. Attach the side pieces, and then, making the seams as flush as possible, glue and nail the porch subroof in place.

Shingles

Use cedar shakes to cut 1½″ × 1½″ squares for the shingles. Cut to fit at the corners and seam lines.

Starting from the bottom, glue a row of shingles in place; then, overlapping ¼″ glue on the next row, stagger placement by about half the shingle width for each row. If necessary, clamp a strip of wood across each row as it is glued to hold the shingles securely in place until they dry. This procedure is more time consuming, but it does make a sturdier, flatter roof.

When you have finished covering the roof, cut a roof cap ¼″ × ¾″ × 9½″ from ¾″ wood. Glue and nail this piece on top of the roof line.

From ⅛″ plywood, cut two ½″ × 5¼″ strips and four ½″ × 6″ strips. Use these to trim the seam lines of the roof. The 6″ strips are used for the hip roof, and the 5¼″ strips for the porch roof.

Chimney

From a piece of two-by-four wood, cut a 2″ × 2½″ block for the chimney. Cut out a section to correspond to the roof line (Illus. 48), and then glue into place.

Painting

Paint the trim, roof, porch railings, and posts with an off-white color. Slate blue is suggested for the house siding. Chimney, shutters, and the porch floor are a brick red color.

Porch railings can give an extra aged charm if you paint them with the crackled finish (see the General Instructions and also page 25).

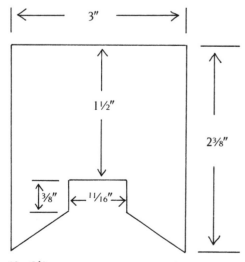

Illus. 48. Chimney

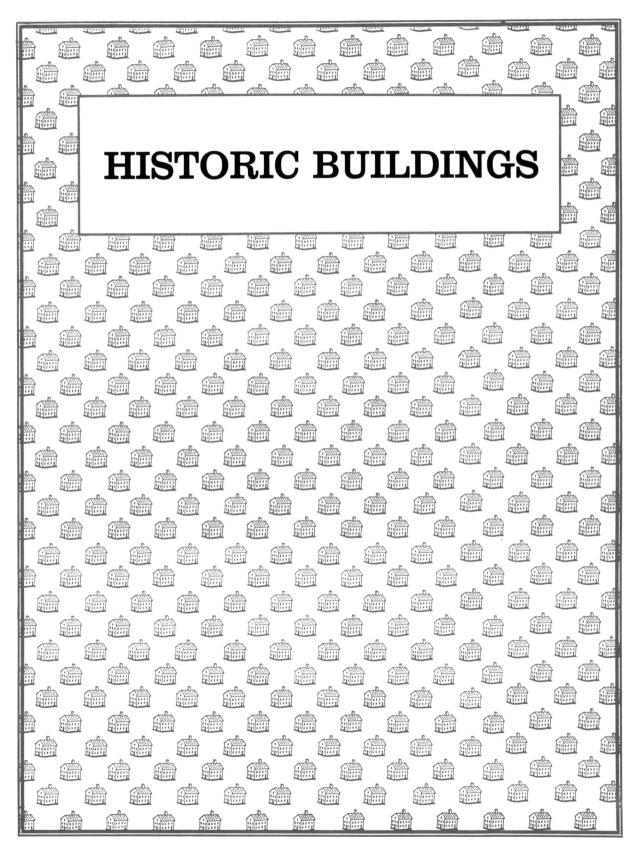

HISTORIC BUILDINGS

❖ Log Cabin ❖

This rustic little log cabin is built from wood dowels—a perfect addition to a little house collection (Illus. 49). Its handsome weathered wood look and the many rich details like the "stone" chimney, windows, and intersecting corner logs help capture the frontier spirit of the settlers.

MATERIALS

Pine, ½" thick, 10" × 28"
Pine, ¼" thick, 10" × 15½"
Pine, ⅝" thick, ⅝" × 17½" strip
Wood two-by-four, one 13" length
Barn wood, ½" thick, 6" × 6' (or other ½" wood)

Illus. 49. Log Cabin

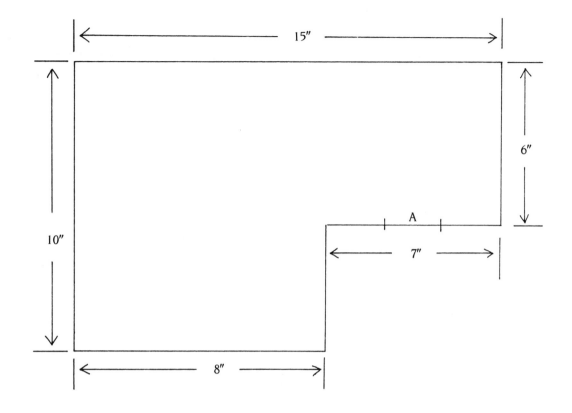

Illus. 50. *Base for the log cabin*

Wood dowels, ⅜″ diameter × 36″, four
Wood dowels, ½″ diameter × 36″, twenty-two
Wood dowel, ¼″ diameter, 1¼ length, one only
Brads, ¾″, No. 17, one box
Stain, 1 pint
Paint, light grey (suggested for the roof if barn
    wood is unavailable)
Sand, 1 oz
Wood glue

TOOLS

Band saw
Table saw
Tack hammer
Penknife
Drill with ¼″ bit

INSTRUCTIONS

Base and Door Frames

From ½″ pine, cut one base piece to the dimensions given in Illus. 50. Also cut six strips, ¼″ × 12″, to be used for the door and window frames (Illus. 51).

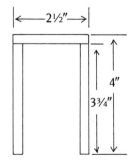

Illus. 51. *Door frame*

From the strips cut two 3¾″ pieces and one 2½″ piece for the door frame. Glue and nail the frame in position adjacent to what is labelled wall A in Illus. 50 since the logs will be built up from the outside of the base edge. Make sure that the corners of the frame are square, and that the door is positioned along the 7″ edge of the base right in the middle of what will become wall A.

Walls

For the first row of logs, cut seven pieces of ½″ dowel to these lengths: one 2¼″, one 3½,″ one 3¾″, one 6″, one 10″, one 11″, and one 18″. Full-length logs that extend beyond the intersecting wall will be 3″ longer than the corresponding base measurement.

Glue and nail the logs to the *SIDE* of the base as shown in Illus. 52. The logs that are longer than the corner will extend 1½″ beyond the adjacent wall.

For the second row, again cut seven pieces but to these lengths: one 1¾″, one 2¼″, one 5½″, one 8″, one 9″, one 13″, and one 15″. Glue and nail these logs on top of the base row.

Alternate sizes (identical to the first row, and then the second row) until you have completed the fifth row on which the window frames will sit.

Window Frames

From ½″ pine, cut six strips ¼″ × 12″. Then cut pieces from these strips to the appropriate lengths for each window.

The front window requires two 1½″ pieces and two 4″ pieces. For the remaining five windows you will need to cut ten 2″ pieces and ten 2½″ pieces.

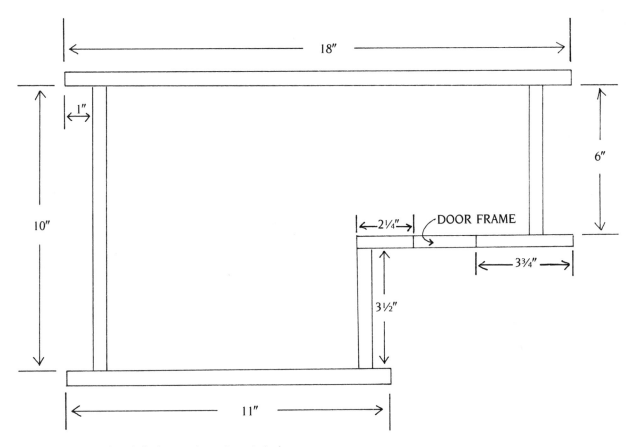

Illus. 52. Glue and nail the logs to the "sides" of the base.

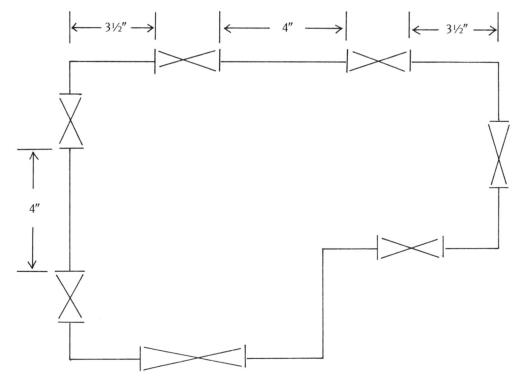

Illus. 53. Position of windows

Glue and nail each window frame, making sure that the corners are perfectly square. The outside dimensions of the window frames are 2″ × 4″ for the front and 2½″ × 2½″ for the side and back.

The exact placement of the windows is diagrammed in Illus. 53. Glue each window frame securely in place. Be sure to leave 4″ between the two side windows on the longest side wall to allow for the chimney.

Add five more rows of logs, one row at a time. Cut the logs to fit the spaces both between and beside the window frames. Notch out the logs that extend across the top of the window frames if the logs are not exactly flush with the top of the frame.

Foundation and Porch

After you have reached the tenth row of logs, add the porch and foundation.

From ¼″ pine, cut three strips 1″ × 15½″, and also cut out a 5″ × 7½″ porch floor. Also cut a 5″ length of ½″ dowel for the porch corner post, which acts as a roof support.

Now cut three foundation sections from the 1″ strips to these lengths: one 5″, one 8¼″, and one 8½″; and for the fourth foundation section use one strip that remains 15½″.

Glue and nail the four foundation pieces and the porch floor to the base of the cabin (Illus. 54). The strips will overlap part of each log (Illus. 55).

From ½″ wood cut a front door step to measurements shown (Illus. 56). Attach the step to the door frame with glue.

Glue the corner post in position making sure it is straight. Then add one more row of logs, the eleventh, with the front log extending over the porch post.

Ridge Braces

Cut two 9½″ ridge braces from ⅜″ thick dowels. Also cut a 15″ length for the roof ridge.

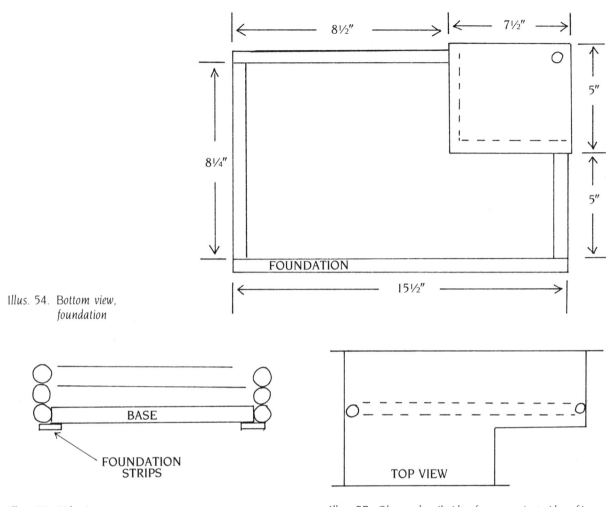

Illus. 54. Bottom view, foundation

FOUNDATION

8½"

7½"

5"

5"

8¼"

15½"

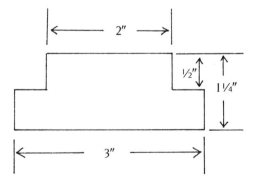

BASE

FOUNDATION STRIPS

Illus. 55. Side view

Illus. 56. Front door step

2"

3"

½"

1¼"

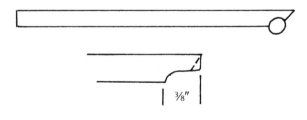

TOP VIEW

Illus. 57. Glue and nail ridge braces against side cabin walls.

⅜"

Illus. 58. Cut a notch into each rafter.

Roof Rafters

From the ⅜" dowels, cut eighteen 9" roof rafters. Cut a notch into one end of each rafter (Illus. 58).

Glue and nail the rafters at each end of the cabin (Illus. 59). Then, in the remaining space,

Glue and nail the braces inside of the cabin, making sure they are plumb (Illus. 57). Glue and nail the roof ridge in place.

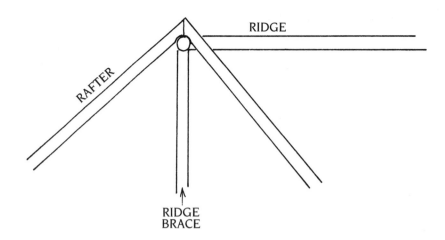

Illus. 59. Roof ridge—end rafters

position and fasten the other 14 rafters, equally spaced, approximately 2" apart.

Finish adding logs to the side walls of the cabin, cutting to fit the angle of the roofline (Illus. 60). Ends can be sanded for a snug fit.

Chimney

To make the chimney, cut the two-by-four to the dimensions given in Illus. 61. With the band saw, make horizontal 1/16" deep, random cuts on the front, sides, and three inches down the back. Use a jackknife or carving tool to make vertical cuts to resemble a stone or brick chimney.

Prepare for attaching the chimney by first drilling a 1/4" hole into the chimney back, approximately 4" from the bottom. Glue and insert the 1/4" diameter dowel (Illus. 62). Drill a corresponding hole into the cabin wall. (Do not attach the chimney until the next step is completed.)

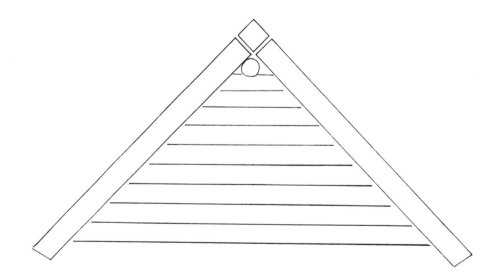

ENDS OF LOGS MATCH ROOF ANGLE

LOG

Illus. 60. Taper logs to form the roof peak.

Staining and Painting

Using either a rag or a brush, stain the inside and outside of the log cabin. Wipe off any excess stain to be sure you'll have a uniform finish.

Paint the chimney with a base coat of grey paint. As this dries, mix a small amount of sand with some grey paint. The mixture should be slightly gritty. Dab this mixture on the drying paint with your fingers. Apply to the front, sides, and the top three inches of the chimney back. Set aside to dry.

Glue the chimney in place when it is completely dry. Make sure it is evenly positioned at the peak.

Roof

From the ½" barn wood, or any other ½" wood, cut six 6" × 8½" roof sections. Notch out two of the sections so that they fit snugly around the chimney. Nail all the sections in place, attaching them to the rafters.

Using ⅝" wood, cut a ⅝" × ⅝" strip that is 17½" long for the roof cap. Glue this in place at the top of the roof line.

If you are using wood other than barn wood, stain the roof a barn-wood grey color or paint it with a thin wash of grey paint (diluted paint). You might want to stain or paint the exposed cut edges of the roof wood even if you have some aged barn wood to work with.

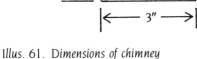

Illus. 61. Dimensions of chimney

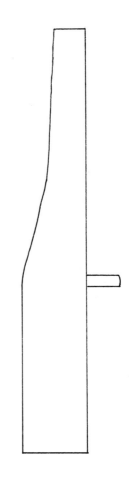

Illus. 62. Side view, chimney

❖ Rex Theatre ❖

The Rex—a must for all house collectors—is reminiscent of the old-time movie theatres (Illus. 63). The wood used for the theatre pictured was weathered barn wood; however, any wood of the proper thicknesses may be used and then stained with a barn-wood grey color. This project would also be quite eye-catching if it were painted in contrasting colors, perhaps a combination of forest green, mustard gold, and tan.

Illus. 63. Rex Theatre

MATERIALS

Wood, ¾″ thick, 12″ × 2′
Wood, ½″ thick, 10″ × 8′
Wood, ⅝″ thick, 8″ × 2½′
Wood, ¼″ thick, 8″ × 12″
Wood, ⅛″ thick, 6″ × 10″
Wood dowel, ¼″ diameter
Plexiglas, ¹⁄₁₆″ thick, 4″ × 5″
Brads, 1″, No. 18, one box
Wood glue
Sandpaper
Barn-wood grey stain (optional)
Acrylic paint: ivory, light green, brick
  (suggested)

TOOLS

Tabletop scroll saw
Table or radial-arm saw
Tack hammer
Drill with ½″ bit and ¼″ bit
Paint brush

INSTRUCTIONS

Basic Cutting

Using either a table saw or radial-arm saw, cut two strips from the ¾" wood, ⅛" × 14". Set these aside to use later as trim for the entrance overhang. Now cut the base piece, 9½" × 13", also from the ¾" wood.

From the ½" wood, cut two sides, 8½" × 9½", and one back, 9" × 12". Cut off the top corners of the back following the dimensions in Illus. 64. Then cut the front roof support to the shape and dimensions shown in Illus. 65.

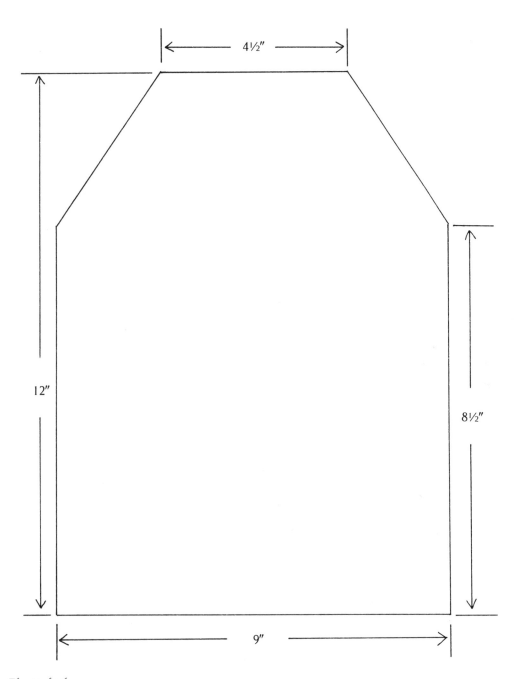

Illus. 64. Theatre back

House Assembly

Cut two ¼″ × ¼″ × 4¾″ pieces, and glue these as spacers between both C sections of the house (Illus. 88). After this has dried thoroughly, glue and nail this and the main house sections together: C to both B sections, and B sections to the largest wall section, A. Refer to Illus. 89 for placement and abutment of these and other sections.

Cut a ¼″ × ¼″ × 6¼″ cross beam, and glue this to the midsections of the top spacer and the top midsection of section A. Illus. 90 shows a plan view of this arrangement.

Connect sections D, E, and F into a wing before attaching them to the other sections. Then glue and nail this wing to the main house, making sure all the corners are square.

Refer to Illus. 89 for the correct position of the turret walls. Sand the inside edges to achieve a mitred fit. Glue them into place.

Cut a roof ridge for the main house sections, ½″ × ½″ × 11¼″. Glue and nail this ridge between both peaks. Then cut a roof ridge for the wing, ½″ × ½″ × 9″. Trim to fit, if necessary, and then glue and nail this piece in place between the roof peak and the other roof ridge (Illus. 91).

Glue and nail the house to the base so that the back of the main house is flush with the base edge as shown in Illus. 89.

Trim

From ½″ wood, cut fourteen feet of strips, ⅛″ × ½″. Cut these strips, to fit, to make window and door trim. Glue these in place so that the inside edges of trim are flush with the inside walls. Also, from ½″ wood, cut six pieces ¼″ × ½″ × 9″ for corner trim. Glue to the front of the B and F sections so that the trim protrudes ¼″ beyond each corner.

Cut one ¼″ × ¼″ × 9″ piece to be used as an inside corner where walls C and E join (Illus. 92). Glue this piece into place.

Siding

From ¾″ wood, cut approximately forty feet of ⅛″ strips for the siding. These may be cut as twenty 24″ pieces, for instance, or forty 12″ pieces.

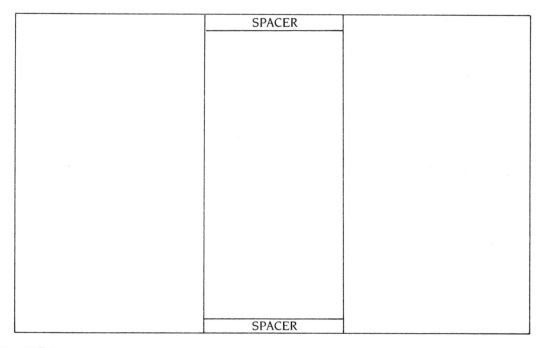

Illus. 88. Wall C spacers

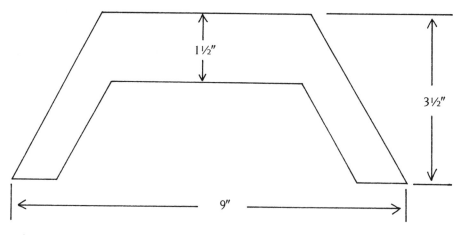

Illus. 65. Front roof support

Roof sections may be cut at this time as well; cut a top section, 5" × 10½", and also cut two side sections, 4¾" × 10½".

Main Structure

Glue and nail the sides to the back, keeping the corners square (Illus. 66). Then, glue and nail the front roof support to the sides.

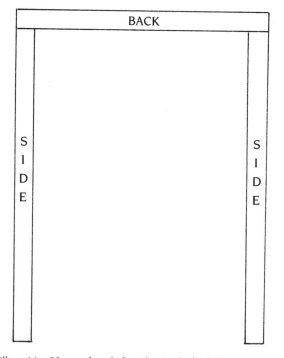

Illus. 66. Glue and nail the sides to the back, keeping the corners square.

Roof

Attach the top roof section so that it is flush with the front. Glue and nail it in place, making sure that it is positioned properly in the middle. Glue and nail the side roof sections in place, also making sure that they are flush with the front.

Now you can fasten the base piece to the structure with glue and nails. The back and sides of the theatre should set approximately ¼" from the edges.

Front Entrance

From ⅝" wood, cut two front pieces, 2" × 6¼". Notch out one corner to the measurements shown in Illus. 67.

Glue and nail these front pieces to the sides. The notched sections will extend over the base piece as you can see in Illus. 63.

Cut two pieces, 3⅝" × 5½", and another piece, 5¼" × 5½", from the ¼" wood. Cut two door openings in the larger piece to the dimensions in Illus. 68. Sand the side edges of this piece at an angle to fit the side pieces as shown in Illus. 69.

The edges of the side pieces that meet the front section will also need to be sanded at an angle. Glue these three pieces together to form the entrance.

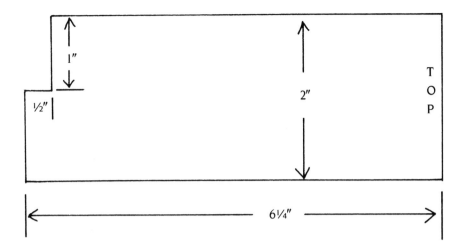

Illus. 67. First floor fronts—cut two.

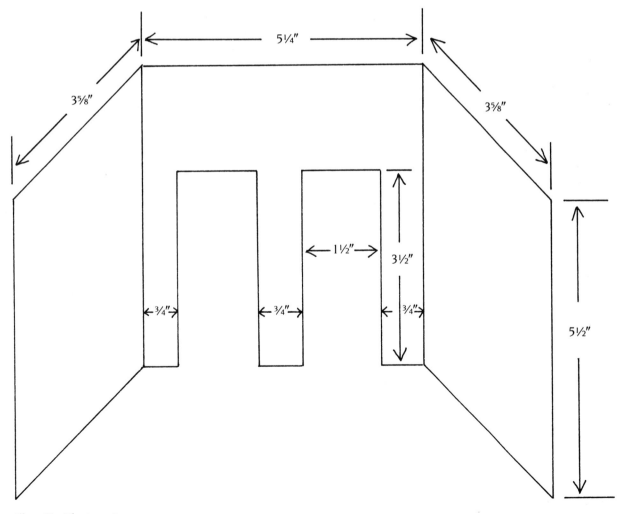

Illus. 68. Theatre entrance

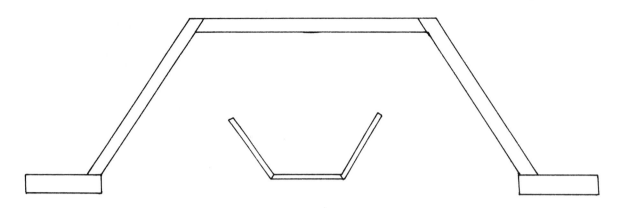

Illus. 69. Top view, entrance

Ticket Booth

Using a scroll saw or band saw, cut two sides, 1⅝″ × 5⅜″, and one front, 1½″ × 5⅜″, from ⅛″ wood. Cut the top and bottom to the shape and dimensions shown in Illus. 70. Also cut a center support to the same dimensions as the top and bottom but following the shape given in Illus. 71.

Illus. 71. Center support

Draw the windows, and then drill a hole into each window section. Detach the scroll saw blade, and insert the saw blade through one of the holes. Reattach the blade, and cut out the window area. Use this procedure to cut out the two remaining windows.

Sand the side edges of the ticket booth pieces so that they will join in a mitred fit (Illus. 72). Glue these pieces together, fitting the top and bottom in place.

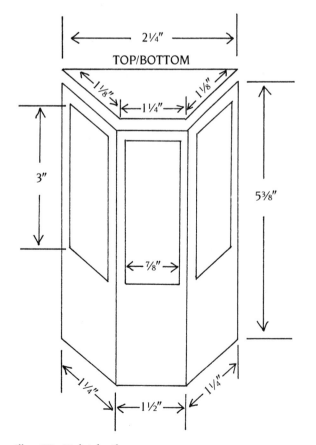

Illus. 70. Ticket booth

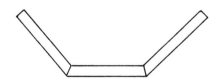

Illus. 72. Top view, ticket booth (mitred fit)

Using the band saw, cut three pieces of ¹⁄₁₆″ Plexiglas, slightly wider than each window opening and approximately ³⁄₈″ longer. Glue these windows inside the booth, and then glue the center support just beneath the bottom edge of the windows.

Spread glue on the bottom of the ticket booth once all joints have dried, and attach the booth to the base. The ticket booth should jut forward approximately ½″ more than the sides of the front section.

Entrance Overhang

For the entrance overhang and ceiling, from ½″ wood, cut a 6¾″ × 9¼″ piece. Then cut out the ½″ notched sections as shown in Illus. 73.

Glue and nail this piece in place so that it rests level, horizontally, on the entrance walls.

Front and Windows

From the remaining ⁵⁄₈″ wood, cut two ⁵⁄₁₆″ × 12″ strips. Cut these into four 2¼″ pieces and four 3″ pieces. Glue and nail these to make the window frames.

Cut twelve ⁵⁄₈″ × ⁵⁄₈″ strips to finish the front; then cut to required sizes shown in Illus. 74. Also cut two small pieces to fit next to the entrance overhang—they should fit flush with the sides. First glue and nail these two pieces in place.

Glue and nail the 11″ piece next, above the overhang. For the next row glue and nail a 2½″ strip, a window, a 1½″ strip, a window, and a 2½″ strip. Continue to build the front wall in this manner, following the pattern of Illus. 74.

For window crosspieces, cut a 12″ length of a ¼″ × ¼″ strip. Then cut, to fit, crosspieces, and glue them into place.

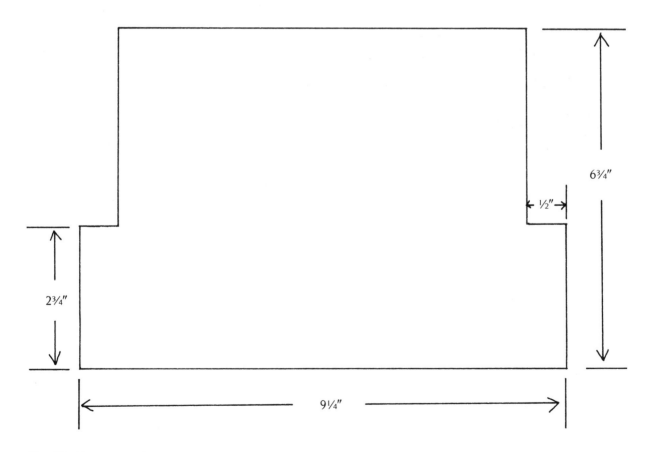

Illus. 73. Entrance overhang

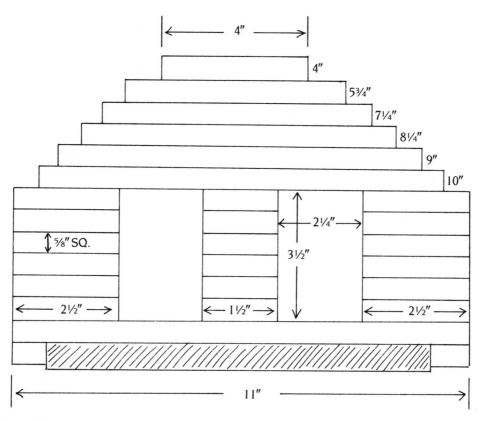

Illus. 74. Front, second storey

Theatre Sign

From ½″ wood, cut a 1¾″ × 6¾″ piece. Round the top corners, using a band saw or a sander, to match the shape in Illus. 75.

Drill two ¼″ holes into one side, positioning one about 1½″ from the top and the other about 1½″ from the bottom. Drill the holes to a depth of approximately ½″.

Cut two ¼″ thick dowel pieces 1¼″ long. Insert these into the holes, and use the projecting ends to determine the placement of holes in the theatre front. The sign piece should be positioned midway between the windows and ¼″ above the entrance overhang. Then drill the holes approximately ½″ deep. Glue the sign and dowels into place.

On ⅛″ wood, draw the letters "REX" twice. These letters should be approximately 1¼″ wide and 1½″ high. Cut out with either a scroll saw or band saw, using a fine-tooth blade.

Glue the letters to both sides of the sign.

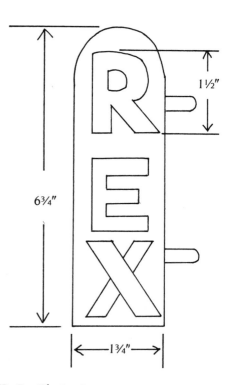

Illus. 75. Rex Theatre sign

Trim

From a ¾" scrap, cut one ⅛" × 9½" strip and two ⅛" × 2" strips. Glue and nail these strips to the front and side edges of the entrance overhang.

An optional detail that you may enjoy adding to give an extra feeling of authenticity is to rip small pieces from a newspaper movie section, and then glue a few scraps to both sides of the front to look like old billboards.

Painting

Paint the sign letters and the entrance walls an off-white. To match the old weathered painted boards used, the ticket booth is painted light green on the bottom half, but brick red on the top half.

❖ Victorian ❖

Reminiscent of days gone by, this two-storey Victorian is certain to draw compliments (Illus. 76). Highlights include a wraparound porch and copper-roofed turret. Gingerbread detailing and the colorful painting of the trim, siding, and window frames in contrasting hues help capture the spirit of an authentic Victorian house.

Illus. 76. The Victorian House

MATERIALS

Wood, ¼" thick, 10" × 5½'
Wood, ⅜" square, 4'
Wood, ½" thick, 10" × 3'
Wood, ¾" thick, 12" × 3½' (Roof caps, shingles, and siding)
Plywood, ⅛" thick, 2' × 2'
Decorative trim, ¹⁄₁₆" thick, ½" × 5'
Copper 0.025 gauge, 5" × 6"
Wood dowel, ⅛" diameter, two 36" lengths
Emery paper, small pieces
Wood glue
Epoxy
Brads, ¾", No. 18, one box
Acrylic paint: off-white, gold ochre, dark green, brick red (suggested)
Stain: medium color

TOOLS

Table, radial-arm, or band saw
Tabletop scroll saw
Tack hammer
Drill with ⅛" and ½" bits
Soldering iron and solder
Metal cutters or tin snips
Flat-end pliers (linesman's)

INSTRUCTIONS

Basic Cutting

Following the dimensions in Illus. 77 through Illus. 82, cut house pieces and an 11¼" × 15½" base from ¼" wood. Note the identification of

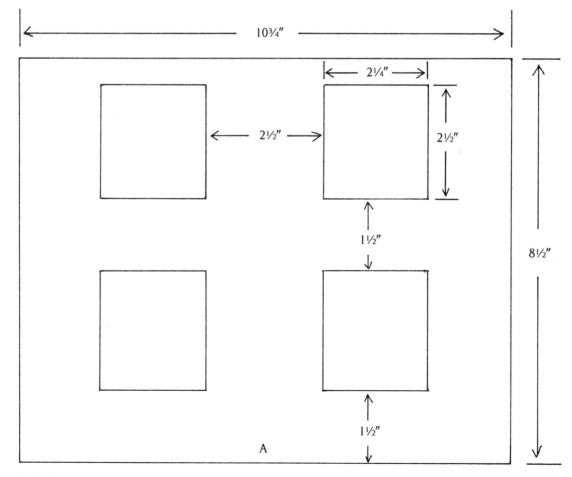

Illus. 77. Wall A

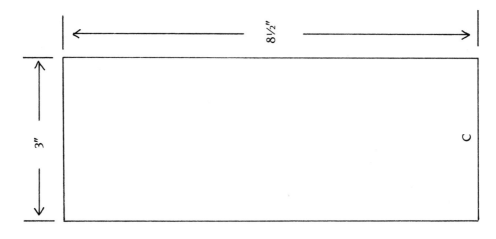

Illus. 79. Wall C

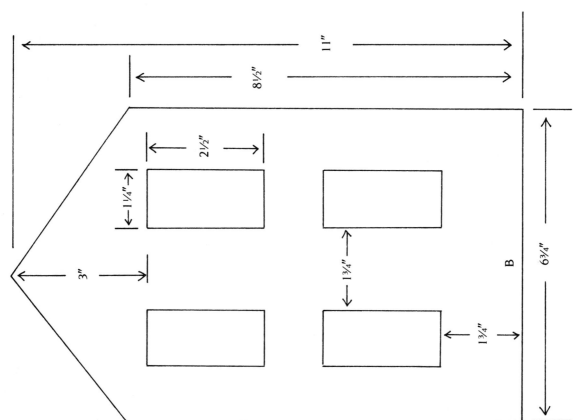

Illus. 78. Wall B

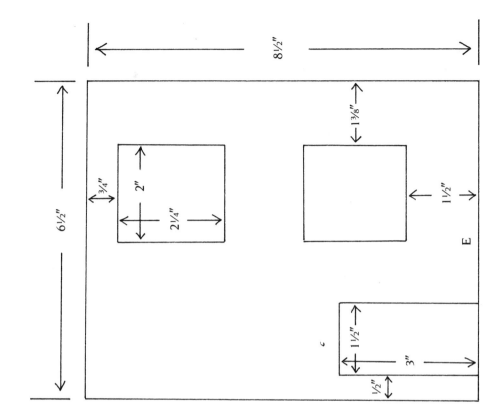

Illus. 81. Wall E

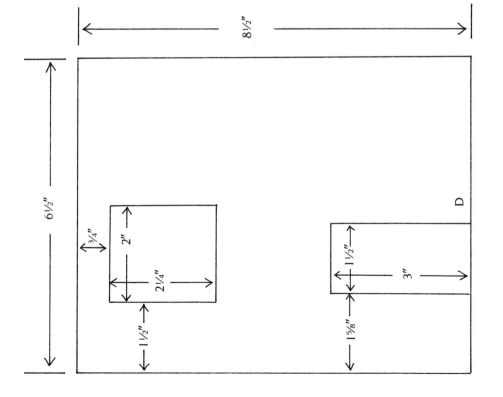

Illus. 80. Wall D

each section, A through F. You will need two C sections and two B sections. Also cut three 1¼″ × 8½″ pieces for the turret (Illus. 83).

From ⅛″ wood, cut out the subroof sections for the house and the porch a shown in Illus. 84, 85, 86, and 87. Do not notch the roof sections until they can be fitted to the turret.

Windows and Doors

Draw the windows and doors onto the house and turret sections. Consult the appropriate diagrams for their dimensions and placement.

With a ½″ bit, drill a hole into the middle of each area where a window is drawn. Using a tabletop scroll saw, cut out the windows. Do this by detaching the blade and inserting it into one of the holes. Then reattach the blade. Make preliminary cuts from the hole to the corners for ease in cutting out the window.

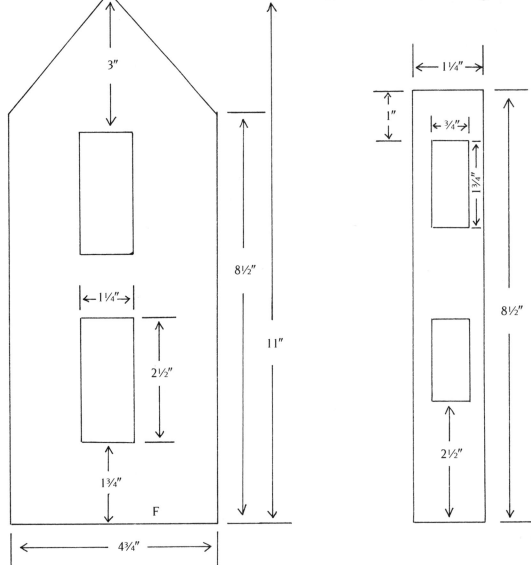

Illus. 82. Wall F

Illus. 83. Turret—cut three.

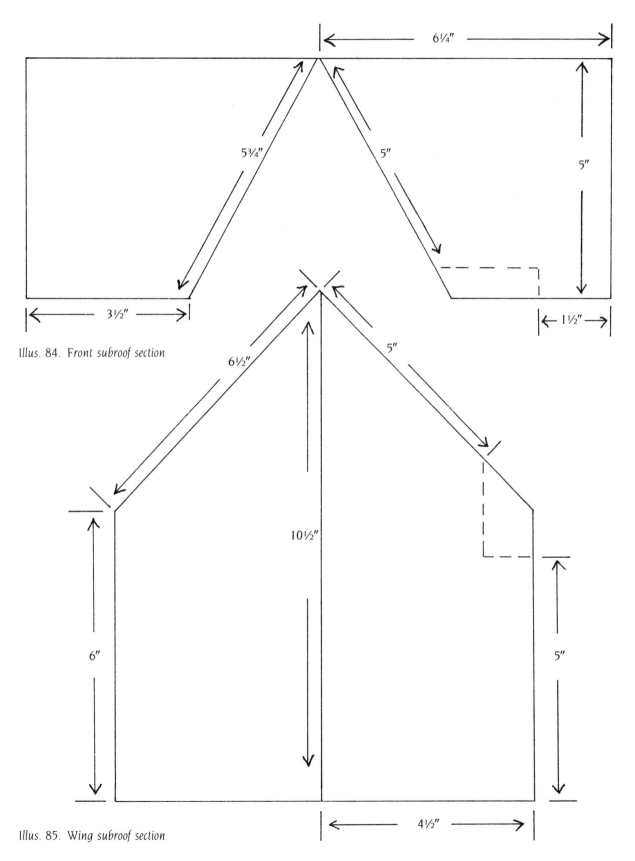

Illus. 84. Front subroof section

Illus. 85. Wing subroof section

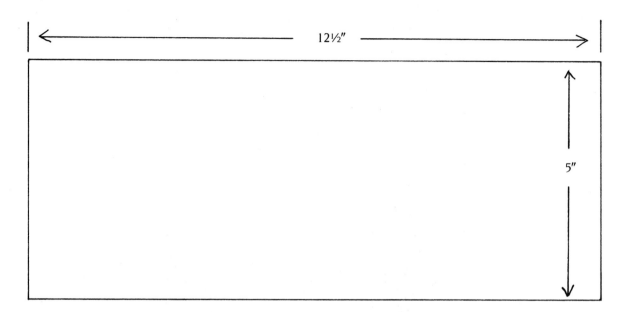

Illus. 86. *Back subroof*

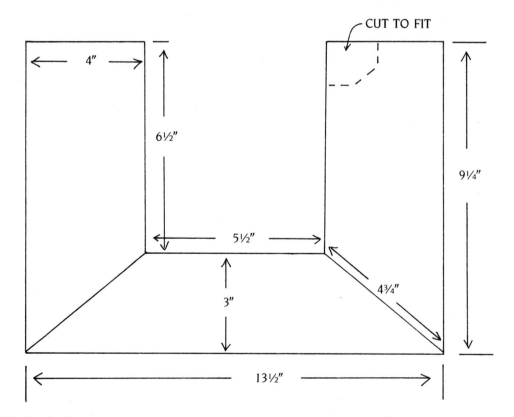

Illus. 87. *Porch subroof*

B

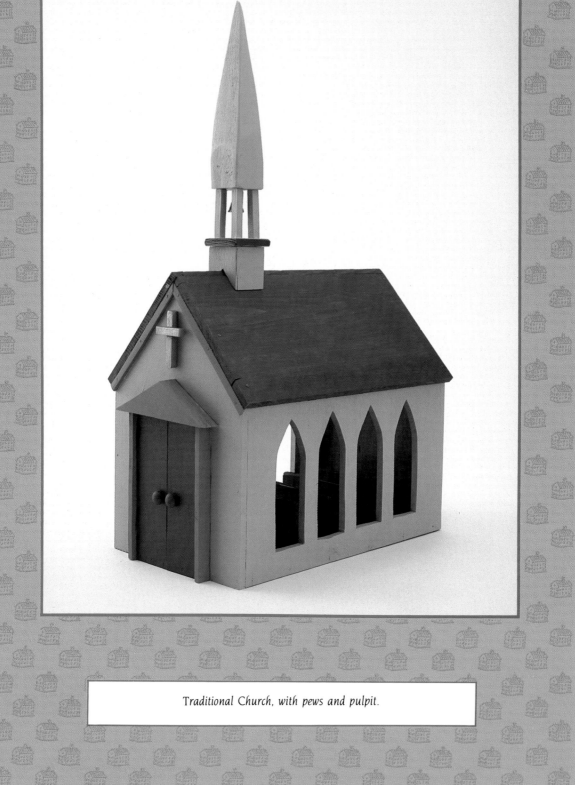

Traditional Church, with pews and pulpit.

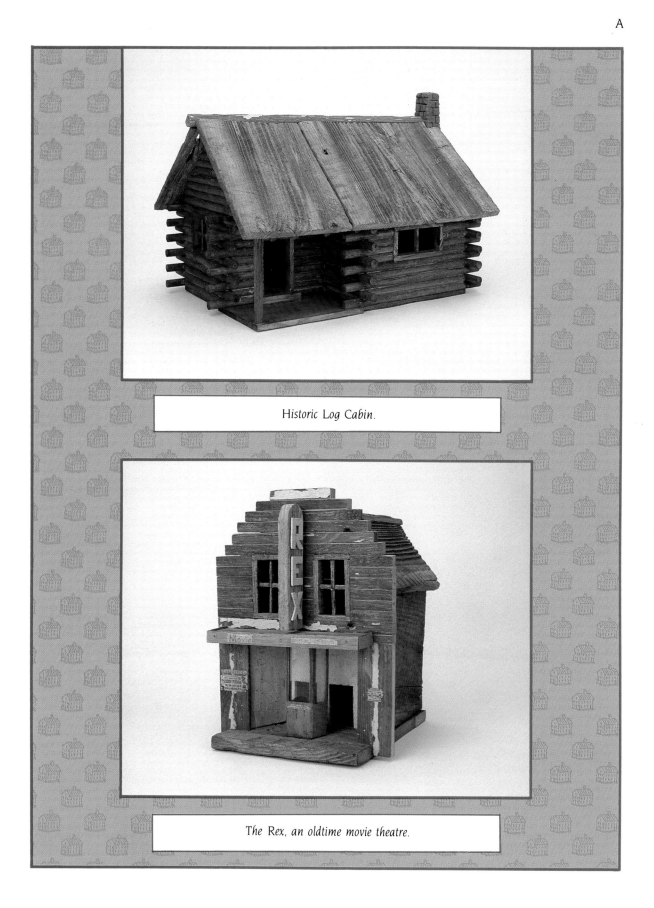

Historic Log Cabin.

The Rex, an oldtime movie theatre.

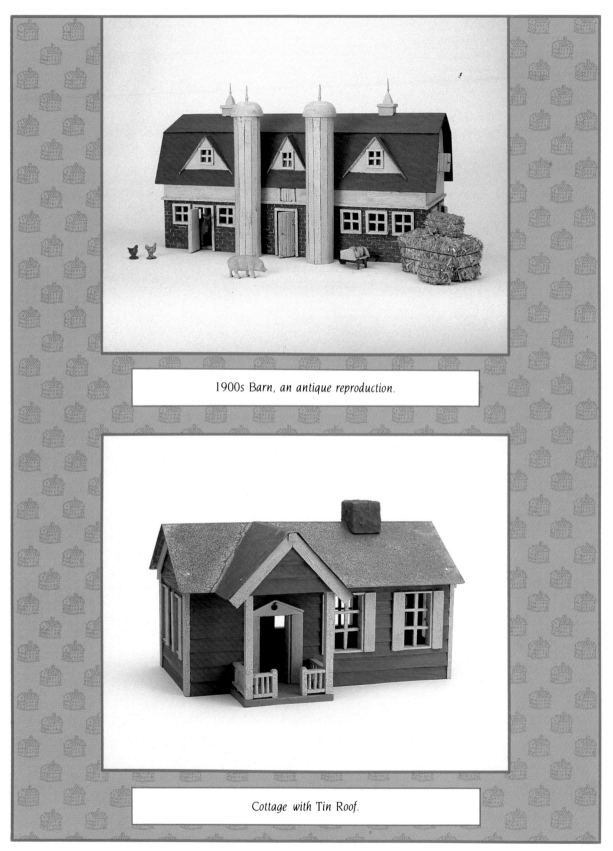

1900s Barn, an antique reproduction.

Cottage with Tin Roof.

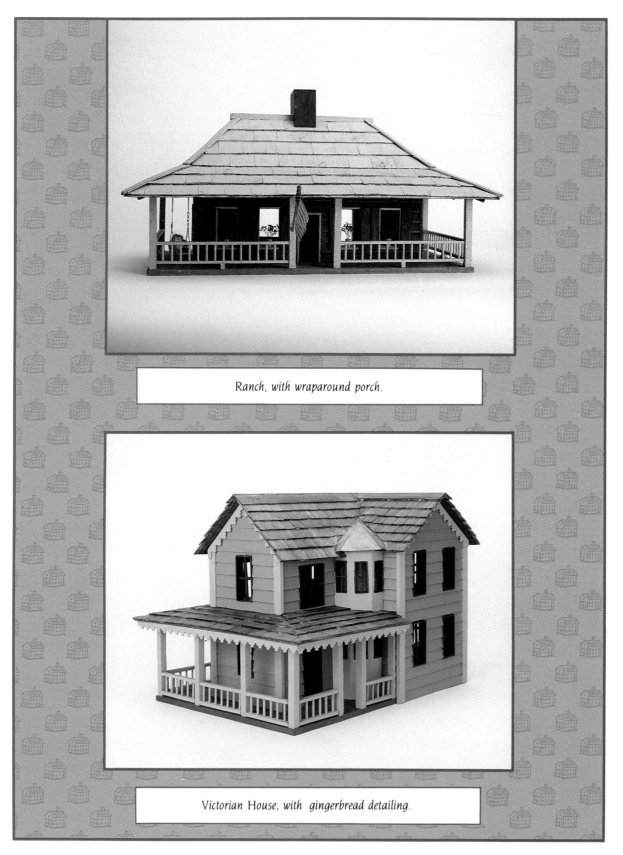

Ranch, with wraparound porch.

Victorian House, with gingerbread detailing.

Two-Storey with Basement.

Three-Storey with Dormers.

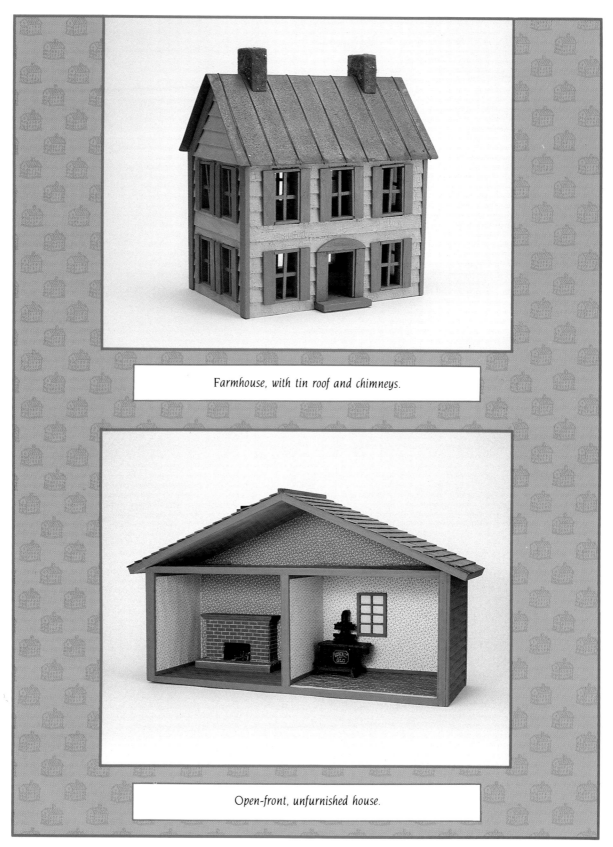

Farmhouse, with tin roof and chimneys.

Open-front, unfurnished house.

House with Picket Fence.

Mission Church.

Block Buildings and Houses.

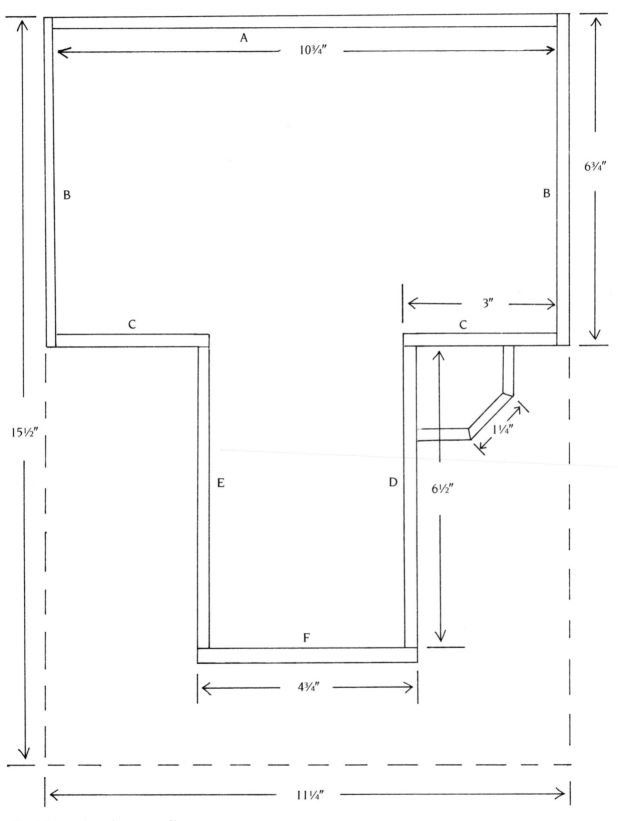

A 10¾″

6¾″

B   B

C   3″   C

15½″

E   D   6½″

1¼″

F

4¾″

11¼″

Illus. 89. Top view—house assembly

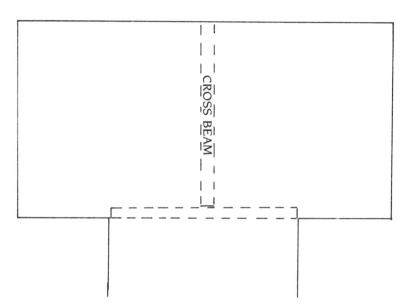

Illus. 90. Glue the cross beam in place.

Illus. 91. After completing the walls, glue and nail the house onto the base.

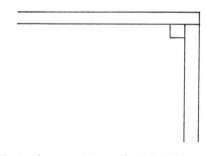

Illus. 92. Inside corner trim at the C & E joint

Cut the pieces of siding, to fit, as you progress in applying each row from the bottom to the top. Starting at the bottom, glue the first piece flush with the lowest part of the wall, working on one side at a time. Start the main house siding right at the bottom of the base to completely cover it.

As you work upwards, overlap each row by ⅛" and glue in place. Notch out areas for windows and doors as necessary.

When you have completed applying all of the siding, it is the most suitable time to stain, paint, or wallpaper the inside of the house. Wallpaper is a particularly appropriate choice, since many Victorian homes had not only elaborate stenciling but also used as many as fifteen different wallpapers in one area, walls and ceiling.

Porch Posts, Rafters, and Railings

Using ⅜″ wood, cut nine ⅜″ × ⅜″ × 4″ posts. Glue and nail these in place, ⅛″ from the porch edge, as you can see in Illus. 76 and in Illus. 93.

Illus. 93. Notch the rafters to fit over the porch supports.

Also from ⅜″ wood, cut one ⅜″ × ⅜″ × 11″ roof support and two ⅜″ × ⅜″ × 8⅜″ supports. Glue and nail these on top of the posts.

Make the porch rafters from ¼″ × ⅜″ strips. You will need a total of 4′, so cut: seven 3½″ pieces (sides); two 4¼″ pieces (corners); and two 2¾″ pieces (front).

Notch the rafters to fit over the supports. Sand the end that will join the house to an angle so that the roof will have a slight slope (Illus. 93). Glue and nail the rafters in place, spacing them evenly.

To make the railings, use ¼″ wood, and cut four 12″ strips ⅛″ × ¼″. Place two strips together, and tack a brad into each end to hold them securely while you are drilling holes for railing supports.

With a ⅛″ bit, drill a hole at each ½″ interval. Repeat this procedure for the other set of strips. Cut the strips into sections to fit between the porch posts, leaving room, of course, at doorways.

Now cut thirty-eight (38) 1¼″ pieces of the ⅛″ diameter dowel. Separate the railings and then apply glue and insert the 1¼″ dowel pieces to make railing sections.

Set the railings aside until the house has been painted.

Subroof

Now is the time to cut the notch into the subroof sections that will adjoin the turret. The subroof should fit snug against the turret wall. Glue and nail the main subroof section in place first, and then attach the wing subroof in the same manner.

Also glue and nail the porch subroof into place.

Copper Roof

From the 0.025 gauge copper, cut three pieces according to the dimensions in Illus. 94—one piece marked with bend lines and two triangles. Mark the bend lines, and then using the pliers make a slight bend where indicated. Test the fit of the copper roof pieces before soldering them together. Make any necessary corrections.

Sand the edges to be soldered with a fine emery paper. This will help the solder adhere to the copper.

First join the front section to one back section, soldering from underneath. Then join the remaining piece. Before actually soldering, always make sure the soldering iron is hot to ensure a good joint.

Fasten the copper roof to the subroof with epoxy.

Shingles and Roof Cap

From ¾″ wood, cut approximately fifty (50) feet of ⅛″ × ¾″ strips. Starting with a few strips at a time, cut them into 1″ pieces for shingles. Glue a row of shingles to the bottom edge of all of the roof sections, extending over the edge of the subroof by ⅛″. Work upwards, overlapping by ⅛″ and staggering each row of shingles.

Cut shingles to fit around the turret. When the entire roof is completed, cut, from ⅛″ wood, two ⅛″ × ¾″ × 13″ pieces to cap the main roof. Glue and nail these pieces into place.

Then cut two ⅛″ × ¾″ × 10¾″ pieces for the wing roof cap, and glue and nail them into place.

Finishing Touches

To make the window crosspieces use ⅛″ × ⅛″ strips. You will need a total length of six feet. Cut these to fit each window, and then glue them in place. Use one horizontal piece and two vertical pieces for each window.

As trim typical of a Victorian, use decorative strips ¹⁄₁₆″ thick that are premade and available at most craft and hobby shops. Approximately five feet of trim is needed. Cut the trim to fit under all three roof peaks. Glue it into place. Also cut trim for under the porch roof. Fasten these strips to the ends of the rafters with glue and an occasional brad.

Painting

One suggested color combination, which was used here, is to paint the siding a gold ochre color, the window and door trim a dark green, and the turret, corner and decorative trim, and porch posts and railings an off-white. The porch floor is painted brick red.

When everything has dried, the only thing left to do is to glue the railings into place.

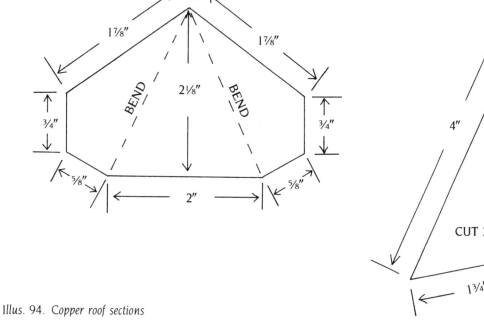

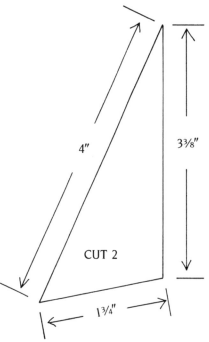

Illus. 94. Copper roof sections

COUNTRY HOUSES

❖ Two-Storey with Basement ❖

Here is an exciting little country house complete with a front and a side porch, both with railings (Illus. 95). Delightful details that add a distinctiveness to this charming but unpretentious house include the front stoop, the side porch steps with lattice work, the double-hung windows, the chimney—and even a faux basement replete with basement windows.

Illus. 95. Two Storey

74

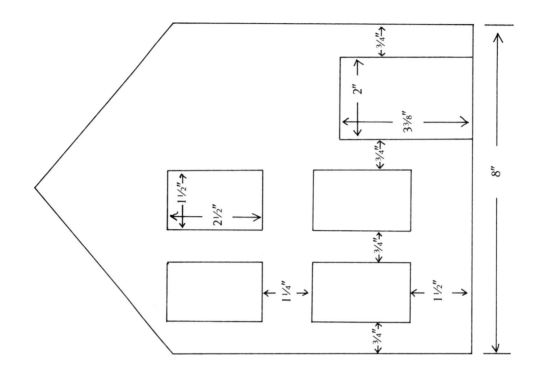

Illus. 97. Right side

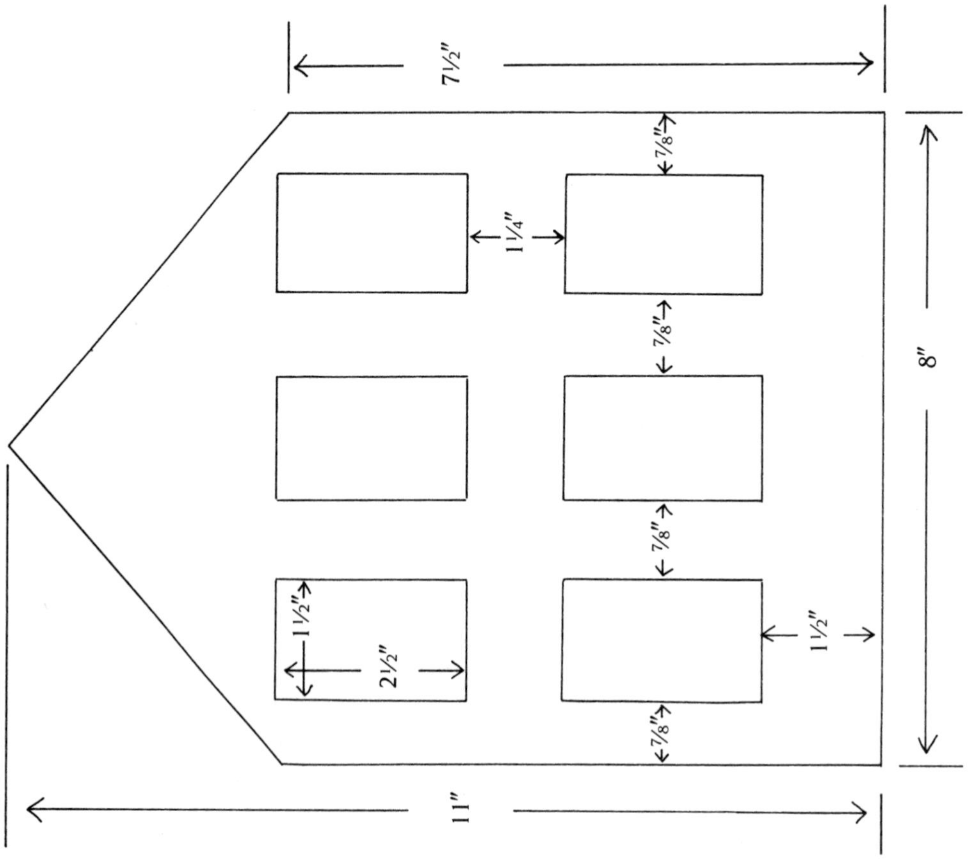

Illus. 96. Left side

MATERIALS

Pine, ¼″ thick, 10″ × 6½′
Pine, ⁵⁄₁₆″ thick, 2″ × 20″
Pine, ½″ thick, 6″ × 24″
Pine, ¾″ thick, 10″ × 20″
Luan plywood, ⅛″ thick, 6½″ × 38″
Wood dowels, ⅛″ diameter, 4′
Brads, ⅝″, No. 18, 1 box
Wood glue
Hide glue
Gesso
Sandpaper
Acrylic paint: antique white, dark brown, brick
   red, grey (suggested)
Sand, ¼ cup

TOOLS

Tabletop scroll saw
Band saw
Table saw or radial-arm saw (lattice work—
   optional)
Tack hammer
Drill or drill press (optional)
Drill bits, ⅛″, ½″
Paint brushes

INSTRUCTIONS

Basic Cutting

From the ¼″ pine, first cut the basic house pieces: one base, 8″ × 11¼″; two sides, 8″ × 11″; and two 7½″ × 11¾″ pieces for the front and back. You can follow the dimensions as given in Illus. 96 through Illus. 99. Also cut two 2″ × 8½″ pieces, one 2″ × 11¼″, three 2″ × 3¾″, and two 2″× 2½″ pieces for the basement foundation.

The porches also may be cut at this time. Follow the dimensions shown in Illus. 100 and Illus. 101.

Cut seven strips from the ½″ wood, ³⁄₁₆″ × 24″, for the window and door frames. Also cut four ¼″ × 7″ strips for the corner trim.

Shingles are cut from the ¾″ wood. Cut sixteen ⅛″ × 20″ strips. Then cut into approximately three hundred (300) one-inch pieces for the individual shingles. Cut twenty-four more ⅛″ × 20″ strips to be used for siding.

Also cut two 6½″ × 13¼″ pieces from ⅛″ plywood for the subroof at this time.

You may also want to cut a chimney piece from ¾″ pine; or you can wait until the structure is essentially complete and then adjust the dimensions to match the final touch you want for your house.

Windows and Doors

Draw the window and door openings as depicted in Illus. 96 through Illus. 99. All of the window openings are the same, 1½″ wide by 2½″ high.

First cut out the doors. Then, drill a ½″ hole into the middle of the area where each window will be cut out. Detach the blade from the scroll saw, and insert it through one of the holes. Reattach the blade, and then carefully cut out the window. Repeat this procedure for each window.

House Assembly

First glue and nail the sides to the base. Then glue and nail the front and back into place.

From ¾″ pine, cut a ¾″ × 11¼″ strip for the roof ridge. Glue and nail this into place between the roof peaks.

Window, Door, and Corner Trim

From the seven previously cut strips, ½″ × ³⁄₁₆″ × 24″, carefully cut and fit pieces to frame each window and door.

Glue this framing in place so that the inside edges of the trim are flush with the inside walls. The trim pieces will protrude ¼″ so that the siding will have room to meet flush against the framing.

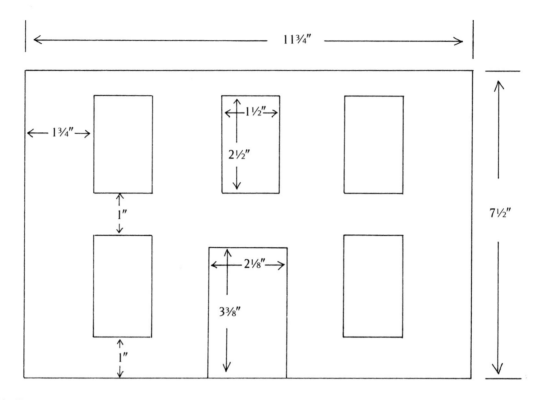

Illus. 98. Front

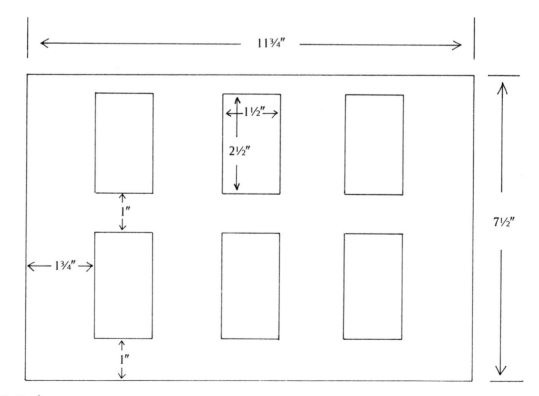

Illus. 99. Back

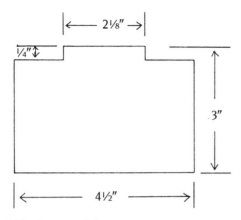

Illus. 100. *Front porch floor*

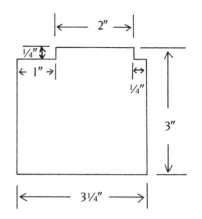

Illus. 101. *Side porch floor*

Cut each corner trim piece and sand the edges to correspond with the pitch of the roof. Glue and nail the four 7″ corner trim pieces onto front and back corners, with each trim piece extending ¼″ beyond the side.

Siding

Using the twenty-four previously cut strips, ⅛″ × ¾″ × 20″, cut and fit siding for one side at a time. Start from the bottom (overlapping the base), and glue on the first piece.

Each subsequent piece should overlap the previous piece. Glue each piece in place working upwards. Cut to fit around windows and doors, notching the piece of siding when necessary.

Roof

Determine the proper placement of the sub-roof sections. The subroof will extend about ½″ all of the way around. Then glue and nail sections into place.

If the shingles have not been cut yet, here is a reminder that it's time to cut the sixteen (16) strips from ¾″ wood that measure ⅛″ × 20″. And as stated before, you then need to cut about three hundred (300) one-inch pieces for the individual shingles.

Start from the bottom roof edge and work up. The bottom row of shingles should extend ⅛″ both below the bottom edge and just be-

yond the side edges of the subroof. Glue the first row in place, and overlap each successive row ¼″ on top of the previous row.

Make the roof cap by cutting two ⅛″ × 13½″ strips from ¾″ thick pine. Glue these in place to finish the top of the roof as can be seen in Illus. 95.

Cut four pieces, ⅛″ × ¼″ × 6¼″, for the peak trim. Cut or sand the ends to fit under the eaves.

Foundation

Assemble your 2″-wide foundation pieces. You should have eight pieces cut. Follow Illus. 102 to determine the placement of the basement windows. All the basement windows are 2″ wide and only 1″ high (Illus. 103). Cut out the windows.

Glue and nail the foundation together according to the layout of Illus. 102. Be careful to check that all the corners are square.

Apply a thin bead of wood glue to the top of the foundation, and then carefully arrange the house on top of it, overlapping the foundation as shown in Illus. 103. Make sure that the front door is above the porch section.

Porches

From ¼″-thick pine, now you will need to cut flooring for the porches, if not already done with the other items covered under Basic Cut-

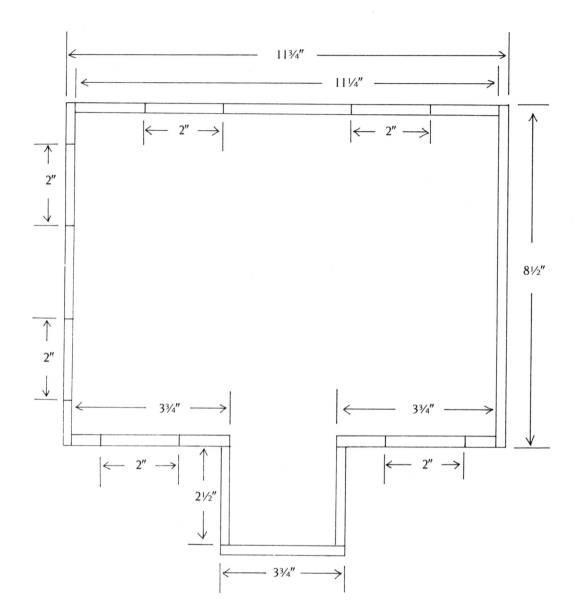

Illus. 102. Foundation

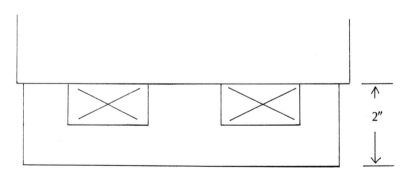

Illus. 103. Side view, house on
foundation

ting. Refer to Illus. 100 and Illus. 101 if you still need to cut these pieces.

For the side porch foundation cut a ¼″ × 2″ × 8″ piece of latticed wood. As an option you can use a piece of prelatticed wood.

To cut the lattice, turn and lock the saw blade at a 45° angle. Using ¼″ wood, make ⅛″-deep cuts. Pull the saw across the wood two times to cut a ¼″-wide gouge. Continue similar cuts every ¼″.

Turn the strip over, and repeat the process at this same angle and depth. This will leave a crisscross pattern.

From the lattice or solid wood, cut two 2″ × 2¼″ pieces and one 2″ × 2½″ piece. Also cut two ⁵⁄₁₆″ × ⁵⁄₁₆″ × 2″ pieces for support posts.

Glue the foundation to the right side of the house, to correspond with the porch flooring, following the diagram in Illus. 104.

Glue and nail both pieces of porch flooring in place.

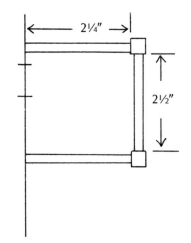

Illus. 104. Side porch foundation—top view

Steps

The dimensions of the stringers for each set of steps are given in Illus. 105 and Illus. 106. Cut two each from ¼″ pine.

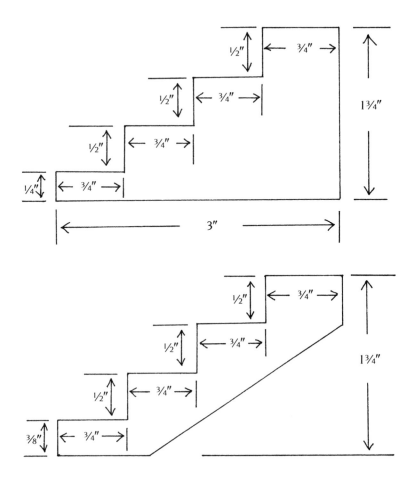

Illus. 105. Stringer, front steps

Illus. 106. Stringer, side steps

For the front porch, from ⅛" plywood, cut four steps, ⅛" × ¾" × 4½", and four risers, ⅛" × ½" × 3¾".

For the side porch, also from ⅛" plywood, cut four steps, ⅛" × ¾" × 2½", and four risers, ⅛" × ½" × 2¼".

Glue the supports in place; next glue the risers and then the steps (Illus. 107).

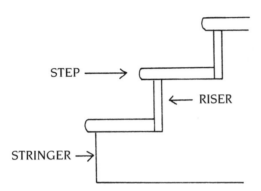

STEP ⟶

⟵ RISER

STRINGER ⟶

Illus. 107. Steps, side view

Handrails and Posts

Using the 5/16" pine, cut four posts, 5/16" × 5/16" × 1½", for the porches themselves, then cut three posts, 5/16" × 5/16" × 2⅛", for the bottom steps.

Also from 5/16" wood, cut two ⅛" × 20" strips to be used for the upper and lower handrails. Place these strips together, and tack a brad into each end to hold securely while holes are drilled for dowels.

With a ⅛" bit, drill a hole at each ¼" interval (Illus. 108). Then cut three 2" sections, one 2½" section, and three 3" sections. Separate the handrails. Then cut the ⅛"-diameter dowel into 1¼" lengths.

Glue and insert the 1¼"-long dowel pieces into the 2" sections and 2½" section, which will be used for the porch railings (Illus. 109).

In order to insert the dowels at an angle for the step rails (the 3" sections), hold a double section at an angle to the drill bit to angle

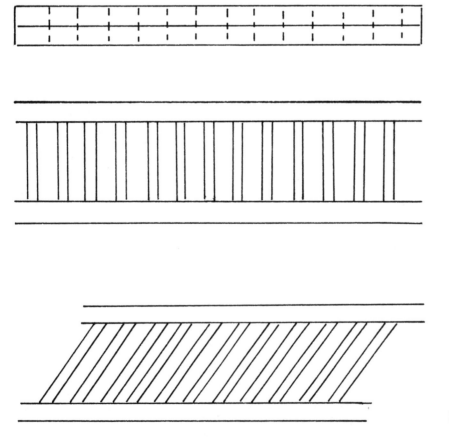

Illus. 108. Handrail assembly

Illus. 109. Railings

slightly the previously drilled holes. Repeat this procedure with each hole. If you have a drill press, it will simplify this step.

Glue and insert the dowel pieces to complete the step rails.

Glue the posts as shown in Illus. 110. Add the completed railings as shown in Illus. 95.

Window Crosspieces

Cut four strips from ¼" pine, ⅛" × 10". From these cut six 1" lengths, and twenty-one (21) 1⅜" lengths.

Sand to fit, and then glue, horizontally, one of the 1⅜" pieces into each opening of the large windows of the house proper.

Glue one of the 1" pieces vertically into each basement foundation window. All of the pieces should be positioned carefully in the middle of the window opening.

As a finishing touch, cut from the remaining siding strips to trim around the front door and above the side door.

Painting

One suggested color combination for paint, used here, is to select dark brown for the siding and antique white for the window and door trim and porch railings. Shingles can be given a grey wash (diluted). You can paint the porches and steps with brick red, and then mix some sand with red for the chimney and basement finish. This may be patted on with your finger or an old brush.

Illus. 110. Glue the porch posts in place.

Three-Storey House
❖ with Dormers ❖

This quaint country house, complete with dormer windows, is sure to be a favorite. Stained trim adds a rustic touch (Illus. 111).

Illus. 111. Three-Storey House

MATERIALS

Pine, or plywood, ¼″ thick, 12″ × 4′
Pine, ½″ thick, 6″ × 12″ (cut fourteen pieces, ⅜″ × ½″ × 12″, for windows)

Pine, ¾″ thick, 6″ × 24″ (cut twenty-two pieces, ⅜″ × ¾″ × 24″, for siding)
Plywood or panelling, ⅛″ thick, 10″ × 18″ (sub-roof)
Corner molding, ½″ × ½″ × 4′
Wood, 1⁄16″ thick, ¼″ × 16″ (peak trim), ⅛″ × 18″ (dormer trim)
Pine, ¾″ thick, 1″ × 9½″ (roof support)

Note: Thin strips, as required, for window trim and crosspieces can be purchased ready-cut at hobby and craft shops or shops that sell materials for making dollhouses and miniatures. Also available are precut shingles.

Wood, ⅛″ × ⅛″ × 10′ (cut to fit for window crosspieces)
Wood, ¼″ × ¼″ × 12″ (for roof dormer supports, dormer caps)
Roof: You will need cedar shakes to cover an area of approximately 10″ × 12″ or pine shingles made from ⅛″ × ¾″ strips (optional: you can substitute tin roof for subroof and shingles)
Brads, ¾″, No. 18, one box
Wood glue
Hide glue
Gesso
Sandpaper
Stain, light color
Acrylic paint: dark green and brick red (suggested)

TOOLS

Tabletop scroll saw
Band saw
Table saw
Tack hammer
Block plane (optional)
Drill
Drill bit, ½"
Paint brushes

INSTRUCTIONS

Basic Cutting

Following the dimensions given in Illus. 112, Illus. 113, and Illus. 114, cut the ¼" wood for the front, back, two sides, and porch.

For the window and door trim, cut the ½" wood into fourteen (14) strips, ⅜" × ½" × 12".

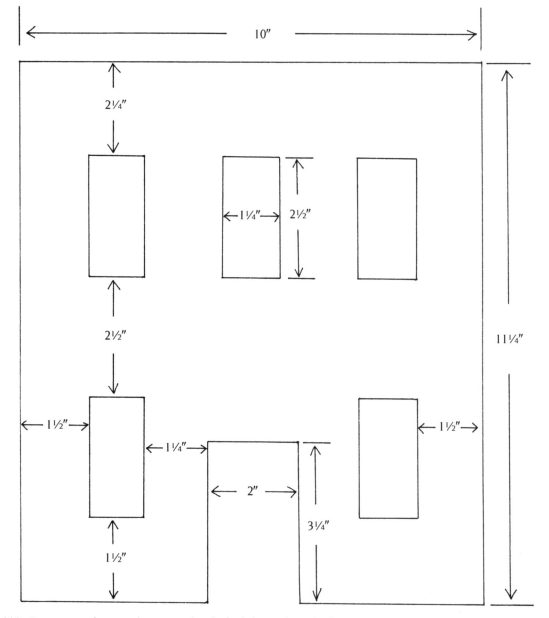

Illus. 112. *Front—use the same dimensions for the back but without the door and with an extra window.*

Then, from the ¾" wood, cut twenty-two (22) pieces, ⅜" × ¾" × 24", to be used for the siding.

From the corner moulding, cut four 11" pieces.

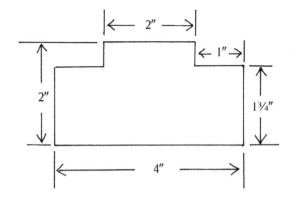

Illus. 114. Porch

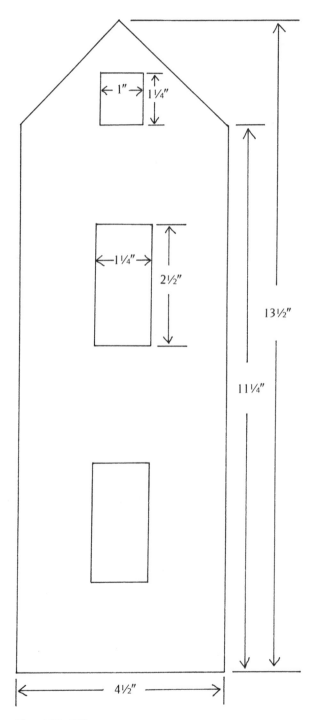

Illus. 113. Side

Windows

Draw the windows and door in place on all the main house sections. Then, using a ½" drill bit, drill a hole into the middle of the area outlined for each window.

Disconnect the blade to the tabletop scroll, then saw and slide the blade through one of the holes. Reattach the blade, and then carefully cut out the window. Repeat this procedure for each required opening.

House Assembly

Spread a thin bead of glue on the side edges of both side sections. Glue the house together so that the sides are inset into the front and back sections. Then nail the joints together using several brads for each corner.

Once the glue has set, place the house on the remaining piece of ¼" wood, leaving an adequate piece from which to cut the dormers. Pencil along the *inside* perimeter of the house, and then cut out this section for the house floor, cutting just along the outside of your pencil line. Glue and nail the floor into place. Also glue and nail the porch floor.

Stain or paint the inside of the house at this point.

Roof Support

Cut a roof support from ¾" wood. The finished piece should measure ¾" × 1" × 9½", but

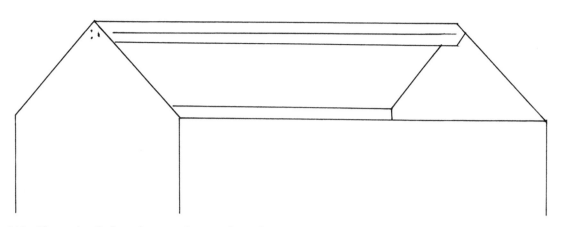

Illus. 115. *Glue and nail the roof support between the peaks.*

carefully measure the inside distance between the roof peaks before cutting.

Using either a band saw or a block plane, trim away the top edges of the support so that the shape coincides with the slope of the roof-top. Glue and nail the support into place (Illus. 115).

Attach the 11″ lengths of corner trim as shown in Illus. 111. These should be glued and nailed into place.

Window Frames

Cut, to fit, four pieces for each window frame from the ⅜″ × ½″ × 12″ strips. When you are gluing the frames, be sure the inside edge of the pieces are flush with the inside walls. Glue the frames only, since the siding remains to be added. Also attach the door frame in the same manner.

Siding

Starting from the bottom, measure and cut, to fit, pieces of siding from the previously cut strips. As you work upwards, overlap each row by ⅛″. Glue the strips of siding into place.

Peak Trim

Cut four pieces of peak trim to fit along the roof line (Illus. 116). These can be cut from remaining window strips; cut two of the strips in half lengthwise using the band saw.

Then cut, to fit, two pieces for each peak. To shape the peak ends for the correct mitred fit, hold each piece at the appropriate angle against a sanding wheel (Illus. 117). Glue into place.

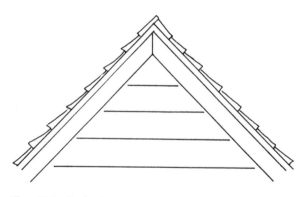

Illus. 116. *Peak trim*

Illus. 117. *Sand one end of the peak trim pieces for a mitred fit.*

Roof and Subroof

If you are going to use pine shingles, then you will need a subroof. Cut two 4½″ × 11¼″ pieces of the ⅛″ wood for the subroof; then glue and nail these in place.

If you are going to have a tin roof rather than the shingles, then there will be no need for the subroof. In that case, attach the dormers directly to the tin roof.

Dormers

From the ¼″ wood, cut four triangular dormer sides to the dimensions given in Illus. 118. Then cut two dormer fronts from the ¼″ wood, using the dimensions in Illus. 119. From ⅛″ wood, also cut four roof sections following the dimensions in Illus. 120.

Using the ½″ bit, drill a hole into the space to be cut for the window for each dormer front. Disconnect the blade to the scroll saw, and slide the blade through one of the holes. Reattach the blade, and then carefully cut out the window. Repeat this procedure for the second window.

Glue the fronts to the sides of the dormers. When dry, sand the bottom edges of the dormer to fit flush with the subroof (or tin roof). Dormer fronts should be parallel to the house front. Cut and glue window trim to fit, and then glue the dormer roof sections in place (sanding as necessary for a flush fit).

A delightful detail, which is purely optional, is to cut thin ⅛″ strips from the remaining siding strips to trim the entire dormer front.

Shingles

If you are using pine shingles, cut ⅛″ × ¾″ strips into 1″ pieces. Starting from the bottom of the roofline, glue shingles in place one row at a time, horizontally. Overlap the next row of shingles by ¼″, continuing upwards with overlapping shingles staggered by about half the width of a shingle. Shingle the dormer roofs in the same way.

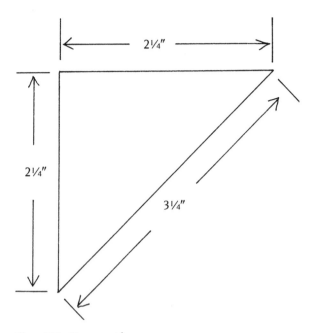

Illus. 118. Dormer side

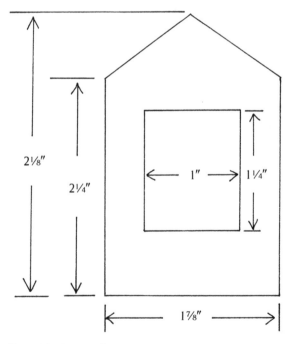

Illus. 119. Dormer front

Roof Caps

Cut two 11½″ pieces from the remaining siding strips. Cap the roof with these, cutting to fit around the dormers. Glue and nail the pieces in place.

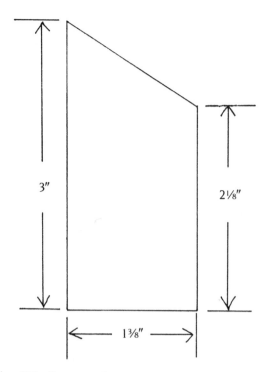

Illus. 120. *Dormer roof*

From the ¼″ × ¼″ piece, cut two 3⅜″ pieces for the dormer roof caps. Sand these to fit, and then glue them in place.

Porch Roof

From the ⅛″ wood, cut a subroof 1½″ × 2¾″. Then cut, from the ¼″ × ¼″ wood, two 1¼″ supports.

Glue the subroof, at a slant, approximately one inch above the door frame. Sand and then glue the roof supports in place as shown in Illus. 121.

When these are dry, add shingles to the porch roof in the same manner as for the main roof.

Window Crosspieces

The window crosspieces are a completely optional feature. But, if you decide to include them, you won't be disappointed by the distinctive charm they bring.

If you have not purchased precut strips for the crosspieces, cut ten feet of ⅛″ × ⅛″ strips.

Measure and cut pieces to fit each window individually, as your windows may vary slightly. Glue the horizontal crosspieces in place first, then the vertical pieces.

Even though this procedure is time consuming, it is just this sort of detail that can add the right finishing touch to the overall look of a house.

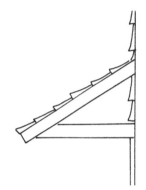

Illus. 121. *Porch roof, side view*

Painting

As a suggestion that was used here, select a dark green color for siding and a brick red color for the porch floor (Illus. 122). Stain all the remaining areas with a light-color stain.

Illus. 122. *Paint with dark green acrylic paint.*

❖ Cottage with Tin Roof ❖

This little vacation cottage features a tin roof and an old-timey front porch (Illus. 123). Try a version without siding for a simpler, more pared-down country look.

Illus. 123. Cottage with Tin Roof

MATERIALS

Pine, ¼" thick, 3½ board feet

Pine, ½" thick, 8" × 12" (cut ten (10) ⅛" × ½" × 12" pieces for shutters, window, and door frames)

Pine, ¾" thick, 8" × 12"

    (cut eighteen (18) ¾" × ⅛" × 12" pieces for siding;

    cut one (1) ¾" × ¾" × 12" piece for roof ridge; and

    cut one (1) ¾" × ¼" × 5½" piece for porch ridge)

Wood, 1½" thick, 1½" × 1½" (chimney)

Tin (or flashing), 10" × 20"

Solder

Brads, ¾", No. 18, one box

Wood glue

Hide glue

Gesso

Sandpaper

Stain, medium color

Acrylic paint: grey-blue, antique white, brick red (suggested)

TOOLS

Tabletop scroll saw

Band saw

Table saw

Tack hammer

Drill

Drill bit, ½"

Soldering iron

Paint brushes

Tin snips

INSTRUCTIONS

Basic Cutting

Following the dimensions given in Illus. 124, Illus. 125, and Illus. 126, cut the ¼" wood for the front, back, and the two sides. Also cut four ¼" × ⅜" × 5" strips for the corner trim. The base piece should be cut to roughly 5½" × 12"; however, be sure to measure the actual

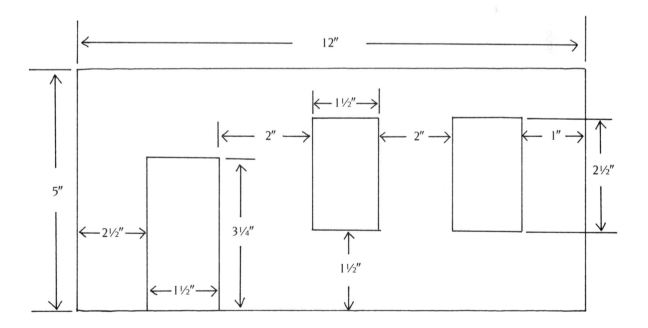

Illus. 124. Dimensions

dimensions of your main structure pieces before you cut the base, to ensure an accurate fit.

Cut the ½" wood into ten (10) strips, ⅛" × ½" × 12", to be used for the shutter, window, and door frames. Cut two additional strips, ¼"

× ½" × 12". Then cut these into four pieces, 3¼" long, for the rafters.

From the ¾" wood, cut eighteen (18) strips, ¾" × ⅛" × 12", to be used for the siding. Then cut a ¾" × ¾" × 12" piece for the roof ridge

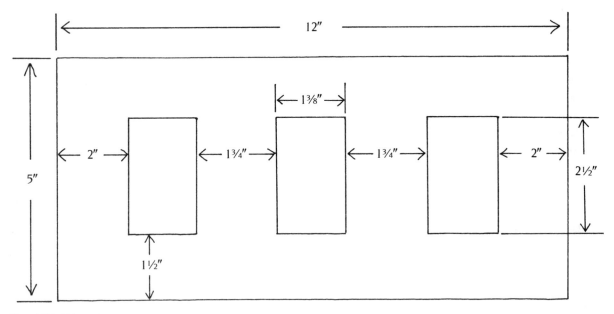

Illus. 125. Dimensions

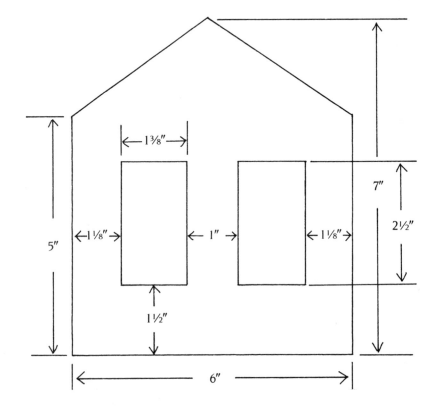

Illus. 126. Dimensions

and a ¾″ × ¼″ × 5½″ piece for the porch ridge.

Windows and Door

Again following the dimensions in Illus. 124, Illus. 125, and Illus. 126, draw the corresponding windows and door in place on all main house sections. Using the ½″ drill bit, drill a hole into the middle of the area outlined for each window.

Disconnect the blade of the tabletop scroll saw, and slide the blade through one of the holes. Reattach the blade, and then carefully cut out the window. Repeat this procedure for each of the windows, and then cut out the door opening.

House Assembly

Spread a thin layer of glue on all the edges of the base piece. Use the ¾″ brads to nail the front and back to the base. Next, spread a thin bead of glue on the side edges of both the front and back sections, and then attach the sides (Illus. 127). Nail the joints together using several brads for each corner.

Fit the ¾″ × ¾″ × 12″ piece for the roof ridge between the peaks. Glue and nail the roof ridge piece in place.

Once you've finished this stage, you are ready to stain or paint the inside of the house.

Corner Trim

Attach the 5″ lengths of corner trim to the front and back corners as shown in Illus. 127. The trim should extend beyond the side by ³⁄₁₆″. Glue and nail each corner trim piece in place.

Window and Door Frames, Siding

Cut, to fit, four pieces for each window frame from the ⅛″ × ½″ × 12″ strips, and cut three pieces for the door frame from the same strips. Glue the frames into place so that their inside edges are flush with the inside walls. You may also want to add window crosspieces at this point, similar to those shown in Illus. 123.

Working from the bottom, measure and cut to fit, pieces of siding from previously cut ⅛″ × ¾″ strips. As you work upwards, overlap each row by ⅛″. Glue each row into place as you go.

Porch

Using the dimensions given in Illus. 128, cut the porch base from ¼″ wood. Glue this piece into place.

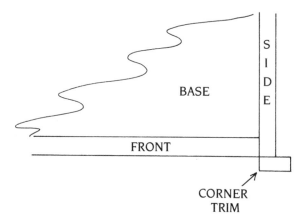

Illus. 127. *Top view of wall construction*

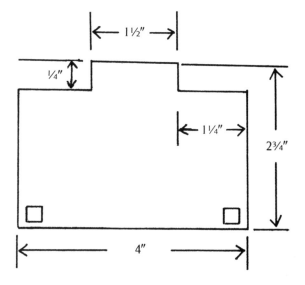

Illus. 128. *Porch base*

92

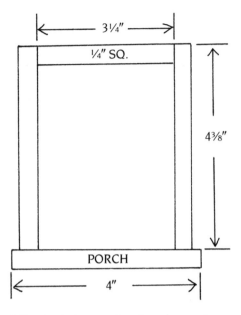

Illus. 129. Front view, porch posts and supports

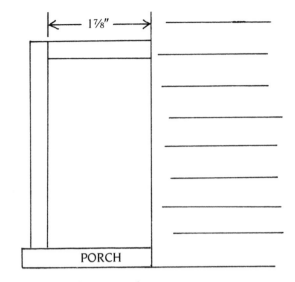

Illus. 130. Side view, porch posts

Also from the ¼" wood, cut two porch posts, ¼" × 4⅜", and the roof supports: two, ¼" × 1⅞"; and one, ¼" × 3¼". Follow Illus. 129 and Illus. 130 to assemble the posts and roof support. Glue and nail them into place.

Rafters and Porch Ridge

Cut a notch in one end of the porch ridge to make a flush fitting with the main roof ridge (Illus. 131). Notch the rafters, as shown in Illus. 132, where they will rest on the cross beams of the porch.

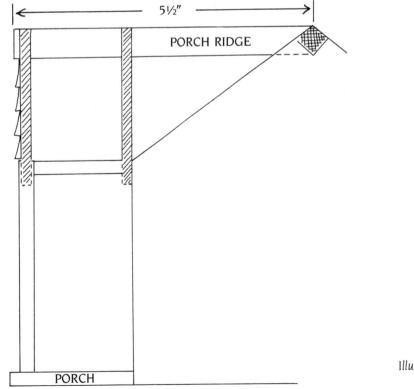

Illus. 131. Side view, porch ridge/rafters

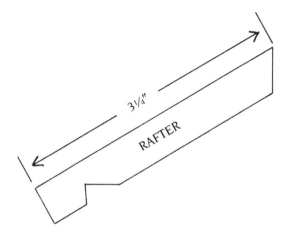

Illus. 132. Notch rafters

Glue the rafters and porch ridge in place. Basically this will be one step, because they will be supporting each other (Illus. 133).

Put siding on the front of the porch peak.

Shutters

From the remaining ½″ × ⅛″ strips, cut two shutters for each window, the length of the windows. Also cut two pieces the length of the door, plus a triangular trim piece for above the door. You can give the triangular trim piece a slight Greek revival flair by drilling a hole just below the crest, as can be seen in Illus. 123. Paint the shutters before gluing them to the house.

Painting

An option that you can consider for this charming cottage is to give the house an old crackled look. First paint the entire cottage with a thin layer of hide glue. Let this dry for four hours.

Illus. 133. Porch ridge without the tin roof

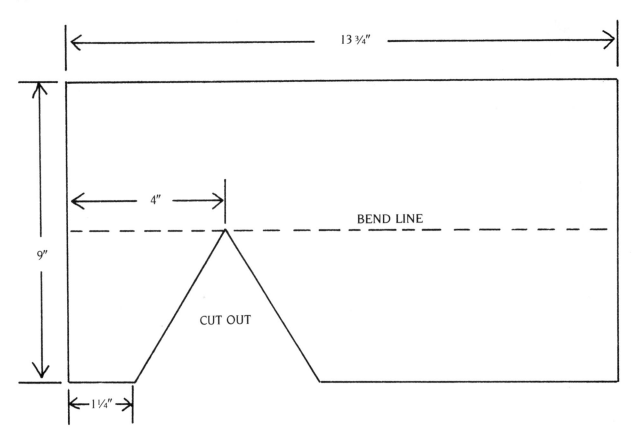

Illus. 134. *Main roof dimensions*

Mix acrylic paint with gesso (2 tablespoons gesso to 1 tablespoon paint). The more gesso you use the smaller the cracks will be.

A suggestion is to paint the house a grey-blue with antique white trim. Paint the chimney and porch floor a brick red color.

When the paint has completely dried, glue the shutters in place.

Roof

Using the dimensions given in Illus. 134 and Illus. 135, cut both of the tin roof sections with tin snips, and then make the appropriate bends to fit the roof ridges. Tack on the large roof section at all four corners. Position the porch roof so that the seams are flush with the main roof, then solder them together (Illus. 136). Tack the front porch roof corners to the supports.

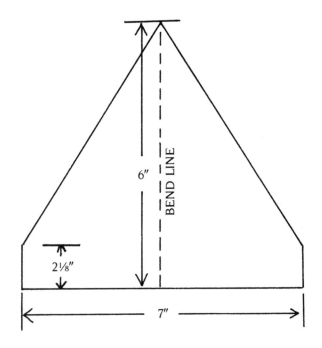

Illus. 135. *Porch roof dimensions*

Illus. 136. Soldering the tin roof

Chimney

From the 1½" × 1½" piece previously cut for the chimney, cut out a "V" to match the roof slope for a proper fit. Using wood glue, attach the chimney to the tin roof.

Porch Railing

Another optional detail that you may enjoy adding is the railings for the front porch. To make the porch railings, follow the instructions for making "Handrails and Posts" in the Two-Storey House with Basement project (page 80). Of course, adjust the dimensions for the handrails to fit the Cottage porch, but the basic steps are all the same.

❖ House with Picket Fence ❖

This is a basic little house that sits on a base surrounded by a white picket fence and a green lawn (Illus. 137). Some delightful touches to this simple but quaint country house are the hinged front and back doors, a "gate" for the picket fence, and decorative trim and an attic window for each gable.

MATERIALS

Wood, ¾" thick, 16" × 16"
Wood, ¼" thick, 10" × 6½'
Wood trim, ¼" square, 8'
Wood trim, ⅛" dental moulding, 2'
Wood, 1" × 1" square, 2¾" length

Illus. 137. House with Picket Fence

Wood glue
Brads, ¾″, No. 18, one box
Hinges, ¾″ brass; four
Flat wood plug, ⅜″; one

Tin, 9″ × 16″
Acrylic paint: off white, dark green, grey, brick
  red, thalo bronze
  (suggested)

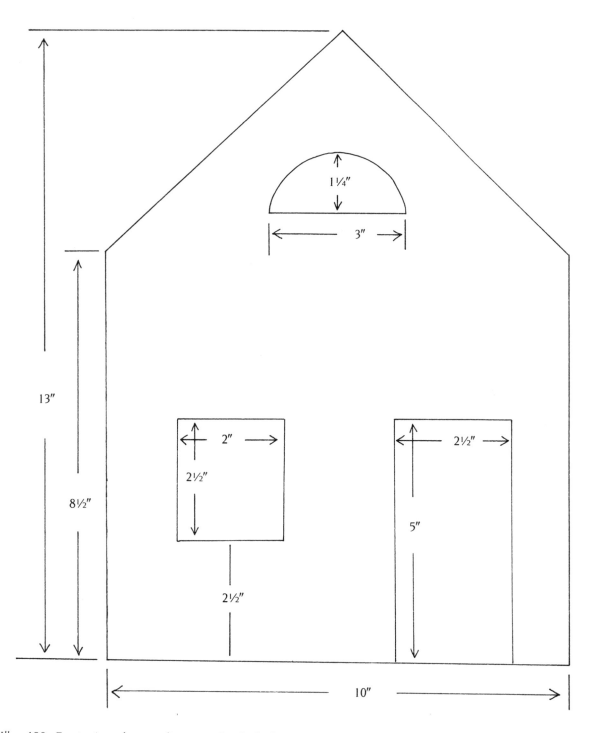

Illus. 138. Front—(use the same dimensions for the back)

TOOLS

Table, radial-arm, or band saw
Tabletop scroll saw
Drill, with ½″ bit, ¹⁄₁₆″ bit
Tack hammer
Jeweler's screwdriver
Tin snips

INSTRUCTIONS

Basic Cutting

From ¼″ wood, cut out the front, back, and the two sides according to the dimensions given in Illus. 138 and Illus. 139. Also cut out two doors, 2½″ × 5″, from this wood.

Cut a base for the fence from ¾″ wood measuring 16″ × 16″.

Windows and Doors

Draw the door and window openings on the house pieces. Then, drill a ½″ hole into the middle of the area drawn for each window opening (Illus. 140). Cut out the openings with the tabletop scroll saw.

To do this, first detach the blade, and then insert the blade through one of the holes. Reattach the blade, and cut out the window area. Repeat this procedure for each window and door.

House Assembly

Glue and nail the sides to the front and back sections (Illus. 141). Then set the structure on a piece of ¼″ wood, and draw a line around the inside perimeter to mark the base piece. Cut this piece out, and then glue and nail it into place.

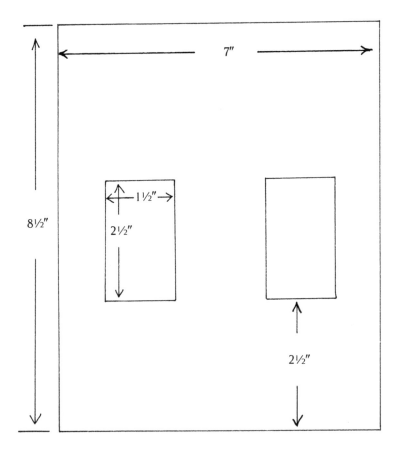

Illus. 139. Side

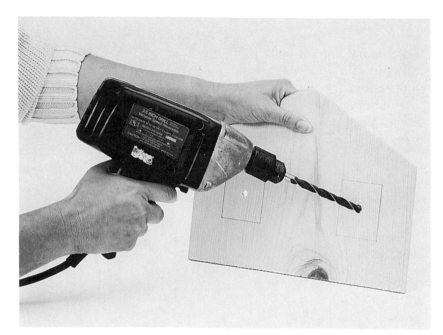

Illus. 140. Drill a hole into each window area.

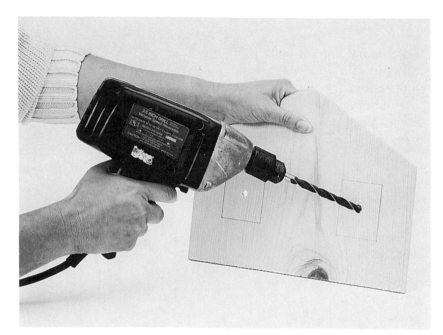

Illus. 141. Glue and nail the sides to the back and front.

Sand the doors to fit, and then attach them to the house with two hinges each. A small jeweler's screwdriver is needed for this task.

Stain or paint the inside of the house at this point.

Fence

To complete the fence, cut sixteen (16) strips of ¼" wood, ½" × 15". Keep four this length, and then cut forty-eight (48) 3½" lengths for the pickets from the remaining twelve strips. Taper these small pieces to a point at one end as shown in Illus. 142.

Glue together four sections of fence using twelve 3½" pieces and one 15" piece for each section. Glue the long crosspiece approximately one inch from the top of the picket points. Let these dry thoroughly, and then glue a section to each side of the 16" × 16" base.

Cut a ¼" strip to glue diagonally across three pickets to look like a gate (Illus. 137).

Roof

Using tin snips, cut a 9" × 16" piece of tin for the roof. Bend this piece in half parallel to the short dimension. This can be accomplished by setting the roof halfway on and halfway off a table or work bench with a sharp, 90° edge, and then pushing down on the unsupported half (close to the bend). Bend the piece partway, and then check for fit.

After you have reached the proper angle for the bend, set the roof on the house. Position it with an equal distance of overhang in the front and the back. From underneath draw a line on the tin against the front and back overhang.

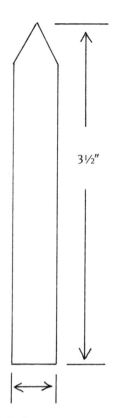

Illus. 142. *Pickets for fence*

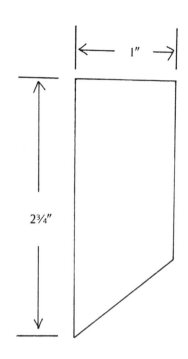

Illus. 143. *Chimney*

This will give you a guide for drilling tiny holes to accommodate the brads.

Drill several holes (1/16" bit) along each line, but about 1/8" in from the line. It is extremely important to check the alignment with the wood before drilling the holes.

Nail the roof in place. Then cut a chimney from 1" × 1" wood, 2¾" long. Cut one corner off to fit the angle of the roof (Illus. 143).

Trim

From the 1/4" dental moulding, cut, to fit, trim pieces for along the front roofline and across the front as shown in Illus. 137.

Use the 1/4" × 1/4" pieces to trim around the windows and door frames. Also cut crosspieces for the windows and dividers for the arched windows. Cut two front shutters from 1/4" wood, 3/4" × 2½". Glue the trim pieces in place.

Painting

Use an off-white color to paint the picket fence and the trim work. A suggested combination is to paint the house grey, the roof a dark green, and the yard a watered-down green.

The house may be glued to the yard, or it can remain freestanding.

HOUSES OF WORSHIP

❖ Traditional Church ❖

This little country church is a unique but classic shape (Illus. 144). Featured are a bell tower, high, arched windows, and an interior complete with pews and pulpit.

Illus. 144. Traditional Church

MATERIALS

Wood, ¼″ thick, 8″ × 8′
Wood, ½″ thick, 6″ × 6″
Wood, ¾″ thick, 2″ × 3″
Wood, 1½″ × 1½″, 9″ length
Wood glue
Brads, ¾″, No. 18, one box
Brass bell, ¾″; one
Wood button plugs, ⅜″, two (doorknobs)
Acrylic paint: ivory, brick, thalo bronze (suggested)
Stain, medium color

TOOLS

Table, radial-arm, or band saw
Tabletop scroll saw
Drill with ½″ bit
Tack hammer
Needlenose pliers

INSTRUCTIONS

Basic Cutting

Cut out the two sides, the front, and the back from ¼″ wood following the dimensions in Illus. 145 and Illus. 146. Also cut out the two 2″ × 5¼″ doors at this time.

Windows

Draw four windows on both of the side pieces. These windows are positioned 1" from the bottom and 1" apart. Use the dimensions in Illus. 146.

Drill a ½" hole into each window area, then, using the scroll saw, cut out each window. To do this, detach the blade and insert it into one of the holes, then reattach the blade. Make preliminary cuts to the corners (backing up to the middle after each cut) for ease in cutting out the windows.

Church Construction

Glue and nail the front and back to the sides. Then set the structure on a piece of ¼" wood. Trace the inside perimeter with a pencil. Cut out this base piece by keeping the saw blade just on the outside of the pencil line. Then glue and nail the base in place.

Pews and Pulpit

From ¼" wood, cut five pews: five 1½" × 4" pieces, and five ½" × 4" pieces (Illus. 147).

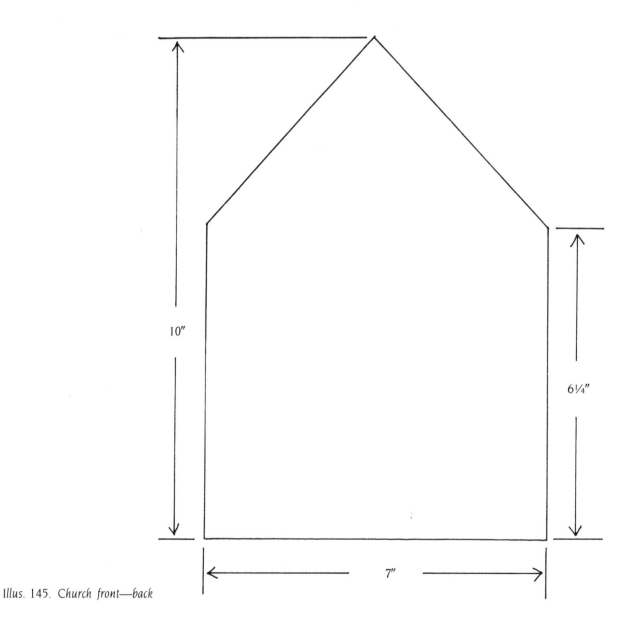

Illus. 145. Church front—back

10"

6¼"

7"

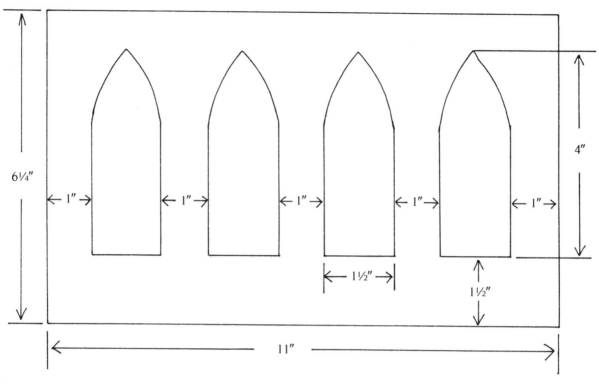

Illus. 146. Side

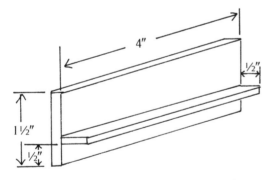

Illus. 147. Pew

Also cut, from ¾" wood, a 1½" × 3" piece for the pulpit. Cut the top at an angle as shown in Illus. 148.

Glue the ½" × 4" pieces (the seats) to the backs of the pews so that the seat is ½" from the floor. Set these aside to dry.

While the pews dry, it is a good time to stain the inside of the church. Using a brush, next paint the pews and pulpit the desired color. The color used for the project shown here is brick red.

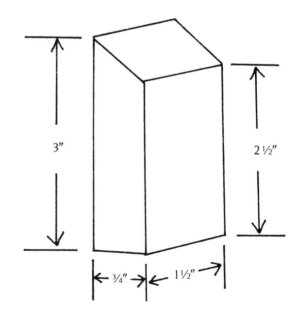

Illus. 148. Pulpit

When the stain has completely dried, glue the pulpit in the front left corner, the end away from where the doors and steeple will be.

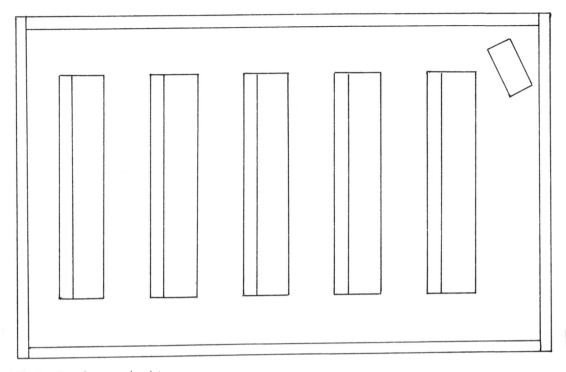

Illus. 149. *Position of pews and pulpit*

Then glue the pews in place, spacing them along the middle of the church (Illus. 149).

Roof

To make the roof, cut two 5½″ × 11¾″ pieces of ¼″ wood. Glue and nail these in place. Do not overlap them at the peak. To fill the gap, cut a ¼″ × ¼″ strip 11¾″ long. This will serve as the roof cap. Glue this strip in place along the roof line.

The Cross and Door Trim

Use ¼″ × ¼″ strips for the cross. Cut a 2″ piece and a 1¼″ piece. Notch out both pieces for a flush fit, and then glue them together.

From ½″ wood, cut trim pieces for around the door. Cut two strips, ¼″ × 5″, and a triangular piece to the dimensions in Illus. 150.

Glue the doors in place, carefully making sure they are right in the middle, and then glue the side trim pieces against the doors. Position the triangular trim piece over the doors, aligned with the roof peak and the mid-

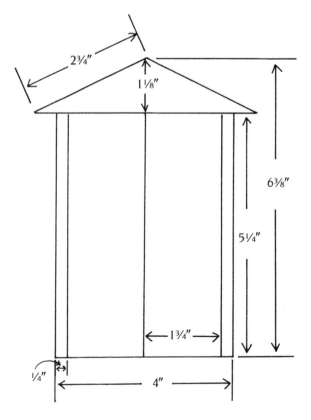

Illus. 150. *Door and trim*

dle of the doorway, and then glue it in place. Also glue the doorknobs in place.

Paint the cross with thalo bronze. Glue the cross above the doors, later, after the church is painted.

Also cut two ¼" × ¼" strips 5¼" long for trim below the roof edge for the end above the doors only. Glue them in place.

Steeple

From 1½" × 1½" wood, cut a base piece 1½" high. Cut out a V-shaped notch congruent with the roof angle. Then cut a 6½" piece from the 1½" × 1½" wood. Starting one inch from the bottom, taper both sides to a point, cutting away the excess with the band saw. Then sand the piece well to get a rounded effect.

Also cut a 1¾" × 2¾" piece from ¼" wood and four posts 1¾" high from ¼" × ¼" pieces.

Glue the notched base to the roof approximately two inches from the front of the roof. Glue the cap in place and then the posts (Illus. 151).

With needlenose pliers, bend a 1" brad on which to slide the bell. Then press the brad into the center bottom of the steeple (gripping the brad with the needlenose pliers). Glue the steeple in place on the posts.

Painting

A suggestion for colors used here is to paint the doors, roof, and roof cap a brick red. The trim is painted gold color. Paint the remainder of the church an ivory white.

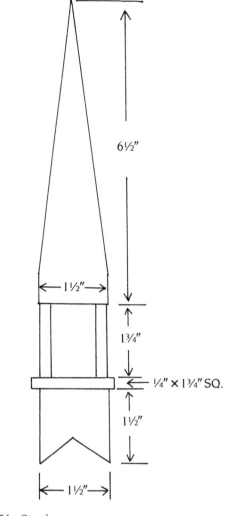

Illus. 151. Steeple

❖ Mission Church ❖

This flat-roofed, adobe church, reminiscent of Southwestern missions, is both delightful and easy to make (Illus. 152). Complete with bell, cross, and arched doors, this little church adds a wonderful accent when displayed with a Mexican folk art collection.

MATERIALS

Wood, ½″ thick, 8″ × 10½″
Wood, ¼″ thick, 8″ × 5½′
Wood, ¼″ × ¼″, 6″
Wood dowel, ⅜″ diameter, 12″

Illus. 152. Mission Church

Wood glue
Brass bell, ¾″ high
Brads, ¾″, No. 18, one box
Wood button plugs, ⅜″, two (doorknobs)
Coarse sand
Acrylic paint: light brick color, white

Tack hammer
Needlenose pliers
Small paint trowel or butter knife

INSTRUCTIONS

Basic Cutting

Using the dimensions given in Illus. 153, cut the front of the Mission Church from the ½″-thick wood. Use either a scroll saw or a band saw to cut out the step design.

TOOLS

Table, radial-arm, or band saw
Tabletop scroll saw
Drill with ½″ bit

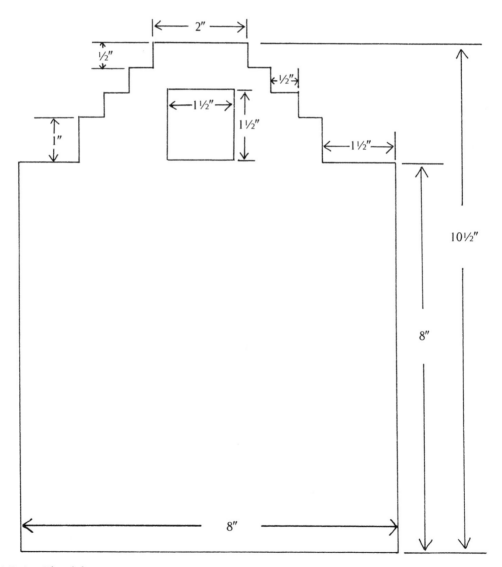

Illus. 153. Mission Church front

From the ¼″ wood, cut the back (Illus. 154), the two sides (Illus. 155), and the two doors (Illus. 156).

Windows and Bell Tower

Draw the windows and the bell tower opening on the pieces according to the dimensions given in Illus. 153, and Illus. 155. Then drill a ½″ hole into the middle of the area for each window and the bell tower.

Detach the blade of the scroll saw, and insert the blade through one of the holes. Re-attach the blade, and cut out the area for the window opening. Repeat this procedure for the remaining windows and the bell tower.

Main Structure

Glue and nail the sides to the back. Then attach the front to the sides, measuring to keep the sides parallel and the corners square since the front extends beyond both sides (Illus. 157). Glue and nail the front to the sides.

Set the church on the remaining ¼″ wood (leaving enough room to later cut out the top), and, with a pencil, trace the inside perimeter of the walls. Keep the saw blade to the outside of the pencil line to cut this piece out. Then glue and nail the floor into place.

Cut a piece for the top from the left over ¼″ wood following the outside perimeter measurements of the wall. The top will rest on the sides and back and will be flush with the front wall. The dimensions are approximately 7¼″ × 11½″, but measure the actual construction first for an accurate fit. Glue and nail the roof in place.

Side Beams

From the ⅜″ diameter dowel, cut ten 1″ lengths. Glue these to the sides, approximately one inch down from the top of the

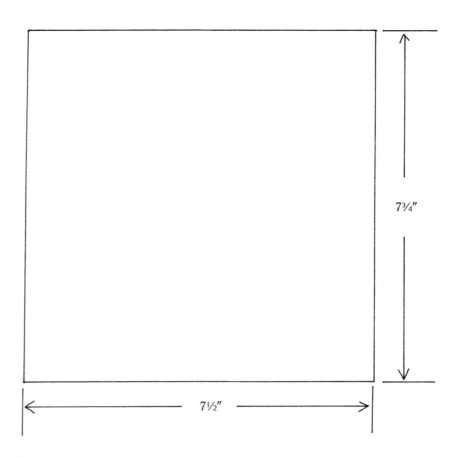

Illus. 154. Back

7¾″

7½″

111

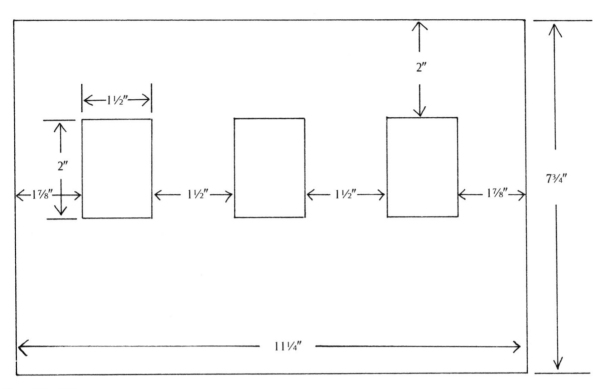

Illus. 155. Side

sides and spaced about 1⅜″ apart. Glue the middle beam first, and then measure outward.

Doors, Bell, and Cross

Cut a ¼″ × ¼″ strip of wood, and then cut it into a 2¼″ length and a 1⅜″ length. Using the band saw or scroll saw, cut a notch from both

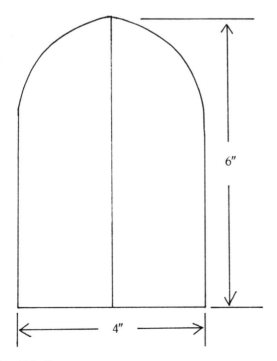

Illus. 156. Door

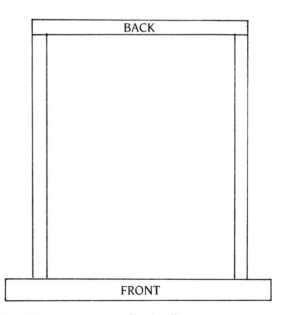

Illus. 157. Top view, assembly of walls

pieces so that they fit flush together to form the cross. Glue the pieces together.

Glue on the two doorknobs, and then paint the doors a coral-brick color along with the cross and beams. Let dry, and then glue the doors and cross in place.

Attach the bell by first bending a 1″ brad, as shown in Illus. 158. Slip the bell on the brad, and then, using needlenose pliers, push the brad into the top of the bell tower as far as it will go.

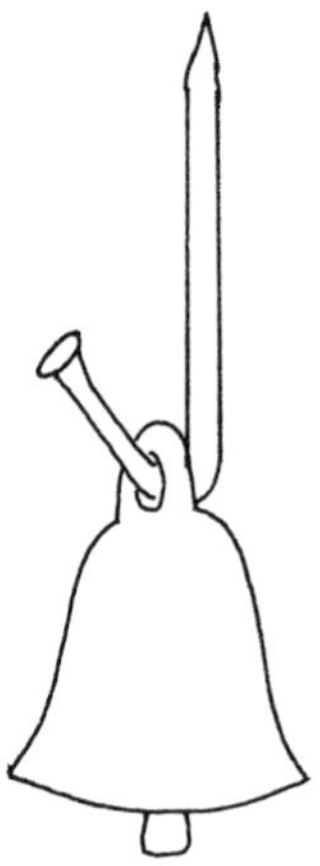

Illus. 159. Apply paint/sand mixture with a flat paint trowel or old butter knife.

Illus. 158. Bend the brad and slide on the bell.

Adobe Finish

Mix a small amount of brick-colored paint with white paint to make a light clay color (¼ brick-colored paint with ¾ white paint). Then mix in coarse sand, using ¼ sand to ¾ paint. Mix thoroughly.

Starting at the top, apply a thin layer, using a paint trowel or old butter knife. Then continue applying the mixture to the walls of the Mission Church (Illus. 159). Be careful *not* to spread it on the doors, beams, or the cross.

Only a thin layer is necessary; however, press and spread the mixture with a firm stroke to ensure adhesion. Work carefully around the bell tower and the window edges. Use a brush as needed.

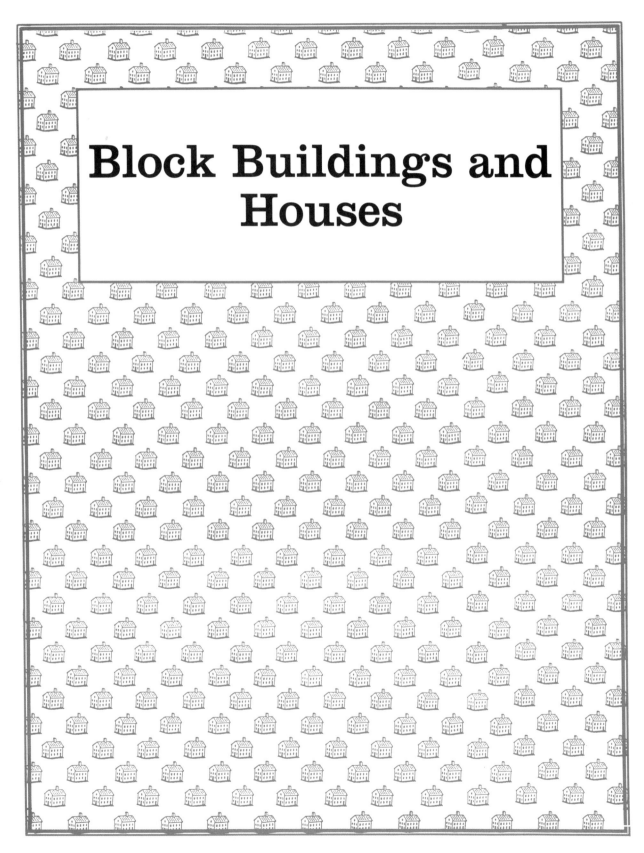

Block Buildings and Houses

❖ Block Buildings (6″–9″ High) ❖

These little buildings are simple to make (Illus. 160). The distinguishing feature is the painting that creates a special character for

Wood dowel, ¼″ diameter, 6″ length
Wood dowel, ⅛″ diameter, 8″ length
Wood, ¼″ thick, 6″ × 14″

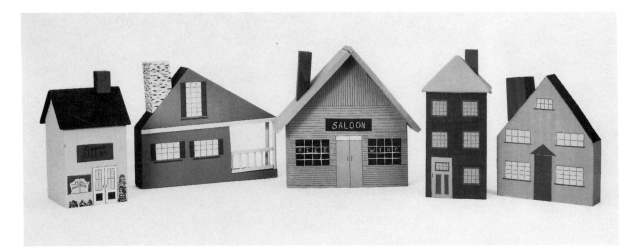

Illus. 160. Block Buildings

each building, which is completed as you wish with details for windows, doors, and signs as well as bushes or stone work.

MATERIALS

Wood, four-by-four (the name, not the actual dimensions): 14″ length
Wood, two-by-ten (the name, not the actual dimensions): 2′ length
Wood scrap, ¾″ thick (chimneys)

Luan plywood, ⅛″ thick, 6″ × 12″
Wood glue
Brads, ¾″, No. 18, one box
Sandpaper
Acrylic paint: assorted colors

TOOLS

Band saw
Tack hammer
Paint brushes
Permanent marker: black fine-tip

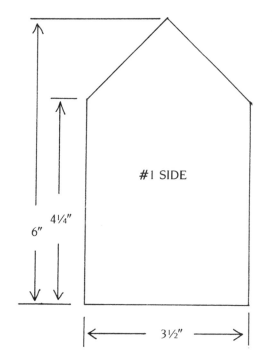

Illus. 161. #1 dimensions

Illus. 162. #1 details

INSTRUCTIONS

Basic Cutting

For this particular grouping of buildings, cut buildings #1 and #2 from the piece of four-by-four wood, according to the dimensions in Illus. 161 and 162, and Illus. 163 and 164, respectively. Use the two-by-ten length for buildings #3, #4, and #5, following the dimensions in Illus 165, Illus. 166, and Illus. 167, respectively.

From 1/8″ luan plywood, cut two 2½″ × 4″ pieces to make a roof for building #1. Cut four triangles for building #2 to the dimensions given in Illus. 168.

Use the ¼″ wood to make the roof for building #5. Cut one piece 4″ × 6″, and another 4″ × 6¼″. When the roof is attached, the longer piece will overlap at the peak.

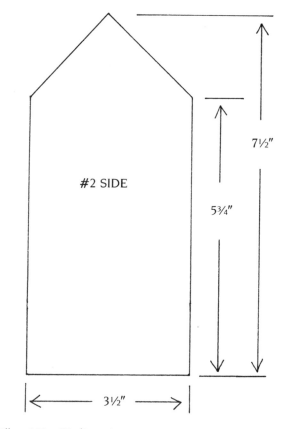

Illus. 163. #2 dimensions

Illus. 164. #2 details

Illus. 165. #3 dimensions—details

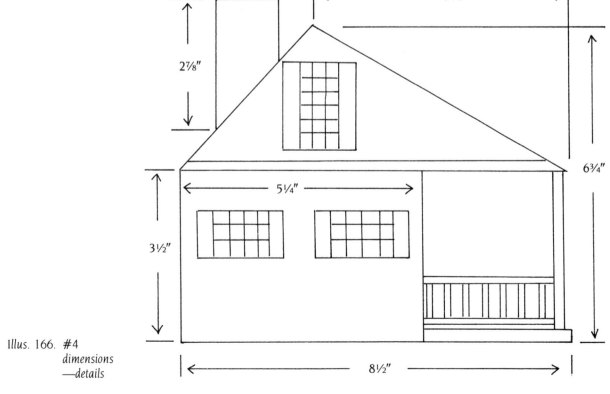

Illus. 166. #4
dimensions
—details

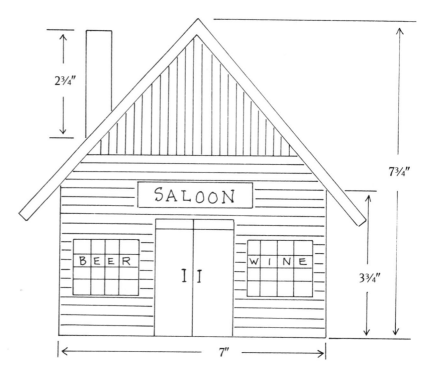

Illus. 167. *#5 dimensions—details*

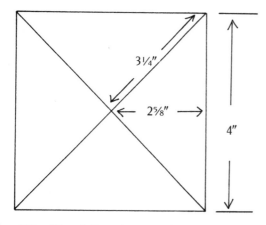

Illus. 168. *#2 roof dimensions, top view*

Roof, Chimney, and Trim

Glue and nail the roofs to buildings #1, #2, and #5. Sand the roof edges well, especially for building #2.

Cut chimneys from scraps of wood ranging from 1¼″ high (building #1) to 3″ high (building #5). Then for building #4, cut two 3″ pieces of ¼″-diameter dowel. Glue these in place as porch posts.

From ¼″ wood, cut two ⅛″ × 3″ pieces. Using a ⅛″ bit, drill six holes, equidistant, into these 3″ railings. Then cut six 1¼″ pieces of ⅛″ diameter dowel, and glue these into the top and bottom railings. When this assembly is dry, glue the railing into place.

Cut a thin strip from ¼″ wood, 1⁄16″ × 8½″, to use as trim across the front of building #4. Glue and nail this strip in place.

Painting

You can paint the block buildings the following suggested colors:

Building #1 — Light grey, black roof, red chimney, red and black trim

Building #2 — Dark green, gold roof, red chimney, red and gold trim

Building #3 — Gold, black roof, red chimney and door, cream windows

Building #4 — Dark grey, red roof, speckled chimney (resembling stone), red and white trim

Building #5 — Tan, tan roof, red chimney, black and white trim

Draw details (window panes, doors, etc.) with a black, permanent, fine soft-tipped marker.

❖ Tiny Block Village (1″–2″ High) ❖

This village is tiny enough that it looks great displayed above a door frame (Illus. 169). Tiny buildings and houses can be made from scraps of wood of any size. These range in size from 1⅛″ to 2″ in height and ¾″ to 1½″ wide.

MATERIALS

Wood scraps, ¾″ to 1″ thick
Wood scrap, ¼″ thick (tree cutout)
Sandpaper
Acrylic paint: assorted colors

TOOLS

Band saw
Paint brush
Permanent marker: black fine-tip (optional)

INSTRUCTIONS

Cutting

Cut small rectangles of wood, of various sizes, from the scraps of wood.

Also cut trees from the ¼″ wood scraps (Illus. 170) and bases for the trees.

Then draw the desired roof slope on the side of each rectangle. Some can be steep, some slight. The church roof, in particular, should be long and steep. Cut away the excess.

Painting

Paint these tiny houses in assorted colors; paint the roofs with contrasting colors.

Illus. 169. Tiny Block Village

Make windows using a very fine paint brush, just touching the tip to the house. If you prefer, you can use a fine-tip permanent marker to draw the windows. Also paint a small door for each tiny building.

Illus. 170. Tiny buildings—tree

Open-Front House

❖ Unfurnished House ❖

This little open house can be furnished simply or elaborately (Illus. 171). It is sturdy and can withstand many hours of play.

MATERIALS

Wood, ½″ thick, 8″ × 9′
Plywood, ¼″ thick, 16″ × 24″
Wood, ¾″ thick, 8″ × 24″

Wood, two-by-four, 2¼″ length (optional chimney)
Wood, ¼″ thick, 4″ × 12″
Wood glue
Printed paper, 8 square feet (dollhouse wallpaper or small print wrapping paper)
Brick sheeting, 7½″ × 11″ (dollhouse brick or substitute a linoleum sample)
Rubber cement

Illus. 171. *Unfurnished open-front house*

Brads, 1", No. 18, one box
Acrylic paint: medium blue, dark red (suggested)
Stain, medium color

TOOLS

Radial-arm or table saw
Band saw
Tack hammer

INSTRUCTIONS

Basic Cutting

From ½" wood, cut: two sides, 7½" × 9"; one floor, 7½" × 23"; one attic floor, 7½" × 23"; one wall, 7½" × 8"; and two roof sections, 8" × 14½".

Also cut a back from ¼" plywood according to the dimensions given in Illus. 172.

Assembly

Glue and nail the sides to the floor and to the attic floor sections (Illus. 173). Then glue and nail the center wall in place, making it equidistant from both outside walls.

Attach the plywood back at this time, also using glue and nails. Join the roof sections to the house after first sanding or angle-cutting the roof section edges so that they will join in a tight fit. The roof sections will overhang the front by about ½" (Illus. 174). Glue the peaks together, while also gluing and fitting the sections to the back. Lay the house on its back until the roof pieces are dry. Then nail the roof pieces from the back.

An option you may want to include is a chimney cut from the two-by-four wood to measure 1" × 1½" × 2¼". Cut this piece to fit the roof slope. Glue the chimney into place.

Next, cut four pieces of ½" wood, ⅜" × 8⅞", to be used as corner trim. Glue this trim to the side corners, flush with the front and back.

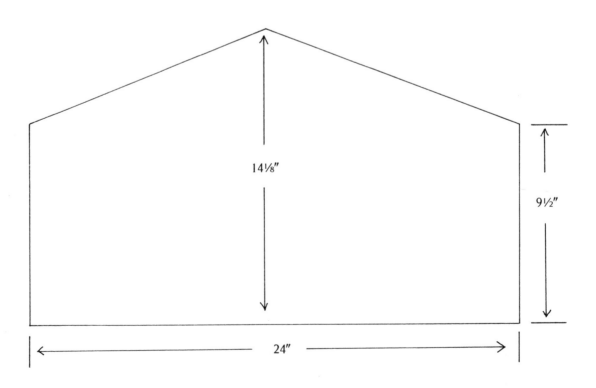

Illus. 172. Back, ¼" plywood

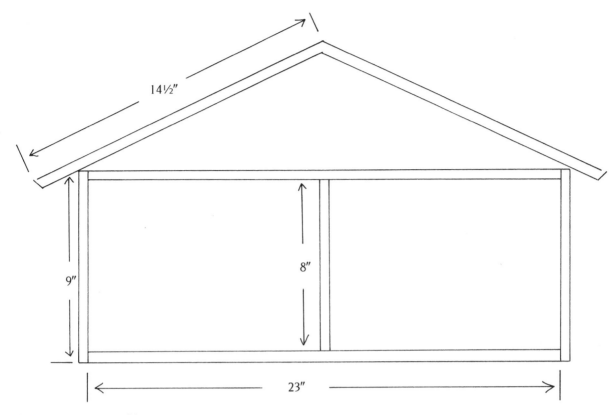

Illus. 173. Front view of house

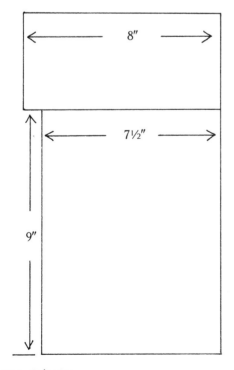

Illus. 174. Side view

Shingles

From ¾″ wood, cut fifteen ¹/₁₆″ × 24″ strips. Then cut these strips into 1″ pieces to be used as shingles for the roof.

Starting from the bottom, glue a row of shingles in place, extending over the lower edge about ⅛″. Glue the next row in place, overlapping the first row by ⅛″. Stagger each row of shingles as you work upwards.

When both sides are finished, cut a roof cap from ½″ wood measuring ¼″ × 8½″. Glue this piece across the roof peak.

Siding

To make the siding, cut ten ⅛″-thick strips from the ¾″ wood, 24″ long. Cut these again into twenty-eight (28) 6½″ strips, measuring first to verify the exact size needed.

Working on one side at a time, glue the first piece of siding flush with the bottom between the corner trim. Overlapping the first piece by ⅛″, glue the next piece in place, and work your way upwards in this manner.

Floors

To begin putting the finishing touches on this open-front house, you can follow the suggestions of staining the attic floor and the floor of the room on the left. To add variety you can put a brick or linoleum floor down in the other room.

Wallpaper and Trim

Cut variously patterned paper to fit all of the inside walls. Then attach the pieces using rubber cement since it will not buckle the paper.

An optional touch that really adds a feeling of finished detail is to add inside trim. From ¼″ wood, cut twelve ¹⁄₁₆″ × 12″ strips. Cut these, to fit, for ceiling trim and baseboard trim. Paint the trim and set it aside to dry before gluing it into place. Use a paint color to set off the trim from your choice of wallpaper.

Painting

One suggestion, used here, is to paint all of the outside walls and edges a medium blue color. The chimney is best painted a dark red to give the impression of brick. As with all of the projects, you may be as creative as you would like with the choice of colors and decorations, as well as with the details you choose to include or add and options you decide to take.

METRIC EQUIVALENCY CHART

MM—MILLIMETRES   CM—CENTIMETRES

INCHES TO MILLIMETRES AND CENTIMETRES

INCHES	MM	CM	INCHES	CM	INCHES	CM
⅛	3	0.3	9	22.9	30	76.2
¼	6	0.6	10	25.4	31	78.7
⅜	10	1.0	11	27.9	32	81.3
½	13	1.3	12	30.5	33	83.8
⅝	16	1.6	13	33.0	34	86.4
¾	19	1.9	14	35.6	35	88.9
⅞	22	2.2	15	38.1	36	91.4
1	25	2.5	16	40.6	37	94.0
1¼	32	3.2	17	43.2	38	96.5
1½	38	3.8	18	45.7	39	99.1
1¾	44	4.4	19	48.3	40	101.6
2	51	5.1	20	50.8	41	104.1
2½	64	6.4	21	53.3	42	106.7
3	76	7.6	22	55.9	43	109.2
3½	89	8.9	23	58.4	44	111.8
4	102	10.2	24	61.0	45	114.3
4½	114	11.4	25	63.5	46	116.8
5	127	12.7	26	66.0	47	119.4
6	152	15.2	27	68.6	48	121.9
7	178	17.8	28	71.1	49	124.5
8	203	20.3	29	73.7	50	127.0

Index

128

REVISED and EXPANDED
10th Anniversary Edition

The New Social Story™ Book

by Carol Gray

FUTURE HORIZONS INC.

Arlington, Texas

All marketing and publishing rights
guaranteed to and reserved by:

FUTURE HORIZONS

721 W. Abram Street
Arlington, TX 76013
Toll-free: 800-489-0727
Phone: 817-277-0727
Fax: 817-277-2270
Website: *www.FHautism.com*
E-mail: *info@FHautism.com*

Cover and interior design © TLC Graphics, *www.TLCGraphics.com*
Cover: Monica Thomas; Interior: Erin Stark

Photos courtesy of *iStock.com*

Publisher's Cataloging-In-Publication Data
(Prepared by The Donohue Group, Inc.)

Gray, Carol.
  The new social story book / by Carol Gray. -- Rev. and exp. 10th anniversary ed.

  p. : ill. ; cm. 1 CD.

  Accompanying CD contains the text of the social stories in both Microsoft Word and PDF formats. Includes bibliographical references and index.
  ISBN: 978-1-935274-05-6

1. People with mental disabilities--Education. 2. Autistic children. 3. Developmentally disabled children. I. Title. II Title: Social story book

LC4717.5 .N48 2010
371.92

Printed in Canada

This book is dedicated to Alex Gilpin,
in memory and celebration of his wonderful
and incredible life story.

In Appreciation: The People of Social Stories™ History

I initiated the Social Story™ approach nearly twenty years ago. Since then, I have met thousands of wonderful, talented, interesting people. I am very impressed by the company that Social Stories™ keep. This book is the sum of their efforts, and I am grateful to each of them. Here, I'd like to describe the contributions of a few of them. I believe they are excellent representatives of the people—from all walks of life and all areas of Planet Earth—who write, read, or support Social Stories™—and add to their history each day.

Eric and Tim. Separated by fifteen years and 150 pounds difference in their silhouettes, Eric and Tim were both on my consultant caseload as the school year began in the fall of 1990. Eric was close to leaving his program at the high school; Tim was entering kindergarten. Eric and Tim never met, yet they each played an important role in Social Story™ history. A conversation with Eric caused me to see things from a far more accurate perspective; it was a paradigm shift. I was determined to put what I had learned from Eric into practice. One week later, I wrote the first Social Story™ for Tim. In my time, I've had many teachers; to date, however, Eric and Tim have been the most influential.

My husband, Brian. In the fall of 1990, I was having a lot of success writing stories for students on my caseload. To say I was hesitant to share that success with others is definitely an understatement. Despite my many protestations, which sprang from my innate shyness, my husband, Brian, encouraged me to share the success of Social Stories™ with others. The result was the first presentation on Social Stories™ in Indianapolis, Indiana. There was plenty of interest in my presentation, but I hid in my hotel room for the remainder of the conference. Two complete days of room service! Brian has been my coach—and, as always, my best friend—throughout the unique twists and turns of Social Story™ history.

Joanna Carnes and Barrett Gray. Brian and I are blessed with two incredible children, Joanna and Barrett. They definitely know—and are a big part of—Social Story™ history. Looking back, I'm impressed by their patient, calm support.

Joanna's maiden name is Gray, of course. She is now married to Mark, and they are the parents of our grandson, Ryan. Joanna may not realize this, but her comments have helped to bring this book to completion. At a critical point in the development of the manuscript, I was beyond overwhelmed; there were too many Stories, not enough minutes in the day—and too many other demands. Joanna listened to my frustration and, with a calm confidence that I will never, ever forget, she said, "You have to set some limits. Sometimes, you just have to say, 'That doesn't work for me right now.'" Suddenly, I saw them: the things that did not work alongside the goal of completing this project. I am very grateful to her, and I have been happily saying, "That doesn't work for me," (at the right times, of course) ever since. She's right. It works.

My son, Barrett, attended some of my earliest presentations. I remember one in particular, in Albuquerque. Barrett had the stack of evaluations in hand as we drove north from the conference. A hazy purple thunderstorm framed the horizon. Barrett was reading the comments on the evaluations to me. The majority of them were great, but it was the critical statements I took to heart. Praise didn't count. Barrett decided to throw the evaluations with negative comments into the back seat. Don't get me wrong—I value constructive criticism and feedback. But whenever I encounter criticism that I think is especially undeserved, in my mind I see a crumpled piece of paper, heading for the back seat, illuminated by flashes of lightning against a purple evening sky. Years later, over a glass of wine in a local bar, Barrett transformed the original Social Story™ ratio into the current Social Story™ Formula.

Joy Garand and Edna Smith, Ph.D. After the first presentation on Social Stories™ in Indianapolis, I met Joy Garand, a young special education teacher from Ohio, and Edna Smith, Ph.D, at the time Director of Missouri's Project ACCESS. Joy had attended my Indianapolis presentation, and she wrote to me a few months later to share her success with Social Stories™. I remember being surprised—not only did Social Stories™ work for me in Michigan, they were now working in Ohio, too! Joy and I co-authored the article, "Social Stories™: Improving the Responses of Students with Autism with Accurate Social Information," and Edna helped us submit it to the journal *Focus on Autistic Behavior*, where it was published in 1993. Meeting Joy and Edna led to the formal introduction of Social Stories™ to the field of autism.

Dr. Tony Attwood was one of the earliest professional supporters of Social Stories™. Tony contacted me for feedback on a portion of his new manuscript, titled, *Asperger's Syndrome: A Guide to Parents and Professionals.* He wanted to be sure that his description of Social Stories™ was accurate. Just as I had been surprised by Joy's success with Social Stories™, I was intrigued that a noted autism professional, from another country, was writing about my work. Not only that, but Tony genuinely understood Social Stories™. His description expanded my own understanding of them. (Today, Tony is a valued friend of mine, and I deeply respect his contributions to our field. I was thrilled and honored when he agreed to write the Foreword to this book.)

Diane Twachtman-Cullen, Ph.D., CCC-SLP introduced me to *Wayne Gilpin,* President of Future Horizons. Diane encouraged Wayne to sit in on one of my earliest presentations. At first, I don't think Wayne believed that stories could have such a positive impact. I was impressed that he stayed and listened to my entire presentation that day … and changed his mind. Ultimately, he offered to print and distribute the very first book of Social Stories™, titled *The Original Social Story Book*—even though it had been turned down by several other publishers.

The Gray Center for Social Learning and Understanding (TheGrayCenter.org) is a non-profit organization that serves people with autism spectrum disorders and those who work on their behalf. Led by Laurel Falvo, Executive Director, The Gray Center has been the official home of Social Stories™ since its inception in 1998. The Gray Center provides many resources and services. Among them is the distribution of accurate information about Social Stories™, and multi-faceted efforts to protect the quality and the integrity of the approach.

Keith Lovett, Director of Autism Independent (UK) brought Social Stories™ to the United Kingdom, and has sponsored Social Story™ workshops ever since. Keith is concerned for the education and welfare of people on the autism spectrum, and that includes protecting the quality of the instructional techniques that are used on their behalf. If Social Stories™ had a dad, it would be Keith. He looks out for the approach, informs me of any misinterpretations of it, and has steadfastly worked to ensure that high-quality Social Story™ workshops are held on his side of the Atlantic.

Team Social Stories™ is an ever-growing number of presenters who work with me to conduct quality workshops worldwide. I remember when I was working for Jenison Public Schools, and I was talking with the personnel director. We were discussing the increasing number of my Social Story™ workshops and presentations. I asked, "How long can it possibly take to teach the world to write a Social Story™? This can't last forever." Now, I think it might. That's why I have recruited help from Team Social Stories™. Today we have Team members in five countries. For a current and complete list of Team Social Stories™ members, visit the Gray Center website listed above.

Melissa Andrews has been involved in Social Stories™ past and present, and will undoubtedly be a part of their future. She and I worked together at Jenison Public Schools. Today we work together in my office, scheduling workshops. Melissa reviewed a draft of this manuscript, and helped keep me sane through its completion. Melissa doesn't know this, but she makes me stop, think, and regroup, better than anyone I know.

My Cottage Friends are reflected in the pages of this book. They were the only "social norm" I had available to me this past summer, at our cottage, where most of the Stories in this book were written. I usually refer to them as the "cottage people," and they helped me research many of the Story topics. Often, I would ask them unusual questions about social concepts and skills. For example: What is the difference between a one- and a two-person hug? My questions led to discussions with little agreement, always framed by the unique personalities and unshakable mutual respect that defines this incredible group. I am blessed to have these friends in my life. I am indebted to them for their candid contributions to this book. I'd like to publicly thank Paul and Pat, Granny, Jim and Maureen, Jeff and Marci, Sheri, Andy and C, Keith and Sandy, and Prudy and Jim. They make life on Planet Earth continually intriguing and interesting, easier, and a heck of a lot of fun. In my next life, I want to have them as my friends again.

The Boy at Barnes & Noble came up to me at a critical point in the development of this book. I wish I knew his name, so that I could thank him properly. Approaching the completion of the rough draft of this manuscript, I had been writing non-stop, eyes-open to eyes-shut, for over two weeks. I needed a change of writing venue, so I decided to head to the Rivertown Crossings Mall near our home. I worked on location. It was there that I wrote the Stories in this book about the up escalator and eating at a food court. I decided to head to Barnes & Noble, to write a Story about eating in a quiet bookstore café. However, the place was wall-to-wall people. I couldn't get to the café. So I sat down in an overstuffed chair, took out my laptop, and wrote the Story, "This Place is Busy!"

That's when he appeared: a boy about nine years old with curly brown hair. He was on his own—with his mother nearby—and approached me. Well, no, he approached my computer. He had many of the qualities of children on the autism spectrum. He read what I had written on the computer screen, looked up and around, and then turned to me and asked, "Does it help you to write a story about what is going on here?"

I was at a loss for an answer. I have it now. Yes, it does. Writing Stories about what is going on helps me because of the wonderful people, the incredible people, that it introduces me to. People like those whom I have listed here, people like the boy at Barnes & Noble, and people whom I have never met … but I know I would like if I did. Social Stories™ do keep the best company, and I have been—and will continue to be—honored to work alongside them.

The New Social Story™ Book, 10th Anniversary Edition
© by Carol Gray, Future Horizons, Inc.

Table of Contents

Foreword

Carol Gray originally developed Social Stories™ in 1991 from working directly and collaboratively with children with autism and Asperger's Syndrome. For nearly twenty years, she has been modifying the guidelines for writing Social Stories™, based on extensive personal experience and feedback from parents, teachers, and the children themselves. The ideas and strategies have matured over the years and Social Stories™ have now been examined independently in numerous research studies published in scientific journals. There is no doubt that the use of Social Stories™ in education and therapy is what scientists describe as "evidence-based practice." Social Stories™ really do work.

Whenever I learn that Carol Gray is working on a new publication, I become quite excited in anticipation of reading her latest insights into how children with an autism spectrum disorders perceive and experience the world. I know that her innovative ideas and strategies will be incorporated into my clinical practice, and that I will be recommending the latest publication to teachers, parents, and colleagues. As I read the manuscript for the *The New Social Story Book*, I thought, "Carol, you have done it again!" She has written another exceptional resource that will improve not only social understanding but also self-understanding. Carol has remarkable insight into the world of autism and the neurotypical world, and her Social Stories™ are for members of both—improving mutual understanding, communication, and acceptance.

This book is complementary to Carol's other publications and provides examples of Social Stories™ that can be used without modification, or adapted and edited to suit a specific child and his or her unique abilities and circumstances. I recommend *The New Social Story Book* for those who are new to the area of autism and Asperger's Syndrome as a parent, teacher, therapist, or psychologist, and also for those with considerable experience writing Social Stories™. I often refer to my copy as a source of guidance and inspiration when I am working with a child who has Asperger's Syndrome.

From her extensive experience of working with children, parents, and teachers, Carol knows the problem areas—the "hot topics." These include coping with change, making mistakes, specific situations (such as attending a birthday party or being an airline passenger), and managing and expressing emotions. Carol chooses her words very carefully. Great thought, wisdom, and talent went into this new publication. There are some parts I will always remember, in particular the statement, "Adults are children who kept getting older," and the Social Story™ for when "some gifts are disappointing." I know that children with an autism spectrum disorder and neurotypical adults alike will enjoy and appreciate the comprehensive explanations and the sage advice in *The New Social Story Book*.

TONY ATTWOOD, PH.D.

How To Use This Book

I wrote this collection of Social Stories™ with you and the child or adolescent in your care (I refer to them as the "Audience" of your Stories) continually in mind. You may use the Stories in a variety of ways. They may be used directly from the book, or as a pattern to develop Stories of your own. This brief introduction will acquaint you with the resources in this book, specifically the Stories, the companion CD, and the Social Story™ 10.1 Tutorials.

This book contains 158 Social Stories™ that I wrote either for students I was working with directly, or for fellow parents and educators. The Stories are divided into chapters according to their subject matter: Learning with Stories, Change, Mistakes, Me and My Feelings, Celebrations and Gifts, People Skills and Friendship, Bullying, Understanding Adults, Home and Community, School, and Planet Earth. Whereas some chapters focus on specific contexts, others focus on some of the most challenging issues facing children with autism spectrum disorders. I did my best to include the Stories most requested by parents and educators, and ones that I felt, from my personal experience, had helped children the most.

Some of the Stories in this book are designed to be used in groups, in sequence. The Fort Able Stories (#30-38) describe an imaginary comfort zone (Come to Fort Able=ComFortAble). Each Fort Able Story describes a "room" in a "fort." The bullying Stories (#74-82) are intended to be read/completed chronologically as well.

One of the most exciting attributes of this revised edition is the companion CD. On the CD, there are two sets of Stories. The first set includes all of the Stories in Adobe PDF format, exactly as the Stories appear in this book. You can print Stories for individual use in the home, or include a Story in a classroom presentation to teach a skill to a group of students—and those are only a couple of examples. (Copyright permissions/restrictions are explained in detail on the CD.)

The second set of Stories on the CD includes all of the Stories in Microsoft Word format, but it does not include the colors and graphics from the book, only the unformatted text. This allows you to select a Story in the book, open the corresponding Word file on the CD, and make changes to tailor the Story to the needs of your Audience. I wish we could have included the photos in this version, too, but copyright restrictions prevented us from doing so. In the end, it will benefit the student if you add *custom* photos and/or images that the student recognizes and can relate to. This can greatly increase the effectiveness of the Story. (I discuss this further in the Social Stories™ 10.1 Tutorials.)

Conversely, be aware that some students' reactions to the imagery can *negatively* impact their understanding of a social situation or skill. They may think that the Story applies to the child in the picture, but not to them. So if your child or student thinks very concretely, and has difficulty generalizing the skills, you may want to use only the Stories in Word format, customized with his or her experiences, and use the pre-illustrated Stories from the book for your reference only.

When you are working from the CD, you will find that the Stories in Word format provide you with the ability to customize in numerous ways. You can:

- Change fonts and/or font size
- Use alternate vocabulary that will be more effective for your Audience
- Add additional text to further describe and/or explain the subject matter, or to cater to your Audience's experiences
- Include references to Audience interests, perhaps using a favorite character to demonstrate Story content (only if you are certain that the fictional character will not be confusing or misunderstood by the Audience)
- Use photos or high-interest images to illustrate your Story
- Incorporate activities or additional visual supports to demonstrate or cue Story meaning

This is not a complete list—the possibilities are endless!

While most of the Stories can potentially be used as they are written, there are some Stories in this book that *have* to be revised before they are shared with your Audience. These are Stories that were written for a fictional character (e.g., Trevor, Mason, Fletcher) that include sample descriptions of past events. You will need to review those Stories for ideas, and then edit the corresponding Word file on the CD, replacing existing details with your Audience's experiences. The individualized Story will make the most sense to your Audience if it is written from a first-person perspective, as though Audience is talking.

Many of the Stories in this book are intentionally "over-written." They may include more text or longer sentences than I typically use when writing for students on my caseload. I did this to provide you with as many ideas and phrasing options as possible, while still maintaining sound Story structure. You, in turn, may review a Story and determine that it's ready to use with the person you are caring for. Or you may decide to revise it, in which case you should have enough text to shorten and/or personalize the Story as you see fit.

To shorten and simplify a Story, I suggest using only the first sentence of each paragraph and deleting the others. (This strategy only works with *some* of the Stories, so use your best judgment.) The one-sentence paragraph structure is great for kids who are younger, chronologically or developmentally (this book is intended for children between the developmental ages of 6 and 12). Other options to simplify a Story include omitting commas to create two separate sentences, or splitting one Story into two or more Stories.

You will undoubtedly have many ideas of your own for developing a Story that will meet the unique needs, abilities, and interests of your Audience. The following Social Story™ 10.1 Tutorials are designed to teach you the art and science of writing a Social Story™. They will help you develop Stories that are not only meaningful, but also enjoyable to work on (for both children and adults!). The tutorial section will be your own Social Story™ workshop, for you to complete at your own pace. It includes an introduction to the tutorials, detailed descriptions of the ten newly revised Social Story™ criteria, and a practice activity for each criterion. Once you've successfully read and completed the activities for all ten criteria, you will be able to write effective Social Stories™ for those in your care. Still, I recommend referring to the criteria often during your writing process for ideas and support. I also encourage you to attend an official Team Social Stories™ training, where you can refine your Story writing and practice your skills with others.

Whether you are a beginner or an experienced author of Social Stories™, this book is designed to support your continued learning. You may decide to research Social Stories™ further on the web, but please use your discretion with regard to content if you refer to Social Stories™ on the internet. Above all else, the 10.1 criteria work to ensure Audience safety. There are only three web addresses that I recognize for Social Story™ information. They are my own website (*CarolGraySocialStories.com*), The Gray Center for Social Learning and Understanding website (*TheGrayCenter.org*), and Future Horizons' website (*FHautism.com*). While other sites may imply my involvement, it simply is not the case. Be sure to look for my name explicitly and the trademarked Social Stories™ to ensure that the information and stories found there reference Social Stories™ as they are defined in this book.

If you find this book helpful, I welcome you to explore its companion resources. *Comic Strip Conversations* uses simple drawings to illustrate interactions and explore social events, concepts, and skills with students. *No Fishing Allowed*, a peer violence prevention program, puts the strategies from the bullying Stories into action. My team and I have also created a DVD titled *Storymovies*™. A Storymovie™ is a Social Story™ illustrated with a short movie. Each is shot on location, merging descriptions of social concepts and skills with footage of live situations. (Stories in this book that have corresponding Storymovies™ available have a "scene slate" icon near the Story number.)

Thank you for your interest in Social Stories™. I am glad that this book has fallen into your good hands! Have fun exploring the Stories, completing the tutorials, and discovering the limitless uses of the CD. I sincerely hope that this resource will come to your aid, like an old friend, when you need support, and become a trusted volume in your library for many years to come. Best wishes to you and your Audience!

Social Story™
10.1 Tutorials

Introduction to the Social Story™ 10.1 Tutorials

Welcome to the Social Story™ 10.1 Tutorials! This chapter is your introductory guide to writing Social Stories™ according to the current 10.1 criteria. You will learn the basics of the approach so that you can write Social Stories™ for those in your care. As you know, I wrote the Stories in this book for students with autism spectrum disorders (ASD). The Stories will also help you. I will be referring to them frequently as you read and complete each tutorial.

A Social Story™ describes a situation, skill, or concept according to ten defining criteria. These criteria guide Story development to ensure an overall patient and supportive quality, and a format, "voice," and relevant content that is descriptive, meaningful, and physically, socially, and emotionally safe for the Audience. The criteria define what a Social Story™ is, and the process that researches, writes, and illustrates it.

In this chapter, the criteria are discussed in a series of ten tutorials. Work through them in sequence. Each tutorial opens with a brief definition of the criterion in italics, followed by a short discussion, activity and answers, and final notes. Answers are discussed in the text immediately following each activity. For this reason, complete each activity before reading further. It's also important to read the closing notes of each tutorial. They are not always a simple summary. As titled, they are final notes. They may contain information not previously mentioned, or suggest an additional exercise. Finally, it is not necessary to complete all of the tutorials in one session. In fact, it may be preferable to spread them out a bit, perhaps completing one each evening.

The 10.1 criteria are titled to make them easy to memorize. This makes it possible for Authors to develop a Social Story™ without having to turn to this book each time.

The 10.1 criteria are:

1. One Goal
2. Two-Part Discovery
3. Three Parts and a Title
4. FOURmat
5. Five Factors Define Voice and Vocabulary
6. Six Questions Guide Story Development
7. Seven Types of Sentences
8. A Gr-eight Formula
9. Nine Makes It Mine
10. Ten Guides to Editing and Implementation

After completing each tutorial, try to list the titles of the criteria that you have completed from memory. Occasionally, I will remind you to do that! By the time you finish all ten tutorials, I am confident that you will have them memorized.

SOCIAL STORY™ VOCABULARY

First, it's important to establish some basic Social Story™ vocabulary. This vocabulary is designed to save time, so that Authors (that's you!) can efficiently focus on the task at hand.

- *Author:* The Author is you, the person who researches and develops a Social Story™. The Author may also be someone else, or a team of parents and professionals. Authors adhere to ten criteria that define each Social Story™ and the process that creates it. Due to the Author's specialized skills, the word *Author* is always capitalized when it is used in reference to Social Stories™.

- *Audience:* The Author writes for a specific *Audience.* This is most frequently a child, adolescent, or adult with an ASD. Each Social Story™ is developed with consideration of several individual factors, including but not limited to the age, gender, abilities, personality, preferences, and/or interests of the Audience. *Audience* is always capitalized when it is used in reference to Social Stories™.

- *Social Stories*™: The definition of Social Stories™ appears in the second paragraph of this introduction. Any time the term *Social Story*™ is capitalized, it refers to a Social Story™ that meets all of the current 10.1 criteria. This distinguishes *Social Stories*™ from "social stories" (lower case) that may not meet the criteria. When the term is used in these tutorials, it refers to Social Stories™ and Social Articles™. Social Articles are the more advanced counterpart of Social Stories™. They are often written for students who are older or academically more advanced. Social Articles adhere to the same criteria as Social Stories.

- *Story:* Any time the word *Story* is capitalized, it refers to a Social Story™ that meets all of the current 10.1 criteria. It is simply a truncated version of the term above, *Social Story*™. Similarly, the capitalized *Story* distinguishes it from other stories (lower case) that may not meet the criteria.

- *Team:* The Team includes parents and professionals, all those working together on behalf of an individual with ASD. Due to the specialized nature of this group, and the unique issues that they encounter and address, *Team* is always capitalized.

ACTIVITY

It is likely that you've already had some experiences with Social Stories™. Maybe you have read one, written one, heard about one, seen one, or been in a room with one. I've developed a short exercise for you. Is this a Social Story™? Complete the activity first, and then continue reading.

Introduction Activity: Is This a Social Story™?

Directions: *Read the Story below. Is it a Social Story™?* ❏ Yes ❏ No

Many people write Social Stories™. You may want to learn how to write Social Stories™, too. Then you will be able to write Stories for the students in your classroom. You'll have fun at the same time!

You may use the tutorials in this chapter to learn about the ten criteria that distinguish Social Stories™ from other visual strategies. Work through each tutorial at your own pace. Have fun!

Answer: This is not a Social Story™. It contains errors that deviate from the ten criteria. Here are three of them:

- Every Social Story™ has a title that represents the topic. In addition, Social Stories™ use sound story construction, using an introduction, body, and conclusion. This story does not have a title, and the delineation of an introduction, body, and conclusion is unclear.

- Social Stories™ contain first- and/or third-person statements. Second-person statements, or "you" statements, are not allowed. This story contains several second-person statements.

- Social Stories™ are accurate and unassuming. Thus, a phrase like, "You'll have fun at the same time," would not appear in a Social Story™. The phrase assumes the experience of the Audience; it is a guess that may or may not be true.

These are common errors. In my work, I have reviewed several stories that people refer to as "Social Stories" that deviate from the criteria, or ignore them altogether. The term *Social Stories* is often used carelessly to refer to anything put into writing for a person on the autism spectrum. As a result, there is a lot of misinformation that ultimately threatens the quality and safety of this important instructional tool.

To get a "feel" for this approach, randomly select a few Stories in this book. As you read them, note the title, introduction, body, and conclusion; the omission of second-person statements, and the overall patient quality of each. The Stories in this book have additional characteristics in common as well. We'll be discussing each of their shared characteristics in the following ten tutorials.

FINAL NOTES

I want to personally thank you for taking the time to learn more about Social Stories™. In doing so, you are helping us protect the quality and integrity of this important educational intervention. I sincerely appreciate your efforts. In return, I will do my best to support you as you work to learn the art of researching and writing Social Stories™.

The 1st Criterion: The Goal

DEFINITION

The goal of a Social Story™ is to share accurate information using a process, format, voice, and content that is descriptive, meaningful, and physically, socially, and emotionally safe for the Audience. Every Social Story™ has an overall patient and reassuring tone.

ACTIVITY

Unlike the other tutorials, this one begins with an activity. Complete the activity. Then, read the answer and the rest of the tutorial.

Criterion 1 Activity: The Goal

Directions: *Reread the definition of the goal in italics at the beginning of this tutorial. Then answer this question:*

Is the goal of a Social Story™ to get the Audience to do what the Author or Team wants him/her to do? Check one: ❑ Yes ❑ No

Answer: The most common misconception is that the goal of a Social Story™ is to change Audience behavior. This has never been the case. The goal of a Social Story™ is to share accurate information meaningfully and safely. Admittedly, it is often a behavior that draws attention to a specific concept, skill, or situation. However, if our goal were simply to change behavior, we would likely focus on "telling the child what to do." The chances are that the Audience has already been told what to do, perhaps many times. Instead, the focus is on the underlying causes of frustration or misinformation. Authors work to identify and share information that supports more effective responses. The theory is that the improvement in behavior that is frequently credited to a Social Story™ is the result of improved understanding of events and expectations.

DISCUSSION

Every Social Story™ has an unfaltering respect for its Audience, regardless of the topic. Read the Story in this book titled, "Why People Take Baths or Showers" (p. 152). Many parents and professionals have difficulty helping the children, adolescents, or adults in their care understand the importance of personal hygiene. This Story addresses that topic with careful phrasing. Third-person statements describe the importance of bathing in general, without pointing an accusing finger at the Audience. Also, the Story incorporates historical facts and a bit of humor, to make the content interesting and fun. Other Stories in this book use similar strategies, all geared to sharing information accurately, respectfully, meaningfully, and safely.

The physical, social, and emotional safety of a Story is an Author's first concern. In terms of physical safety, consider the following example. A mom writes a story for her son, Harrison, about swimming at the beach. She includes a photo of Harrison in the water. There is no one else in the photo. Dad was right next to the child when the photo was taken, although he was out of the range of the viewfinder. Interpreted at face value—through the eyes and mind of Harrison—the photo may seem to give him permission to swim alone. To be discussed later, Authors of Social Stories™ work to develop literally accurate text and illustrations. This supports clarity and meaning. As demonstrated in the story for Harrison about swimming, literal accuracy is important to his physical safety as well.

Social safety is equally important. Mrs. Barnes, a first-grade teacher, writes a story for Adam, age six. She includes the following statements about her class: "We're all friends here. Friends cooperate with friends." Adam reads the story and goes out to recess. Two "friends" from his class approach him, and tell him to pull down his pants. Working from the information in the story, that these two classmates are friends and friends cooperate with one another, Adam complies with their request. He's confused as they turn, laughing, and walk away. Adam's story was inaccurate. Classmates in a classroom are not all friends. Mrs. Barnes did not write a Social Story™. With all good and noble intentions, she wrote a socially unsafe story.

In my experience, among the most frequent Author mistakes are statements in a story that threaten emotional safety. Here are some examples from the story archives: "I often interrupt," "Sometimes, I hit other children," and, "I often don't listen when people are talking to me and that's rude." To be discussed in greater detail later in the 5th Criterion Tutorial, self-deprecating statements, or negative references to the Audience, are not allowed in a Social Story™. They threaten self-esteem in the immediate sense, without providing the Audience with any information about alternative responses, and the rationale behind them. In addition, using the Audience voice —i.e., first-person statements—in reference to negative behavior models the use of self-deprecating statements, and is at the same time disrespectful of the Audience.

FINAL NOTES

The goal that supports every Social Story™ is representative of the remaining criteria. The 2nd, 3rd, and 4th criteria refer to the process of researching, developing, and implementing a Story with sound Story content, construction, and a meaningful format. The voice of every Story is defined by the 5th criterion, and is directly related to its characteristic patient and reassuring tone. The descriptive quality of every Social Story™ is the focus of the 6th, 7th, and 8th criteria. Meaning is critically important in a Social Story™, and the 9th criterion contributes to it by engaging Audience interest. Finally, the 10th criterion ensures that the process that carefully researches and develops every Story is reflected in its implementation. In the remaining tutorials, each of these criteria will be discussed in more detail.

The New Social Story™ Book, 10th Anniversary Edition
© by Carol Gray, Future Horizons, Inc.

The 2nd Criterion:
Two-Step Discovery

DEFINITION

Keeping the goal in mind, Authors gather relevant information to 1) improve their understanding of the Audience in relation to a situation, skill, or concept, and/or 2) identify the specific topic(s) and type(s) of information to share in the Story.

DISCUSSION

Social Stories™ are documents that are worthy of the trust of their Audience. To accomplish this, Authors need to complete two steps. First, they gather accurate information. (Sometimes, in the process of gathering information, an Author discovers a solution and a Social Story™ is not needed.) Next, they identify the topic and types of information that will be shared in the Story.

Unfortunately, this criterion is frequently dismissed or overlooked. Many Authors fail to realize how this criterion can make the difference between an ineffective story, and a Social Story™ that "hits the nail on the head." In addition, among the ten criteria, this one is a "lead domino" that contributes to Story quality early in the writing process. It has a direct impact on the remaining criteria.

GATHER INFORMATION

The original rationale for Social Stories™, now increasingly supported by first-hand accounts and research, is that a child or adult with an autism spectrum disorder (ASD) may frequently perceive social events differently. This requires Authors to "abandon all assumptions" in favor of considering Audience learning style, abilities, interests, and challenges, and their collective impact on social understanding. In other words, Authors try to determine what an event may look, feel, smell, or sound like—or how a concept may be perceived—from the Audience point of view.

It is important to gather information prior to identifying a specific topic. Prematurely deciding on a topic threatens to limit the search for information far too early in Story development. Instead, Authors begin with a general targeted situation or topic area, gather information, and then discover the specific topic and Story focus within it. Getting the sequence right on this one—gathering information first, prior to identification of a specific topic or title—saves the Author time and the Audience frustration.

The Team is an important source of information. The Author discusses the targeted situation, concept, or skill with all Team members. Each member of the Team is likely to have different and valuable expertise and perspectives. Involving the Team early in Story development keeps everyone "on the same page," and avoids duplicate efforts. It's certainly okay, and often necessary, for the Author to write the Story on his or her own. The Team will be consulted once again to provide feedback on a draft of a story prior to implementation.

At least two observations are required. The first, from a third-person "fly on the wall" perspective, gathers information about the relevant cues that define a situation or concept. The second observation places the Author ("I") in the middle of the action, where the experience is continually considered in terms of Audience perception and cognition.

In the course of gathering information, a topic is often discovered. Topic discovery is preferable to topic invention. When a topic is "discovered," the roots of Audience confusion, misinformation, or challenge become readily apparent, and the topic is obvious. Invented topics, in contrast, are an informed guess that is based upon gathered information. Sometimes, Authors have no other choice but to use an invented topic. As the following example describes, however, topic discovery is preferred.

Andrew, a student in Mrs. Clark's first-grade class, struggled in math. Only once had he raised his hand for help. As his consultant, I was curious as to why Andrew had given up on the hand-raising process. I decided to try drawing a picture with Andrew to learn more. We drew about what happened when Andrew raised his hand. While doing so, Andrew said, "I'm never going to raise my hand again. My teacher doesn't know anything about math." I asked why he felt that way. "Well, I raised my hand. Mrs. Clark came over and said, 'Okay, Andrew, what's the first number?' Mrs. Gray, she doesn't even know her numbers!" The Story topics became clear. I wrote two of them. One described what his teacher knows. It included copies of her diploma and first-grade math assignments that she had completed. The second Story explained why teachers ask questions when they already know the answers. Immediately after reading both Stories, Andrew began raising his hand once again. Based upon my experience, discovered topics are, quite frankly, the absolute best! They tailor Author efforts and often result in Stories with an immediate and positive impact.

A final important note about topics: 50% of all Social Stories™ must applaud what the Audience is doing well. In this book, the Story, "Using 'Excuse Me' to Move Through a Crowd" (p. 101) is an example. The rationale is simple. Given that Social Stories™ are helpful in teaching new concepts and skills, they may also be just as powerful in adding meaning and detail to praise. What a wonderful way to build self-esteem! These ten criteria apply to Stories that praise, the same as they do to other Stories, including the requirement to gather information. If Authors write stories that describe only challenging situations, concepts, or skills, they are ignoring an important and required part of the writing process. They are not writing Social Stories™.

TYPES OF SOCIAL STORY™ INFORMATION

There are three types of Social Story™ information: *The News, Ways to Think about the News,* and *Connections and Implications.* There is definite overlap among them. For our purposes, it's important to distinguish them from one another. Each has a specific focus and role in a Social Story™.

The News is objective information that describes the targeted situation, concept, or skill. The News often introduces a Story topic, and also describes relevant cues throughout the text. For example, a Social Story™ about an invitation to a birthday party may start with: "I am invited to Angela's birthday party. She is going to be six years old." Later, we will talk about Descriptive Sentences. They are objective statements. As fact-oriented, assumption-free messengers, Descriptive Sentences are perfect for describing The News.

Ways to Think about the News is information that describes how to effectively process The News, including cognitive processing, problem solving, and/or conflict resolution strategies. Continuing with the example of an invitation to a birthday party, Ways to Think about the News retrieves relevant past experience: "To guess what we will eat and do at Angela's party, I may try thinking of other parties. Last year I went to Tracey's party. There was a cake. We played games." In addition to mentioning relevant past experience, this type of information may also describe strategies to help a student relax, stay in control, and/or work through challenges effectively.

Connections and Implications is information that describes the relationship between past, present, and future experiences and learning. The concluding statements to the birthday party Story draw upon past experience to make a "logical" guess about what may happen at Angela's party: "There is often a birthday cake at a birthday party. At Angela's party, there may be a _____. There are often games at a birthday party. At Angela's party, there may be _____." To build Connections and Implications into a Social Story™, an Author asks, "What has the Audience experienced that is similar to this in the past, how does that help now, and what are the future implications?" Whenever past, present, and future line up, Connections and Implications are at work.

The New Social Story™ Book, 10th Anniversary Edition
© by Carol Gray, Future Horizons, Inc.

ACTIVITY

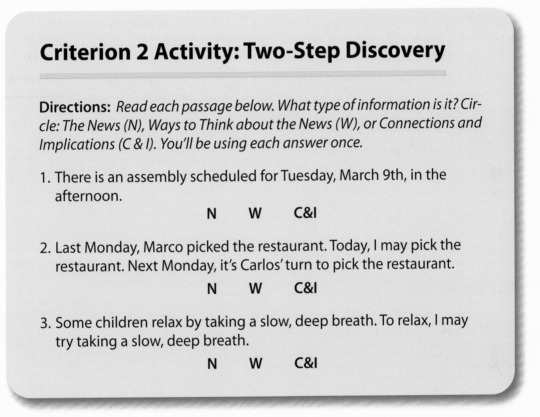

Criterion 2 Activity: Two-Step Discovery

Directions: *Read each passage below. What type of information is it? Circle: The News (N), Ways to Think about the News (W), or Connections and Implications (C & I). You'll be using each answer once.*

1. There is an assembly scheduled for Tuesday, March 9th, in the afternoon.

   N   W   C&I

2. Last Monday, Marco picked the restaurant. Today, I may pick the restaurant. Next Monday, it's Carlos' turn to pick the restaurant.

   N   W   C&I

3. Some children relax by taking a slow, deep breath. To relax, I may try taking a slow, deep breath.

   N   W   C&I

Answer: The activity contains a representative of each of the three types of information. "There is an assembly scheduled for Tuesday March 9th, in the afternoon," is a genuine newsboy, and an accurate one at that. The word *scheduled* acknowledges that while an assembly is planned, something unforeseen could happen. It's The News (N), and it is accurate. In the passage about the selection of restaurants on Monday, the past (last Monday), present (this Monday), and future (next Monday) line up. A relevant connection is demonstrated between three events that occur at different points in time. It demonstrates Connections and Implications (C&I). The final sentence describes a relaxation strategy. It does so carefully, with mention that it works for some children, without risking accuracy by implying that it will, in fact, work for the Audience. In terms of information, it's Ways to Think about the News (W).

FINAL NOTES

Two-Step Discovery is a welcome newcomer to the Social Story™ criteria. Information is its mission. It reflects the importance of gathering information prior to identification of a topic, and reminds us of the different types of information that can contribute to Story quality. Supported by the Social Story™ goal that emphasizes the importance of meaning and safety, Two-Step Discovery ensures that Authors "take great notes." Like the voice recorder of a news reporter, Two-Step Discovery helps us get the Story right, the first time.

The 3rd Criterion: Three Parts and a Title

DEFINITION

A Social Story™ has a title and introduction that clearly identifies the topic, a body that adds detail, and a conclusion that reinforces and summarizes the information.

DISCUSSION

Similar to all good stories, Social Stories™ have roots in sound structure and organization. Each one has a title and introduction, a body, and a conclusion. Recognizing the purpose of a Social Story™ and its unique Audience, these "story basics" take on increased importance. Select two or three Stories in this book to review, and note how each includes these important story elements.

Writing with the introduction, body, and conclusion in mind helps Authors efficiently identify (introduction), describe (body), and reinforce (conclusion) the most important concepts in a Social Story™. The introduction includes a clear topic sentence. For example, "If I lose a toy, people can help." Sometimes, an Author may include a sentence to recruit the Audience's attention first, prior to introducing the topic, as in, "My name is Jeremy." The body immediately follows the introduction. It adds further description and/or explanation with statements like, "Mom or Dad knows how to find my toy. We will try to think and look." The conclusion refers the Audience back to the beginning—the concepts, situations, and/or achievements that initiated the Story. It restates the original purpose with the benefit of additional information, "People can help me look for my toy." Collectively, the introduction, body, and conclusion guide the development of Social Stories™, regardless of their complexity or length.

In addition to organizing and sequencing an Author's thoughts, the structure provided by the title, introduction, body, and conclusion clarifies information for the Audience. For a typical child, knowing what a story is about first (the title and introduction) provides a frame where all subsequent details (the body) can be placed. As the story draws to a close, important details are reinforced. The same is true of Social Stories™, with one difference. The Audience has an inherent difficulty conceptualizing, sequencing, "getting the gist" or seeing the bigger picture, and applying information to their own experience. This increases the critical role of clear organization within each Story.

ACTIVITY

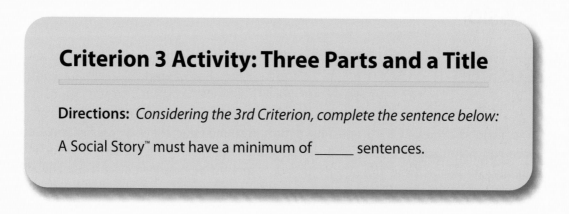

Criterion 3 Activity: Three Parts and a Title

Directions: *Considering the 3rd Criterion, complete the sentence below:*

A Social Story™ must have a minimum of _____ sentences.

Answer: In order to have a clear and meaningful introduction, body, and conclusion, a Social Story™ has a minimum of three sentences. The title, of course, doesn't count.

FINAL NOTES

Before moving on, stop a moment and try to recite the first three criteria. Yes, now—before reading a word further. They are: One Goal, Two-Part Discovery, and Three Parts & a Title. To this point, we've discussed the goal, and explored what is meant by Two-Step Discovery. We've also covered basic story structure, and discussed why every Social Story™ has Three Parts & a Title. FOURmat is next!

The New Social Story™ Book, 10th Anniversary Edition
© by Carol Gray, Future Horizons, Inc.

The 4th Criterion: FOURmat!

DEFINITION

A Social Story™ has a format that clarifies content and enhances meaning for the Audience.

DISCUSSION

In a Social Story™, the word "format" refers to the individualization, organization, and presentation of text and illustration. There are several ways to tailor text and illustration to the needs of the Audience. Several individualized factors are considered, including the length of the Story, sentence structure, vocabulary, font style/size, and the organization of the text and illustration. The art and science of every Social Story™ is selecting the format elements that are most likely to be meaningful for the Audience. In other words, format is developed from an understanding of the Audience, so that, in turn, it may help the Audience understand.

AGE AND ABILITY

The age and ability of an Audience is central to format considerations. For a younger child, the time required to peruse each page—or an entire Story—needs to be brief! Generally, a Social Story™ for a young child will contain three to twelve short sentences (eliminating commas to create two or more shorter sentences is often recommended). This matches the duration of many of their other interactions and activities throughout the day. Shorter Stories are among the most challenging to write. A struggle often ensues between the opposing goals of covering the topic, while at the same time keeping the Story brief. A good solution is to "write everything down" first, then edit the text to the desired length. Sometimes a topic will be impossible to cover in a short Story. To meet the demands of the topic and respect the attention-span of the child, information can be broken down into two or more shorter Stories. Called Social Story™ Sets, this format limits the length of each Story while making it possible to include important details and link concepts.

Longer Stories are often more suitable for older or more advanced Audiences. These Stories will contain twelve sentences or more—up to and including extensive Social Articles. Considering the often complex topics that accompany increased age and skill, having more time to explain the "ins and outs" that are involved is a welcome and necessary freedom! In this case "twenty-five words or less" isn't desirable or necessary; covering the topic takes a higher priority.

REPETITION, RHYTHM, AND RHYME

Repetition, rhythm, and rhyme may be an excellent match for an Audience who thrives on routines and predictability. These elements can capture attention, as well as infuse familiarity into a new or difficult topic. For these reasons, many Social Stories™ use rhythmic and repetitive phrasing: "On the playground, I may play on the swings, I may play on the slide, I may play on the monkey bars, or I may play with something else." Rhyme is often overlooked as Stories are developed, despite the important role that it can play. Rhyme does not have to be used throughout a Story to be effective. It may be used to emphasize just one idea. For example, "Feeling angry is okay. It's important what I do and say." Despite the potential benefits of incorporating repetition, rhythm, and/or rhyme into a Story, it's important to consider Audience preference as well. Some Audiences may regard these elements as "babyish" and thus, insulting. This brings up an important rule of thumb: never risk insulting the Audience.

ILLUSTRATION

Illustration plays a critical role in many Social Stories™. For our purposes here, illustration refers to the use of visual arts to support the meaning of text. Illustration options include but are not limited to: actual objects, photos, videos, drawings, PowerPoint presentations, figures, charts, and diagrams. At their very best, illustrations highlight and summarize information, captivate interest, and improve Audience comprehension.

The New Social Story™ Book, 10th Anniversary Edition
© by Carol Gray, Future Horizons, Inc.

Authors are as cautious with illustration as they are with text. They look for anything that may mislead or confuse the Audience. If an Audience makes frequent literal interpretations of words and statements, he or she may do the same with drawings in a Social Story™. For example, Thomas has a toileting Story. It contains plenty of eye-catching color and detail. The boy depicted in the illustrations wears a crayon-yellow shirt and blue pants, and the pictured bathroom has two small, symmetrical windows. Thomas concludes with some relief that should he ever get a yellow shirt and find himself in a bathroom with two small symmetrical windows, he may be asked to try to use the toilet. Imagine his distress with those who ask him to use a toilet without those factors in place! Thomas' literal interpretations of illustrations will not be an issue for all Audiences. For Thomas, though, minimizing the use of color or extensive detail in the illustrations may reduce the likelihood of misinterpretation.

Photographs are often used to illustrate a Social Story™. The benefit of photographs is that they 1) are accurate; 2) may communicate meaning where drawings have failed; and 3) are fast and easy to create, particularly if digital cameras are used. However, a photo may be too accurate. The Audience may assign irrelevant meaning to extraneous detail. Photographs work best when the subject is clear, and the background is free of competing detail. Black and white photographs may be more helpful than color photos, as they contain interesting subject details and minimize extraneous factors (color, for example). In addition, circling important details on a photograph can help to focus Audience attention on the most relevant aspects of an illustration.

Several factors determine the selection of illustrations for a Social Story™. Similar to choosing appropriate text, it is equally important to match illustrations to a child's ability and interests. For example:

1. Does the Audience have the prerequisite skills to use this form of illustration?

2. Will the Audience understand the representational meaning of a simple drawing?

3. Would a chart or a graph "work harder" with this content, and would the Audience understand its meaning?

4. Has the Audience previously demonstrated interest in this type of illustration?

5. Has this method of illustration captured this child's attention in the past?

6. Would a combination of two or more forms of illustration work best with this Audience?

Keeping several illustration options in mind, and considering the questions listed above, helps Authors select a method of illustration that will match the learning profile of the Audience.

ACTIVITY

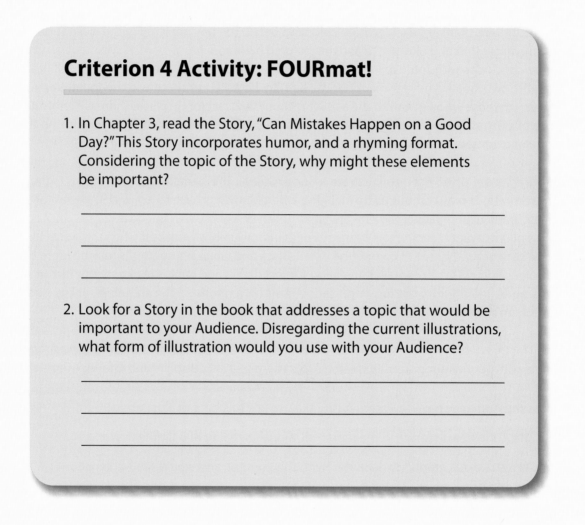

Criterion 4 Activity: FOURmat!

1. In Chapter 3, read the Story, "Can Mistakes Happen on a Good Day?" This Story incorporates humor, and a rhyming format. Considering the topic of the Story, why might these elements be important?

_____

_____

_____

2. Look for a Story in the book that addresses a topic that would be important to your Audience. Disregarding the current illustrations, what form of illustration would you use with your Audience?

_____

_____

_____

Answer: Accepting and responding effectively to change is difficult for many people, and that is especially true for many people on the autism spectrum. For this reason, "Can Mistakes Happen on a Good Day?" uses the elements of humor, rhythm, and rhyme to surround the topic with a predictable format.

FINAL NOTES

If the ten Social Story™ criteria were the United States, the 4th Criterion would be Alaska. It's big. There are many possible formats and variations, countless ways that an Author can improve the odds of effectively reaching the Audience. Creative Authors will discover—as they translate each new topic into a meaningful format—that despite the required adherence to ten criteria, writing Social Stories™ offers unlimited possibilities. The best Authors understand this potential, and discover something new about the approach with every Story that they write.

The 5th Criterion: Five Factors Define Voice and Vocabulary

DEFINITION

A Social Story™ has a patient and supportive "voice" and vocabulary that is defined by five factors. These factors are:

1. *First- or Third-Person Perspective*

2. *Positive and Patient Tone*

3. *Past, Present, and/or Future Tense*

4. *Literal Accuracy*

5. *Accurate Vocabulary*

DISCUSSION

In the last tutorial, the 4th Criterion focused on tailoring a Story to the Audience, including the arrangement of text and illustration. The 5th Criterion picks up where the 4th Criterion leaves off, listing five additional factors that relate to Story "voice" and vocabulary. These five factors contribute to the characteristic patient and reassuring quality that distinguishes Social Stories™ from social scripts and other similar visual strategies.

FIRST- OR THIRD-PERSON PERSPECTIVE STATEMENTS

Selecting an effective perspective from which to share the information in a Social Story™ is important, and a pre-requisite to placing any words on paper. A few factors impact this decision, and ultimately determine the Story's voice.

Many Social Stories™ are written in a first-person voice, as though the Audience is describing the situation, event, or concept. This presents information from an Audience vantage point. This increases Author responsibility. It's important to take extreme care not to carelessly "put words into the mouth" of the Audience, particularly when it is not representative of the Audience's experience. For this reason, statements like, "I will like recess," are presumptuous and potentially inaccurate, and not suitable in a Social Story™. Even though a Story is written in the first-person voice, it is quite likely that it will contain both first- and third-person perspective statements.

A Social Story™ may be written from a third-person voice, similar to a newspaper article. These Stories, referred to as Social Articles, may borrow format elements from newspapers, using columns, advanced vocabulary, and/or Times New Roman font to minimize any "babyish" or insulting quality in the text. Social Articles are often developed for an older or more advanced Audience.

POSITIVE AND PATIENT TONE

A Social Story™ uses positive language. This is very important in descriptions of behaviors, especially those that are typical or desirable in a given situation. A person with an autism spectrum disorder (ASD) is more likely to be challenged, corrected, and re-directed far more frequently than his or her peers. By clearly describing desirable responses and the rationale behind them, Authors provide suggestions about what to do in a given situation.

Social Stories™ keep the self-esteem of the Audience safe. For example, sentences like, "I have difficulty listening to my teacher," or "Sometimes when I am angry, I hit people," provide little usable information. Authors never use the Audience voice in reference to his or her negative behavior. Instead, an Author may describe a specific negative behavior in general, without "pointing a finger" specifically at the Audience. In addition, information about learning more effective responses is also included.

For example, an Author may write, "All children have difficulty with interrupting at times. With practice, they learn when to talk and when to listen." This maintains a positive tone, even in light of a negative topic. It helps to build and preserve the positive self-esteem of the Audience, while sharing what may be new social information.

PAST, PRESENT, AND/OR FUTURE TENSE

People readily use information from their past to build self-esteem, solve problems, and anticipate likely outcomes. In Chapter 1 of this book, the Story "Learning with Stories" (p. 6) describes three positive past experiences of the Audience to demonstrate that stories teach. Past experiences are also important to problem solving, where previous solutions may apply to a current challenge.

Finally, just as "history repeats itself," the past helps us make predictions about what may happen next, important in relieving anxiety and being ready for the next task or activity. For these reasons, Authors may include references to the past, and use the past, present, and/or future tense in a Social Story™.

LITERAL ACCURACY

An Author selects words, phrases, and sentences that are accurate, even if interpreted literally. Many people with ASD make "face value" assessments of phrases and statements, without the additional meaning that social insight provides. For this reason, a Social Story™ contains the clearest language possible, where there is no difference between intended and stated meanings. If the meaning of a word or phrase changes if it is interpreted literally, it is not used. The only exception to the requirement of literal accuracy relates to the use of metaphors and analogies. Metaphors and analogies may be used in a Social Story™ if they are meaningful for the specific Audience. Outside of analogies and metaphors, a Social Story™ clearly and accurately describes its topic.

ACCURATE VOCABULARY

Authors use the most accurate, hard-working vocabulary possible. In a Social Story™, *accurate vocabulary* refers to words that most efficiently represent the Author's intended meaning. Two considerations apply. The first is related to the use of positive language. Positive verbs are preferable to their negative counterparts. For example, instead of:"I will try not to run in the hallway," it is better to use:"I will try to walk in the hallway." Second, verbs are notorious for the subtle but critical contrasts between them. Consider the difference between, "Dad will get the milk at the store," and "Dad will buy milk at the store." People who *get* milk may be shoplifting. We want Dad to buy the milk!

An Audience may demonstrate strong emotional reactions to specific words. For example, words like *change*, *new*, or *different* may be associated with negative situations, causing the Audience to feel uncomfortable or uneasy. The use of alternative vocabulary helps to keep Audience attention relaxed and focused on the topic at hand. Instead of the word *new*, for example, *another* may be used. Though the use of alternative vocabulary should always be a consideration, it may not be necessary for all Audiences.

ACTIVITY

The 5th Criterion includes several writing considerations:

1. Exclusive use of first and/or third person statements (with omission of all second person statements)

2. Maintenance of an overall positive and patient tone regardless of topic

3. Consideration of the potential value of present tense information, as well as relevant past experiences or future implications to enhance meaning, build self-esteem, and/or support generalization

4. Literal accuracy to help to ensure accurate meaning

5. Selection of the most accurate and comfortable vocabulary for the Audience

To complete the following activity, consider all of the above factors simultaneously to determine which sentences are okay—and which would never be used—in a Social Story™.

Criterion 5 Activity:
Five Factors Define Voice and Vocabulary

Directions: *Which of the sentences may be used in a Social Story™? Place a "Y" for "YES!" and an "N" for "NEVER because then it wouldn't be a Social Story™!"*

1. _____ I shouldn't run in the house.

2. _____ I will keep the paint on the paper.

3. _____ You'll have fun at recess.

4. _____ Veterinarians know a lot about dogs, cats, and other animals.

5. _____ Because our plans are up in the air, this is no time to decide on an itinerary.

Answer: There is one sentence we can save for use in a Social Story™, and that is #4. All of the others, as written, are unacceptable. Here's how each of them could be acceptably revised:

1. Many times, it's important to walk in the house.

2. I will try to keep the paint on the paper.

3. At recess, I have a choice. I may play on the swings. I may play with the ball. Or, I may decide to play something else.

4. When Dad knows the dates for his vacation this year, our family will plan a trip to California.

FINAL NOTES

This marks the half-way point in the tutorials! Take a moment to recall the titles of the first five criteria. In addition, randomly select a few Stories to read, noting in particular how the first five factors are used, and how they overlap.

The 6th Criterion: Six Questions Guide Story Development

DEFINITION

A Social Story™ answers relevant "wh" questions, describing the context (where); time-related information (when); relevant people (who); important cues (what); basic activities, behaviors, or statements (how); and the reasons and/or rationale behind them (why).

DISCUSSION

Basic information about a specific topic (situation, interaction, concept, or skill) is needed to write a Social Story™. Basic, that is, with plenty of details! The six "wh" questions (who, what, when, where, why, and how) can serve as an outline that identifies where and when a situation occurs, who is involved, how events are sequenced, and what occurs. Next, the "obvious" details are considered. What cues or concepts may the Audience have missed? Often, this is also the answer to the last "wh" question, why. While it is not necessary to answer all "wh" questions, all of them are considered as Story content when the text is developed.

At face value, looking to "wh" questions to describe the basic features of a situation or concept seems quite simple. Occasionally, this is where an Author's greatest challenge may lie, especially in terms of why. One of my first Social Stories™ was developed for a kindergarten student to describe "lining up" at school. I sat a long time trying to figure out why it was so important to have children stand and walk in lines, a little desperate that if I couldn't come up with the rationale, how could the Story support the practice? Rest assured that thousands of Social Stories™ and many years later, only once have I been at a loss to figure out why. It was for a Story to describe a child's kindergarten routine. I couldn't make sense of the eight adults and seven locations that were his Wednesday routine! What

The New Social Story™ Book, 10th Anniversary Edition
© by Carol Gray, Future Horizons, Inc.

was I to write? "Sometimes, adults design overwhelming programs for innocent children. This is okay." Unable to describe in good conscience this student's schedule, I abandoned writing the Story in favor of making the needed changes in his school day. The process of answering "wh" questions, coupled with the collective accuracy and sincerity required by the other criteria, renders it impossible to write a Social Story™ to describe or "sell" an unwise idea, strategy, or plan.

A Story can efficiently answer several "wh" questions. For example, a single, opening sentence can answer many "wh" questions: My family (who) is going (what) to the beach (where) today (when). This may be followed with a brief statement that answers how the trip to the beach will occur: "We'll ride in our car to the beach," or a sentence that explains why this activity is planned: "Many families have fun when they visit the beach." In this way, a Social Story™ succinctly identifies who is involved, where and when a situation occurs, what is happening, how it happens, and why. While not all "wh" questions are answered in every Story, they are all considered.

ACTIVITY

Criterion 6 Activity:
Six Questions Guide Story Development

Directions: *Read the Story, "Absent Today? This is okay!"*

Which "wh" questions are answered in this Story?

Answer: There are several "wh" questions that are answered in this Story. Here are a few of them:

- Who is absent from school?

- What did my parents say about being absent?

- When will I be back in school?

- Where do sick children need to be?

- Why are students sometimes absent from school?

- How will I get my assignments?

Your questions may be slightly different. This is okay! As mentioned earlier, a single statement in a Social Story™ may hold the answers to several questions.

FINAL NOTES

Thank goodness for "wh" questions! They can save Authors from staring at a computer screen or blank piece of paper. When an Author is at a loss for where to begin, how to get started, or what to write, thinking of the important "wh" questions that need to be answered provides a quick rescue. These questions, used in combination with the seven sentence types described in the following tutorial, help to structure the task of writing Social Story™ text.

The New Social Story™ Book, 10th Anniversary Edition
© by Carol Gray, Future Horizons, Inc.

The 7th Criterion: Seven Types of Social Story™ Sentences

DEFINITION

A Social Story™ is comprised of Descriptive Sentences (objective statements of fact and/or the information that "everyone knows"), with an option to include any one or more of the following sentence types: Perspective Sentences (that describe the thoughts, feelings, and/or beliefs of other people); Three Sentences that Coach [that identify a) suggested responses for the Audience, b) responses for his or her team, and/or c) self-coaching statements]; Affirmative Sentences (that enhance the meaning of surrounding statements); and Partial Sentences (developed from any sentence to encourage Audience participation and check for comprehension).

DISCUSSION

There are seven possible types of sentences that may be used in a Social Story™. Descriptive Sentences are the only required sentences; all of the others are optional. In this section, each is briefly described, followed by three sample sentences. Many of the sample sentences are from Stories in this book.

DESCRIPTIVE SENTENCES

Descriptive Sentences are factual, objective, assumption-and-debate-free statements that are required in every Social Story™. Collectively they describe 1) context and/or 2) the relevant but often unspoken aspects of a situation, person, activity, skill, or concept. The best place to start when learning to write Descriptive Sentences is to pretend that you are looking through the lens of a camera.

This describes context. What do you see? In addition, Descriptive Sentences also describe information that a camera doesn't record—the information that many people often mistakenly assume that everyone knows and understands.

Sample Descriptive Sentences:

1. There are many vacation days during the year.

2. Some vacations are long, and others are short.

3. Wrapping hides a gift, and helps to keep it a secret.

PERSPECTIVE SENTENCES

A Social Story™ Article may contain Perspective Sentences. Perspective Sentences are statements that accurately refer to, or describe, a person's internal state, or their knowledge, thoughts, feelings, beliefs, opinions, motivation, or physical condition or health. Authors may be prone to making mistakes when guessing the Audience perspective. For this reason, Perspective Sentences are rarely used to describe the internal status of the Audience. The only exception to this occurs when the Audience's own references to positive thoughts or feelings are used (e.g., "I often say, 'I really love to swim.'") or the content of the sentence is a "pretty safe bet" that is likely to be true of all people (e.g., "Sleeping helps me feel rested."). Most of the time, Perspective Sentences refer to the internal status of another person or group of people.

Sample Perspective Sentences:

1. Many people think that nice surprises are fun.

2. Adults may think it's polite to wait a while before opening a gift.

3. Many students want to help our substitute teacher, Mr. McCuen.

The New Social Story™ Book, 10th Anniversary Edition
© by Carol Gray, Future Horizons, Inc.

SENTENCES THAT COACH

A Social Story™ may contain Sentences that Coach. Sentences that Coach gently guide the behavior of the Audience or the members of his or her Team. They describe a suggested response, a choice of responses, or describe self-coaching strategies (also referred to as Coaching Sentences).

In my experience, Authors misuse and abuse Sentences that Coach the Audience more than any other sentence type. It is here where many Author errors are made. Protecting Audience self-esteem, and ensuring the safety of the Social Story™, is paramount. This requires Authors to use careful phrasing to describe more effective Audience responses. Sentences that begin with, "I will try to" or "I will work on" place the emphasis on Audience effort. Sentences that Coach the Audience may also include a list of Audience options, as in, "At recess, I have a choice. I may choose…."

Sample Sentences that Coach the Audience include:

1. I will try to follow Mrs. Jones' directions to the class.

2. I may choose to play on the swings. Or, I may choose another recess activity.

3. I will try to keep the paint on the paper.

A Social Story™ may contain Sentences that Coach the Team. These sentences identify what others will do to assist the Audience. Parents and professionals play an important supportive role. Sentences that Coach the Team define that role, and may also ensure a consistent response by a variety of people to a situation or behavior. In addition, the Audience has information about what others on their Team will be doing in advance. Thus, any changes in the responses of others are expected.

Sample Sentences that Coach the Team include:

1. Mrs. Clark will try to give me more time to complete each science test.

2. My mom will be with me in the doctor's office.

3. Mom or Dad will be with me in the water.

A Social Story™ may contain Self-Coaching Sentences. These statements are written by the Audience to identify personal strategies to recall and apply information. The Audience takes "control" of the information in a Story by identifying a personal strategy to recall and apply its content in practice. Because they are written by the Audience, Self-Coaching Sentences often reflect his or her interests or preferred writing style. Self-Coaching Sentences provide an opportunity to teach students to "self-talk," a strategy that is important in emotion regulation and independent recall of important information.

To develop a Self-Coaching Sentence, the Author writes the entire Story, reviews it with the Audience, and then asks, "Is there a sentence that you could add to help you remember the information in this Story?"

Sample Self-Coaching Sentences include:

1. When someone says, "I changed my mind," I can think of a caterpillar turning into a butterfly.

2. To help me stay calm, I may try thinking about the next fun activity. For example, I may think, "After the test, it's time for recess."

3. I can use a paper chain to help me keep track of the number of days until my birthday.

AFFIRMATIVE SENTENCES

A Social Story™ may contain Affirmative Sentences. Affirmative Sentences enhance the meaning of surrounding statements, and often express a commonly shared value or opinion within a given culture. Specifically, the role of an Affirmative Sentence is to stress an important point, refer to a law or rule, or to reassure. Usually, Affirmative Sentences immediately follow a Descriptive, Perspective, or Coaching Sentence. In the following sample, the Affirmative Sentences are italicized.

The New Social Story™ Book, 10th Anniversary Edition
© by Carol Gray, Future Horizons, Inc.

Sample Affirmative Sentences

1. People wake up. Sometimes they are happy to wake up. Other times they would like to be able to sleep longer. *That's Life on Planet Earth.*

2. Sometimes a student is absent. *This is okay.* The teacher will help them get their assignments, so that they can finish their schoolwork.

3. To stay safe, children take turns going down the slide. *This is very important.*

PARTIAL SENTENCES

Partial Sentences are statements that incorporate the familiar fill-in-the-blank format. They are used to check comprehension, or to encourage the Audience to make guesses regarding the next step in a situation, the response of another individual, or his/her own response. Partial Sentences are often introduced into a Story after it has been reviewed several times. In a Social Story™, a Descriptive, Perspective, Coaching, or Affirmative Sentence may be written as a Partial Sentence. A selected portion of a sentence is replaced with a blank space. For example, following a series of sentences describing why children have to walk in lines at school, a Partial Perspective Sentence may conclude with: Sometimes, teachers tell students to walk in a _____. Filling in the blank encourages a child to retrieve critical concepts, an important step toward applying the information at school. In this way, Partial Sentences provide an opportunity for a child to participate in the review of a Story while increasingly taking ownership of its contents.

Sometimes, an Audience may review a Story and fill in the blank with a word or phrase that was not found in the original Story. If the meaning is the same, there's no need for correction. If the child's meaning is different from that of the original text, it may need to be checked, revised, and/or corrected.

Sample Partial Sentences:

1. Wrapping hides a gift, and helps to keep it a _____.

2. Many people think that nice surprises are _____.

3. To stay safe, children take turns going down the slide. This is very _____.

For new Authors, the seven sentence types may seem overwhelming. With experience, their individual contributions to a Social Story™ become more apparent, as well as how well they work together to describe social situations, concepts, and skills.

ACTIVITY

Criterion 7 Activity:
Seven Types of Social Story™ Sentences

Directions: *What type of sentence is it? Indicate Descriptive (D), Perspective (PE), Coaching (C), Affirmative (A), or Partial (PA).*

1. Many students in my group have ideas for our project. _____

2. That's Life on Planet Earth. _____

3. My bed will be moved to our new home. _____

4. Many children want to be first in line. _____

5. I will try to stay calm when another student is first in line. _____

Answer: "Many students in my group have ideas for our project," is a Perspective Sentence. The phrase, "have ideas" refers to the thoughts of other group members. "That's Life on Planet Earth," is an Affirmative Sentence, introduced for the first time in this book and used frequently in many of its Stories. "My bed will be moved to our new home," is a reassuring Descriptive Sentence. It describes information that most people would assume, or take for granted. "Many students want to be first in line," is a Perspective Sentence, and an important one at that! Finally, "I will try to stay calm when another student is first in line," is a Coaching Sentence.

FINAL NOTES

There is a lot of information in this tutorial. Feel free to challenge yourself and create your own activities. This will help you gain practical control of these new ideas and skills. Try writing several sample sentences of your own. Or look at the stories that you may have already, and identify the different types of sentences in each. With time and experience, you'll begin to feel comfortable with the different types of sentences and the process of writing a Social Story™.

The 8th Criterion:
A GR-EIGHT Formula

DEFINITION

One Formula and Seven Sentence Types ensure that every Social Story™ describes more than directs.

DISCUSSION

The Social Story™ Formula is an equation that defines the relationship between the different types of sentences in a Social Story™. It ensures that every Story focuses on describing interactions or events, and that it also includes, where applicable, an explanation of the rationale that underlies what people think, say, or do. The Formula provides for an unlimited number of Descriptive, Perspective, and Affirmative Sentences in a Social Story™. At the same time, the Formula limits the number of Coaching Sentences (Figure 1).

The New Social Story™ Book, 10th Anniversary Edition
© by Carol Gray, Future Horizons, Inc.

Figure 1: The Social Story™ Formula

of Descriptive + Perspective + Affirmative Sentences (Complete or Partial) =
# of Sentences that DESCRIBE

$$\frac{\text{\# of Sentences that DESCRIBE}}{\text{\# of Sentences that COACH}} \geq \mathbf{2}$$

(Complete or Partial)

Knowing how to use the Formula is essential to writing a Social Story™. The seven types of Social Story™ sentences are divided into two groups, sentences that DESCRIBE and those that COACH. Descriptive, Perspective, and Affirmative Sentences DESCRIBE. Coaching Sentences COACH. To use the formula, an Author counts the number of each type of sentence, adds their totals, and then divides the total number of sentences that DESCRIBE by the total number of sentences that COACH. To be considered a Social Story™, the answer must always be greater than or equal to two.

ACTIVITY

Criterion 8 Activity: A GR-EIGHT Formula

Directions: *Randomly select three Stories from this book. In each Story, identify and count the total number of Descriptive, perspective, and Affimative Sentences. Add their total (DESCRIBE). Count the total number of Sentences that Coach, and add their total (COACH). Divide DESCRIBE by COACH. Compare the results. The Answers will vary, though they always will result in a number that is greater than or equal to two.*

FINAL NOTES

If a Social Story™ had a heart, the Social Story™ Formula would be it. The Formula definitely contributes to the patience and unassuming quality that distinguishes Social Stories™ from other visual strategies. It is a Gr-eight Formula that reminds Authors to take time to share information, including that which people often assume "everyone knows." It provides a guarantee, of sorts, that every Social Story™ will describe more than direct.

The New Social Story™ Book, 10th Anniversary Edition
© by Carol Gray, Future Horizons, Inc.

The 9th Criterion: Nine Makes It Mine

DEFINITION

Whenever possible, a Social Story™ is tailored to the individual preferences, talents, and interests of its Audience.

DISCUSSION

As readers, we all choose books that are in line with our interests and abilities. Few of us want to read information that is very difficult or hard to understand. It's frustrating, uninteresting, and … it puts us to sleep. It's important for Authors to keep in mind that "social" is their most frequent topic, and it is a topic that is exceedingly difficult for the Audience. For this reason, Authors try to make the information interesting and fun, to increase the likelihood that a Story will be effective.

The 9th Criterion personalizes Story content and format. Whereas many of the other criteria ensure that information is individualized to Audience needs and ability, the 9th Criterion personalizes a Story. The 9th Criterion considers Audience experiences, important relationships, interests, and preferences in the development of content, text, illustration, and format. Also included in this criterion are highly creative elements that reflect, and in some cases demonstrate, Story content. The 9th Criterion increases Audience enthusiasm for a Story, as well as comprehension and potential ownership of concepts and information. It also increases the likelihood for generalization of concepts and skills.

There are countless examples of the 9th Criterion at work. One grandmother embroidered a Social Story™ about what love means on a quilt for her grandson's bed. A mother pasted a Social Story™ about buying new shoes on the top of a shoe box, placing photos of the exact shoes her child would try on in the box (taken the day before with a digital camera and the store manager's permission). For a child with an interest in the United States Postal System, Stories arrived via the mail, in interesting containers with postmarks from new locations. Frustrated by the behavior of an entire classroom, a music teacher wrote a Story that identified the rules, and then set it to music to open each lesson. These ideas serve as inspiration of the potential for building additional meaning and fun into Social Stories™.

A word of caution: the 9th Criterion can unleash Author creativity, but don't get carried away! You still need to practice caution and consideration. Whenever an idea is "over the top," it threatens the Social Story™ goal of safety and meaning. What seems fun and cute to the Author may be confusing or even frightening to the Audience. A case in point: An enthusiastic and well-intended dad wanted to prepare his son, Dustin, for the costumes and activities surrounding Halloween. Dad approached his son to introduce the Story. But something stood in the way of their success—a big, furry, bright blue monster, which turned out to be a head-to-toe costume that poor Dad chose to wear. Dustin screamed and refused to read the Story, even after the costume was removed. The Story was then and forever to be known as The Monster Story.

Creativity—with careful consideration and cautious restraint—results in Stories that can indeed captivate the Audience and promote learning. The key is for Authors to understand the positive potential, and the need for caution, that the 9th Criterion requires. Once that is in place, the 9th Criterion can be the difference between a story that is read by the Audience and tossed aside, and a Social Story™ that is affectionately taken to bed.

ACTIVITY

Criterion 9 Activity: Nine Makes It Mine

Directions: *Select a person to be the Audience of the next Story you write.*

How might you use the 9th Criterion to personalize information?

FINAL NOTES

Congratulations! You've completed nine of the ten Tutorials. Recall their titles from memory. Select an Audience and, using the nine criteria that you have learned to this point, research, develop, write, and illustrate a rough draft for a Social Story™. You will be using this draft as a work in progress, as you read and complete the final criterion.

The 10th Criterion, Ten Guides to Editing and Implementation, ensures that the care that is put into creating each Social Story™ is also reflected in its implementation. The 10th Criterion will help you edit and revise your rough draft to its final form, and support your efforts to introduce and implement the Story with your Audience.

The 10th Criterion: Ten Guides to Editing and Implementation

DEFINITION

The Ten Guides to Editing and Implementation ensure that the goal that guides Social Story™ development is also evident in its editing and use.

DESCRIPTION AND ACTIVITY

The 10th Criterion has a focus that is different from the other nine. The first nine criteria define the process that researches each Story, as well as the characteristics of the final product. The final Criterion guides implementation. However, you will note similarities. This is because all of the criteria are rooted in the same philosophy and guided by the same principles, with concern for Social Stories™ that are—from first step to last—patient and reassuring, positive, and socially, emotionally, and physically safe.

The Ten Guides to Editing and Implementation are each briefly described in this section. In the previous tutorials, you read the description section prior to completing the activity. For this tutorial, the Discussion and Activity sections merge, and are to be completed simultaneously. You will need a rough draft of a story that you have written. This tutorial will help you to determine if it has the required characteristics of a Social Story™, and will guide you in developing a plan to introduce and implement the Story with your Audience.

1. Edit!

The effort to ensure Social Story™ clarity, meaning, and interest begins with research and topic identification, and continues throughout story development and editing. An Author uses the resources of the Team to review each story. This is critically important to keep everyone "on board" and to catch regrettable errors early, prior to implementation. Team members carefully check the text and illustration for compliance with the Social Story™ criteria, suggest revisions, and bring the Story one step closer to a final draft. Activity: Compare your story against the Social Story™ criteria, and make needed revisions, if necessary.

2. Plan for Comprehension

Authors of Social Stories™ plan for comprehension. This is an opportunity to look one last time at the text and illustration, specifically with comprehension in mind. Might questions be developed to go with the Story? Once the Audience is familiar with the Story, would Partial Sentences be helpful? An Author sets up a plan to build Audience comprehension. Additional ideas identified in the next guide, Plan Story Support, may overlap with this effort.

3. Plan Story Support

Story Support includes resources and instructional techniques to support a Story as it is implemented. Is there anything that may support the Audience? Might placing the Story on PowerPoint be helpful? What about creating a poster for the classroom that contains an important phrase from the Story? There are many possibilities, each depending upon the specific Audience and Story topic. Activity: Consider your Story. How might you support Audience comprehension and participation as this Story is implemented?

4. Plan Story Review

The review of a Social Story™ reflects the patience, positive attitude, and sound thinking that created it. A Social Story™ is always reviewed in a comfortable setting with a positive tone. Never (never, never, never) force review, or use a Social Story™ as a consequence for misbehavior. Common sense dictates how frequently a Story is reviewed. Establish a predictable review schedule that is frequent enough to be effective, and infrequent enough to avoid needless repetition. Authors consider both the Audience and topic factors to develop a workable plan. Keep in mind that the Audience may not always need—or want—the Author or another adult present to review a Story. Activity: Develop a tentative plan for Story review. Where will the Story be introduced and subsequently reviewed? Considering your Audience and the Story topic, decide how frequently the Story will be read.

5. Plan a Positive Introduction

Every Social Story™ is introduced with the same matter-of-fact and unassuming quality of its text.

An Author may begin with quiet confidence, "This is a story that I wrote for you!" For younger children, it often works well to sit at their side on a comfortable chair or the floor, focusing attention on the Story in front of you both. There are a variety of ways to introduce a Story; the key is to be calm and comfortable. Activity: Introduce your Story to your Audience.

6. Monitor!

Once a Story is in place, Team members monitor its impact. It's important to look for Audience responses that may indicate an interpretation of the text or illustration that is different from what the Author intended. In addition, Authors are highly curious about success. If all is going well, why is that? How might those elements be used in future Stories, to expand upon the current topic or to address a new one?

7. Organize Stories

One Story does lead to another. It's important to keep them organized. A three-ring notebook with a personalized clear plastic cover works well. Stories may be sorted with dividers, to make them easy to retrieve as needed. Activity: Organization is easier when it is present from the beginning. Find a notebook, and insert your Story into it!

8. Mix and Match Stories to Build Concepts

There are many topics to write about. It is not uncommon for one Audience to acquire a sizable number of Stories within a short time! Topics often reappear, too. Keep in mind that Stories may be copied to place in specialized notebooks. For example, all of the Stories about parties—birthday parties, family holiday parties, block parties, etc.—may be placed in a special notebook titled, "Parties!" Within this notebook, dividers may sort the Stories by type, or perhaps year, while the notebook helps to demonstrate the larger concept of "party."

9. Story Re-Runs and Sequels

There may be no such thing as a "retired" Social Story™! Long after it has been set aside, a Story may be reintroduced, like a re-run on television. Your Audience may also benefit from Story Sequels. For example, a Story about friendship at age six may be retrieved and updated with information about friendship at age eight. In this case, the Audience may appreciate the familiarity of elements of the original Story, while benefitting from the updated information the current Story contains. This also helps to tangibly demonstrate the important ties between past and present topics.

10. Recycle Instruction into Applause

Recycling is gaining in popularity. Social Stories™ may be "recycled" too! A Story that originally introduces new skills, for example, may later be recycled into a Story that applauds their mastery. Social Stories™ are easily saved and organized when they are developed on a computer. This makes it easy to transform a Story from instruction to applause. Simply pull up the original Story and save it under a new, related title. Then revise it into a Story that praises the Audience for his or her newly acquired skills. Proudly review it with the Audience!

VERY FINAL NOTES

Social Stories™ have a relatively short but active history. Originally fueled by grassroots enthusiasm, and later studied and confirmed as an evidence-based practice, they have earned the respect of parents and professionals and the trust of their Audience. You are their newest Author. I personally wish you all the best, and invite you to expand your skills by attending a Team Social Stories™ presentation or workshop. May the Stories that you write inform, guide, and inspire your Audience.

CHAPTER 1

Learning with Stories

I Wrote These Stories for You

A LETTER FROM CAROL GRAY

Dear _____,

My name is Carol Gray. Until I was twenty-two years old, my name was Carol Schuldt. Getting married changed my last name.

My mom's name was Viola Schuldt. She really liked to take photographs. She especially liked to take photos that tell a story. She would take five or six photos, and display them together. People would know "the story" behind the photos, even without words. Sometimes, just one photo tells a story, or reminds us of one.

This is a photo of me at three years of age. It was taken in 1955. In the photo, I am at my Aunt Jeannie's home. It's a birthday party for my sister, Marilyn. That's Marilyn, smiling at the cake. I am sitting on Aunt Jeannie's lap. That's me on the bottom right edge of the photo. I remember this party, especially the doll cake. Look at my face. I really loved that cake. I was a little sad that it wasn't mine. My mom is standing, holding my sister, Elaine. Looking at Elaine's face, I think that maybe Elaine felt like I did. I think she loved the cake, too, and felt a little sad that it wasn't hers, too.

This photo (below, left) was taken in 1958. I am six years old. I am with my Grandma and Grandpa Schuldt. It was their anniversary. They had a big, important party. Everyone wore their nice clothes. My dress was scratchy around my waist. After a while, the headband I wore hurt, too. At the moment that this photo was taken, I was tired of wearing my nice-looking-but-uncomfortable clothes.

When I look at these photos, it reminds me of one thing that I have learned about parties. Many people think that parties are fun. I like them, too. A person may have sad or confusing moments, though, even during an activity that is mostly fun. I think it's helpful to remember things like that, and to share it with other people. That way, those people won't be surprised if it happens to them.

This was my home on Dorais Street in Livonia, Michigan. I lived here from 1956 until 1968. I grew up here. It is where I wrote my first story when I was six. My bedroom was on the first floor, across from my parents' bedroom. I had a journal that I would write in each night before I went to bed. I would write letters to me, to read when I got older and became an adult, so that I wouldn't forget what it was like to be a child.

The New Social Story™ Book, 10th Anniversary Edition
© by Carol Gray, Future Horizons, Inc.

I am much older now. I'm still writing stories. I try to remember—always—what it is like to be a kid. I keep reading stories, too, and listening to the stories that people tell me. That's how I have learned much of what I know.

I wrote the stories in this book for you. They describe people and places, and other topics, too. I hope that you like these stories, and that you may learn from them.

I wish for you a wonderful life story,

Carol

Learning with Stories

People learn from stories. People often tell one another their experiences. As they listen, they learn.

Once, my mom was teaching me to tie my shoes. She told me a story about how her grandfather taught her to tie her shoes. I tried it, practiced it, and learned how to tie my shoes.

Another time, I was afraid to go down the slide on the school playground. I wanted to try it. I stood and watched other children climb the stairs of the slide, sit on the top, and slide down. I wondered if I could do that. My kindergarten teacher, Mr. Burns, came up and stood next to me. He told me a story. When he was a boy, he was afraid of going down the slide, too. "Did you try it?" I asked. He said he did. Mr. Burns said it really helped to look up as he climbed the stairs. I thought that might work for me. I went down the slide, and it was okay!

Last Tuesday it was raining. I didn't want to wear my raincoat. My sister, Madison, said it might be better to "just wear it." Then she told me a story. One day last year, it was raining. She didn't wear her raincoat to school. She got wet. Madison was cold, damp, and uncomfortable for the first hour of class. I decided to wear my raincoat to be dry and comfortable.

I am learning each day. People keep telling me their stories. I will try to keep listening, and learning. ■

The Stories in This Book

The stories in the book were written for me.

This book has stories about me and my feelings. It has stories about growing, and a place called Fort Able. There's also a story titled "Maybe I Could Do That!"

This book has stories about people and places. This book has stories about my family, home, and school. It has stories about adults and children.

This book has stories about mistakes. Everyone makes those. It also has stories about changes. Changes happen all the time.

This book has stories about what people think, and what they say and do. It has stories about sharing, playing games, and how to win and lose.

This book has a story about Thomas Edison, and three stories about chewing gum.

This book has stories about Planet Earth. That's my home planet. It also has stories about wild-fires and air travel. There are even stories about the evening news, and why people watch it.

There are other things, too, such as what people mean when they use the word *thing*. That's in the glossary.

There are many stories in this book. One hundred fifty-eight Stories to be exact. They describe life here on Planet Earth. ■

CHAPTER 2

Change

Change

People live on Planet Earth, and Planet Earth is always changing. As it does, people change, too.

There are many changes that people know will happen. Leaves fall to the ground. Water evaporates into air. Daylight darkens to night. People *expect* these changes.

Expected changes often form routines for people. Leaves fall to the ground; people rake them up. Water evaporates; people check if their plants need water. Daylight darkens to night; people go to bed. Expected changes form plans that become routines.

There are other changes that people try to *predict*. People know these changes may come, but they don't know for sure. So, they gather information. Then, they make their best guess. A sunny day changes with a thunderstorm. The night sky changes with a meteor shower. An earthquake breaks the surface of the earth. People try to predict when changes like these will happen.

The changes that people try to predict can *change* their plans. A thunderstorm causes people to have a picnic indoors instead of outside. A meteor shower causes people to watch the night sky instead of going to the movies. An earthquake causes a baseball game to be canceled. People try to predict the changes that can change their plans.

People live on Planet Earth, and Planet Earth is always changing. As it does, it helps people form routines, make plans, and causes people to change those plans, too. That's Life on Planet Earth. ■

The Changes That Form Our Routine

Day changes to night, and night changes to day.
Stoplights change from green, to yellow, to red.
Changes happen around me as I sleep, work, or play,
From the time I get up, 'til I get into bed.

Day changes to night, and night changes to day.
Change happens all around me, but still it may seem,
It's really *surprises* that get in my way,
And *changes* that form my routine. ■

The New Social Story™ Book, 10th Anniversary Edition
© by Carol Gray, Future Horizons, Inc.

A Theory about Change

Here is a theory: Expected and welcome changes are the easiest. Unexpected and unwelcome changes are the most difficult.

Life may seem simple by looking at a calendar. There's a box for each date. People often write their appointments and activities on a calendar. They finish the schedule for one day and then move on to the next.

For many people, changing from one day to another is easy. People go to bed expecting a new day, and welcome it the next morning. For many people, expected and welcome changes are the easiest for them to handle.

Unexpected changes are surprises. Some surprises are nice. For example, seeing a rainbow after it rains. Unexpected but *welcome* changes are often good surprises. ▶

Some unexpected surprises are *unwelcome*. A flat tire on a car is an unexpected and unwelcome surprise. Unexpected and unwelcome surprises often mean that people have to do something they'd rather not do. Unexpected and unwelcome surprises are the most difficult changes for people to handle.

Life may seem simple by looking at a calendar. But each day isn't just the activities and appointments that are listed there. Some of life's most challenging events are those that are never written on a calendar. ■

The New Social Story™ Book, 10th Anniversary Edition
© by Carol Gray, Future Horizons, Inc.

My Theory about Change

Here's a theory: Expected and welcome changes are the easiest. Unexpected and unwelcome changes are the most difficult.

For many people, changing from one day to another is easy. It's an expected and welcomed change. One change that I like and expect is:

_____

For me, this change is (circle one):   EASY   CHALLENGING   DIFFICULT

Unexpected changes are a surprise. Some surprises are nice. For me, one unexpected but nice change (surprise) is:

_____

For me, this change is (circle one):   EASY   CHALLENGING   DIFFICULT

Some unexpected changes are also *unwelcome*. Unexpected and unwelcome changes often make people do something that they would rather not do. For me, an unexpected and unwelcome change is:

_____

For me, this change is (circle one):   EASY   CHALLENGING   DIFFICULT

Life may seem simple by looking at a calendar. But each day isn't just the activities and appointments that are listed there. Some of life's most challenging events are those that are never written on a calendar. ■

The New Social Story™ Book, 10th Anniversary Edition
© by Carol Gray, Future Horizons, Inc.

The Transformers around Us

BUTTERFLIES

Life is full of real transformers. They change their form—and how they look—following a biological plan.

A butterfly is a real transformer. Its life cycle is a biological plan with four stages. First, there's an egg that is laid on a leaf near butterfly food. It isn't an egg for long.

Second, the egg becomes a caterpillar. Caterpillars may have stripes or patches. They eat and grow. Their skin becomes too small. They shed it. A caterpillar grows fast. It may have to shed its skin four or more times.

The third stage is a pupa (also called a chrysalis or cocoon). This is the transformation stage. On the outside, a cocoon looks still. It's silent. On the inside, a lot is happening. The caterpillar is changing into a butterfly.

The fourth stage is the adult butterfly. Many butterflies have colorful wings. They can fly. They lay eggs, near food, that grow into caterpillars, and then cocoons, to become butterflies.

Some of the changes around us are transformations that follow a plan, over and over again. They are quiet transformations that are an important part of Life on Planet Earth. ■

The New Social Story™ Book, 10th Anniversary Edition
© by Carol Gray, Future Horizons, Inc.

The Transformers around Us

FROGS

Life is full of real transformers. They change their form—and how they look—following a biological plan.

A frog is a real transformer. Its life cycle is a biological plan with three stages. First, there's an egg that is laid in the water and covered with special jelly. It isn't an egg for long.

Second, the egg hatches. It's a tadpole! Sometimes, tadpoles are called polliwogs. Tadpoles eat and grow in the water. The top of the pond often looks still and silent. Under the water, a lot is happening. The tadpoles grow back legs, then front legs, and their tails shrink.

The third stage is a frog. People often think of frogs as green. A frog may be other colors, too. Some frogs change colors. Frogs lay eggs that grow into tadpoles, to become frogs.

Some of the changes around us are transformations that follow a plan, over and over again. They are quiet transformations that are an important part of Life on Planet Earth. ■

The New Social Story™ Book, 10th Anniversary Edition
© by Carol Gray, Future Horizons, Inc.

The Transformers around Us

LADYBUGS

Life is full of real transformers. They change their form—and how they look—following a biological plan.

A ladybug is a real transformer. Its life cycle is a biological plan with four stages. First, there's an egg. Ladybugs lay their eggs on the underside of leaves near ladybug food. They aren't eggs for long.

Second, the egg hatches. Larvae come out. Larvae look like insects, with six legs and tiny hairs on the side. They eat and grow for about twenty-one days. Then they begin to change.

The third stage is a pupa. This is the transformation stage. On the outside, a pupa looks still. It's silent. On the inside, a lot is happening. The larva is changing into a ladybug.

The fourth stage is the adult ladybug. They are red with black dots. They lay eggs, near food, that grow into larvae, and then pupa, to become ladybugs.

Some of the changes around us are transformations that follow a plan, over and over again. They are quiet transformations that are an important part of Life on Planet Earth. ◼

The New Social Story™ Book, 10th Anniversary Edition
© by Carol Gray, Future Horizons, Inc.

I Am a Transformer

Butterflies, frogs, and ladybugs, too,
Are life's real transformers, I know.
Another one lives in our house, in my room.
Just watch me transform as I grow! ■

The New Social Story™ Book, 10th Anniversary Edition
© by Carol Gray, Future Horizons, Inc.

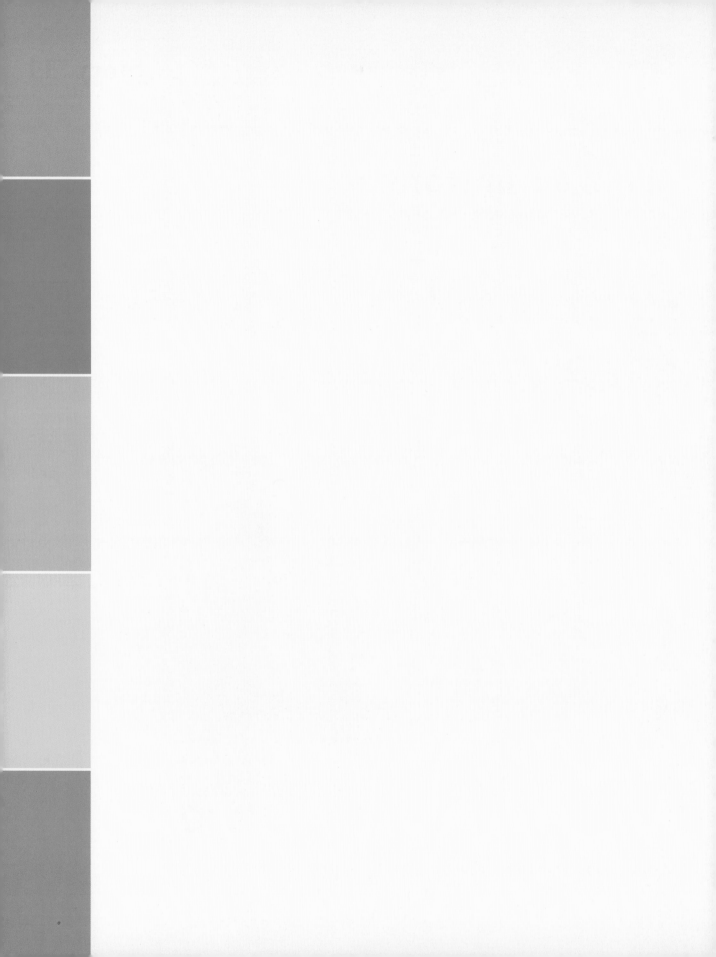

CHAPTER 3

Mistakes

What Is a Mistake?

A mistake is an answer, idea, or act that is an error. When someone says or does something that is not right, it's a mistake.

There are many examples of mistakes. It's a mistake to misspell a word. It's a mistake to leave a jacket at home on a very cold day. It's a mistake to forget to turn in finished schoolwork. People make many other kinds of mistakes, too.

As people grow, they learn from their mistakes. They may not make the same mistake again. However, people are always growing, and having new experiences. For this reason, people are always making new mistakes.

Sometimes, people know they have made a mistake. Other times, they learn that they made a mistake from others. Once in a while, a mistake is made and no one notices it.

Most people try to answer questions correctly. They try to have good ideas. They try to do the right thing. As hard as people may try, though, they still make mistakes.

Mistakes are a part of Life on Planet Earth. That is okay. ■

Thomas Edison and Mistakes

Thomas Edison stayed calm, so he could do his best thinking and learn from his mistakes. He helped to invent the light bulb, the first motion picture (movie) recorder, and he invented a way to make electricity available in people's houses. He invented many other things, too. As an inventor, he *expected* to make many mistakes. For inventors, mistakes are an important part of their work.

It's difficult to invent something. Thomas Edison made over 700 mistakes when he tried to make a practical light bulb. With each mistake, he learned what would *not* work. This brought him closer to knowing how to make a safe light bulb that would work well.

It's smart to know how to handle mistakes. Staying calm is important. A calm body helps a brain think and solve problems efficiently and effectively. (In this case, *efficiently and effectively* means that the brain is working at its very best!)

Many students learn to stay calm when they make a mistake. This helps them think well, and solve their problems efficiently and effectively. That way, like Thomas Edison, they can learn from mistakes.

A brain works best in a calm body. Like many other students, I am learning to stay calm when I make a mistake. This will help my brain to work at its best! ■

The Mistakes Survey

A *survey* is one way to get information about something. In many surveys, people are asked the same question or questions. Then, their answers are studied. I have a survey about mistakes.

Has anyone ever had a day without any mistakes? A survey is one way to learn what people think about this question.

My survey is titled The Mistakes Survey. I may use the survey to learn more about mistakes. My teacher knows how to use a survey. He may be able to help me.

The Mistakes Survey is for adults. To use the survey safely, it's important to give the survey to adults that I know, people who are not strangers. My teacher can help me to make a list of people to take the survey.

To take the survey, each adult will read this (it's at the top of the survey):

A mistake is an error. There are big mistakes, and little ones, too. Some examples of mistakes are:

- Doing something wrong, like making a wrong turn while driving or putting something together wrong

- Forgetting something, like being unable to remember someone's name or today's date

- Losing something, like important notes, keys, a shoe, etc. ▶

- Dropping an item

- Making a calculation or writing error, including "typos"

There are many, many mistakes that people make.

Then they answer this question:

- Do you think that you have ever had a day without a mistake?

I will try to have five adults take The Mistakes Survey. After that, my teacher and I can talk about the answers on the survey. Together, my teacher and I may learn more about people and the mistakes that they make! ■

The New Social Story™ Book, 10th Anniversary Edition
© by Carol Gray, Future Horizons, Inc.

The Mistakes Survey

This is a survey about mistakes. Please read below and follow the directions.

A mistake is an error. There are big mistakes, and little ones, too. Some examples of mistakes are:

- Doing something wrong, like making a wrong turn while driving or putting something together wrong

- Forgetting something, like being unable to remember someone's name or today's date

- Losing something, like important notes, keys, a shoe, etc.

- Dropping an item

- Making a calculation or writing error, including "typos"

There are many, many mistakes that people make. ▶

Please write your name, and circle YES or NO to answer the question.
Write comments if you wish.

Do you think that you have ever had a day without a mistake?

Name   Circle One

1. _____   YES   NO

Comment: _____

2. _____   YES   NO

Comment: _____

3. _____   YES   NO

Comment: _____

4. _____   YES   NO

Comment: _____

5. _____   YES   NO

Comment: _____

The New Social Story™ Book, 10th Anniversary Edition
© by Carol Gray, Future Horizons, Inc.

Mistakes Can Happen on a Good Day

I am learning that mistakes can happen on a good day.

Each day, many people make mistakes as they work and play. For example, they may forget their lunch, trip going up steps, or dial a phone number incorrectly. There are more than a million other mistakes that people can make, too!

As people grow, they learn about mistakes. They learn that making a mistake is okay. A mistake is a mistake, and it's still a good day.

Most mistakes can be fixed. When I make a mistake, adults like my mom, dad, or teacher may be very helpful. They were children once and made a lot of mistakes. They may have made a mistake like the one I am trying to fix!

There's a lot of time in a day—24 hours, or 1,440 minutes, or 86,400 seconds to be exact. Usually, mistakes happen quickly. That leaves plenty of time to fix mistakes, and for other parts of the day to go well.

I am learning that mistakes can happen on a good day. ■

Can Mistakes Happen on a Good Day?

Can mistakes happen on a good day?
I guess it's possibly true.
With so many mistakes that people can make,
It's likely we'll each make a few.

So, do mistakes happen *every* day?
If people wake up, then yes.
But what if they all were to stay in their beds?
Well, *that's* a mistake, I guess.

Can mistakes happen on a good day?
It seems that maybe they do.
People make mistakes and *still* they say,
"Yes, I had a good day, and you?" ■

CHAPTER 4

Me and My Feelings

My Story Album

I have a Story Album with photos of my life story.

I may choose to have photos of me in my album. I am the main character in my story.

I may choose to have photos of favorite people in my album. They are important in my story.

I may choose to have photos of my favorite places in my album. They are the settings of my story.

I may choose to have photos of my favorite toys and things. They are the tools of my story.

I may choose to have photos of fun times in my album. They make fun memories in my story.

I may add photos to my Story Album, too, as I grow.

I may look at My Story Album to look at me, favorite people and places, nice toys and things, and fun times. ■

Children Grow Kind Of Slow

Children grow. Sometimes, an adult will look at a child and say, "You're growing up so fast!" If children really grew really fast, their feet would be farther away every time they looked down!

Compared to many of the animals on Planet Earth, children grow kind of slow. Their bodies change little by little. Hamsters are adults at six months of age. Kittens become cats within one to three years. Puppies become dogs between two and three years of age. Most people become adults between eighteen and twenty-five years of age.

Children are busy people. So, they may not notice that they are growing. Then, one day their clothing or shoes are too small. When this happens, being bigger may seem a little surprising.

Getting bigger is a part of growing up. Compared to some animals, children grow rather slow. That's why children often don't notice getting bigger until their clothes are too small. ■

The New Social Story™ Book, 10th Anniversary Edition
© by Carol Gray, Future Horizons, Inc.

Why Do I Need New Clothes?

I'm a child, and I am growing taller and bigger. All children grow. Their clothes stay the same size. For this reason, children's clothing fits for a few months or so.

The time comes when clothing is too small. Shoes may fit tight and toes may feel crowded inside shoes. Or, pants are tight or short. Sometimes, shirts get hard to button.

It's time for new clothes.

I need new clothes because I get bigger, and my clothes stay the same size. ■

The People on Trevor's Team

Trevor is eight years old. These are photos of Trevor's Team. Every person on Trevor's Team loves and cares for Trevor. They want Trevor to be safe, comfortable, and happy. They teach Trevor, and want to help him grow to be a healthy and happy adult.

There are photos of My Team, too. Every person on My Team loves and cares for me. They want me to be safe, comfortable, and happy. They teach me, and want me grow into a healthy and happy adult. My mom and dad can help me find Team photos to put in My Story Album. ■

The New Social Story™ Book, 10th Anniversary Edition
© by Carol Gray, Future Horizons, Inc.

What Is Comfortable?

Comfortable is a nice, safe feeling.

Comfortable may mean that nothing *on* my body hurts, scratches, itches, or stings. I don't feel cold or hot, I feel just right. My skin feels good. The skin on my head, nose, fingers, and toes feels good.

Comfortable may mean that nothing *in* my body hurts or aches. No headache or stomachache. No sprains or broken bones. No bad noises. Nothing that tastes bad. I feel good inside.

Comfortable may mean that my *feelings* all feel good. I am not worried. I am not afraid. I do not feel sad, bad, anxious, or confused. Knowing what to do, and how to do it, is comfortable. I feel happy, calm, and *comfortable*. My feelings feel good.

Comfortable may mean that a place or thing feels good and safe. There are things and places that feel nice and safe, like a chair or a comfortable room.

Comfortable may mean that it feels nice and safe to be around another person.

Sometimes, everything in me and around me feels good. When that happens, I am *completely comfortable*. Comfortable is a nice, safe feeling. ■

What Is Comfortable for Me?

Comfortable is a nice, safe feeling. What is comfortable for me?

Comfortable may mean that my skin feels good. I have clothes that are comfortable. Pajamas are often comfortable. Three types of clothing that are comfortable for me are:

_____

_____

_____

Comfortable may mean that I feel good inside. There are *comfort foods*. Comfort foods taste good and make people feel happy. Three of my comfort foods are:

_____

_____

_____

The New Social Story™ Book, 10th Anniversary Edition
© by Carol Gray, Future Horizons, Inc.

Comfortable may mean that my *feelings* feel good. There are things that I like to do. I often feel happy when doing those things. Three things that I like to do are:

_____

_____

_____

Comfortable may mean that a place or thing feels good and safe. There are things and places that feel nice and safe, like a chair or a comfortable room. Three places or things that are comfortable for me are:

_____

_____

_____

Comfortable may mean that it feels nice and safe to be around another person. Three people that are comfortable for me are:

_____

_____

_____

Sometimes, everything in me and around me feels good. When that happens, I am *completely comfortable.* Comfortable is a nice, safe feeling. ■

Happy Is a Comfortable Feeling

There are things that make me feel *happy*. Happy is a comfortable feeling.

I often feel happy when I play with my toys. Some toys that I like to play with are:

_____

_____

I often feel happy about my favorite topics. A *topic* is a subject to think, talk, draw, or write about. Some topics that I like to think, talk, draw, or write about are:

_____

_____

Some people are very important to me. They try to keep me comfortable and happy. The people who are important to me are:

_____

_____

_____

I am often happy and comfortable. ◼

The New Social Story™ Book, 10th Anniversary Edition
© by Carol Gray, Future Horizons, Inc.

Looking for Smiles

Sometimes people smile when they are happy. If I were to look for smiles, where would I find them?

I may find them on children playing.

I may find them on moms reading stories to children.

I may find them on dads coming home from work.

Happy can happen almost anywhere, and a smile is often found there. ■

Smile! Why?

Most people like smiles. When people smile, the corners of their mouth go up and their teeth show. If their teeth don't show, that kind of smile is called a grin. Most of the time, when someone smiles, it means something nice.

A smile may mean, *I'm happy to see you.*

A smile may mean, *I'm having fun.*

A smile may mean, *I'm happy.*

A smile may mean, *I'd like to talk with you* or *I'd like to play with you.*

A small, gentle smile may mean, *I wish you felt happier.*

A smile may have other meanings, too.

Most of the time, when someone smiles, it means something nice. ■

The New Social Story™ Book, 10th Anniversary Edition
© by Carol Gray, Future Horizons, Inc.

What Is Uncomfortable?

Uncomfortable is a bad, sometimes-unsafe feeling.

Uncomfortable may mean that somewhere on my body hurts, scratches, itches, or stings. Bee stings, poison ivy, cuts, or scrapes can make skin feel uncomfortable.

Uncomfortable may mean that somewhere *in* my body it hurts or aches. A headache, stomachache, flu, a cold, sprained ankle, broken bone, or food that tastes bad can be uncomfortable.

Uncomfortable may mean that I feel worried, afraid, angry, sad, or bad. Feeling confused is uncomfortable, too.

Uncomfortable may mean that a place or thing is not comfortable to be near or around. Some people feel uncomfortable in a very small place. Other people feel uncomfortable on roller coasters. For many people, very loud, busy, or crowded places may be uncomfortable.

Uncomfortable may mean that it feels unsafe to be around another person. It often feels uncomfortable to be around a person who is angry or out of control. Sometimes, it may feel uncomfortable to be around a person who is doing something that most people don't do in that place, or in that way.

Uncomfortable is a bad and sometimes-unsafe feeling. ■

What Is Uncomfortable for Me?

Uncomfortable is a bad, sometimes-unsafe feeling.

Uncomfortable may mean that somewhere *on* my body hurts, itches, or stings. Scratchy clothes may be uncomfortable. Three other things that can make my clothes uncomfortable are:

_____

_____

_____

Uncomfortable may mean that somewhere *in* my body hurts or aches. A headache is uncomfortable. Three things that can make my body feel uncomfortable inside are:

_____

_____

_____

The New Social Story™ Book, 10th Anniversary Edition
© by Carol Gray, Future Horizons, Inc.

Uncomfortable may mean that I feel worried, anxious, afraid, angry, sad, or bad. Crying is uncomfortable. Three feelings that are uncomfortable for me are:

_____

_____

_____

Uncomfortable may mean that a place or thing is not comfortable to be near or around. Very hot weather is uncomfortable. A very cold bath is uncomfortable. Three places that can be uncomfortable for me are:

_____

_____

_____

Uncomfortable may mean that it feels unsafe to be around another person. It often feels uncomfortable to be around a person who is angry or out of control. Sometimes, it may feel uncomfortable to be around a person who is doing something that most people don't do in that place, or in that way. A time when I felt uncomfortable around a person was:

_____

_____

_____

Uncomfortable is a bad and sometimes-unsafe feeling. ■

It's Okay to Feel Sad, but Feeling Happy Is Better

Sad is an unhappy and uncomfortable feeling. It's okay to feel sad. All people feel sad sometimes. People may cry when they feel sad. When a person feels sad, it's important to find a way to feel better.

Brooke had an ice cream cone. Some of her ice cream fell in the dirt. She felt sad, and cried.

Connor had a problem. He left his stuffed monkey, Elroy, at his friend Luke's house. He felt sad.

Aaron's cat, Orson, ran away. Aaron and his family love Orson. They all felt sad.

When people feel sad, they try to look for a way to feel better.

Sometimes, people feel better when they see that *all* isn't lost. Brooke still had the cone in her hand, and there was some ice cream in there, too. She ate that and began to feel happier. ▶

The New Social Story™ Book, 10th Anniversary Edition
© by Carol Gray, Future Horizons, Inc.

Sometimes, telling someone else about a problem helps. Connor told his mom that his stuffed monkey Elroy was at his friend Luke's house. Connor's mom helped Connor get Elroy. Connor was so happy to see Elroy again!

Sometimes, working with others can help. Aaron's family looked for Orson right away. They found him under the back porch. They were all very happy to find Orson!

Sad is an uncomfortable feeling. It's okay for people to feel sad. When people feel sad they try to find a way to be happy again. That's Life on Planet Earth. ■

What Is a Gift?

A gift is something special that one person gives to another person. A gift is often given to celebrate a birthday or holiday.

If I give a gift to my mom, my mom owns the gift. If I give a gift to my dad, my dad owns the gift. If I give a gift to a friend, my friend owns the gift.

A gift is something special that one person gives to another to keep. ■

The New Social Story™ Book, 10th Anniversary Edition

Everyone Has a Fort Able

There's a place called Fort Able. Fort Able is a very strong and safe place. It is a place in each brain where there's calm, comfort, and control. People are able to do their best there.

Each person builds their own Fort Able as they grow. Each person is unique; each Fort Able is, too. There's a lot that is up to the builder of each Fort Able, although others can certainly help. In front of every Fort Able, there are three steps that lead to the door. That's how the builder gets in. ▶

The New Social Story™ Book, 10th Anniversary Edition
© by Carol Gray, Future Horizons, Inc.

- In every Fort Able, there's a photo gallery. Photos of favorite people and fun times hang there.

- In every Fort Able, there's a media room. Favorite songs, movies, electronic games, and videos of fun times are stored there.

- In every Fort Able, there's a scrapbooking room. It's a room with anything and everything with a comfortable meaning or memory.

- In every Fort Able, there's a gymnasium. Healthy thoughts get exercise there. My Team and I will try to make a list of healthy thoughts for that room.

Every Fort Able comes with people who love the builder. They stand guard, and try to be ready to help in hard times, and cheer in good ones.

I have a brain, and a Fort Able, too. I'll try to draw you a tour, and be your guide through. ■

WELCOME TO FORT ABLE—SAMPLE (optional)

Welcome to Fort Able!

Welcome to Fort Able, the strong and safe place in my brain. This is the first stop on the tour. I'm the builder and owner of the place. I'm able to do my best thinking here. I'd like it if you could see it as I do, but it's not possible to squeeze you in through my ears, mouth, or nose. So, I will try to draw it for you, with three steps in front leading to the door.

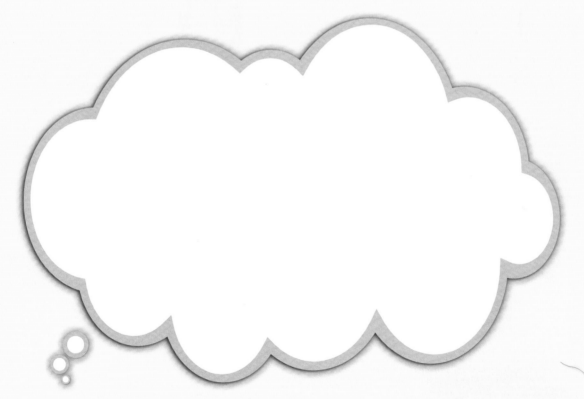

Many forts are built with strong materials like wood, blocks, or cement. In the brain, people build with ideas and imagination. This is Fort Able from the outside. Of course, the goal is to stay *inside* the Fort. ■

THE PHOTO GALLERY—SAMPLE (optional)

The Photo Gallery

This is the Photo Gallery. Photos of favorite people and fun times hang here. ■

THE MEDIA ROOM—SAMPLE (optional)

The Media Room

In my Fort Able, this is the Media Room. Favorite songs, movies, electronic games, and videos of fun times are stored here. ■

THE GYMNASIUM—SAMPLE (optional)

I am really good at soccer.

My parents love me a lot.

My teacher says I am a good student.

The New Social Story™ Book, 10th Anniversary Edition
© by Carol Gray, Future Horizons, Inc.

The Gymnasium

This is the gymnasium. Healthy thoughts get exercise here. ■

THE PEOPLE ON MY TEAM—SAMPLE (optional)

The People On My Team

These are the people on My Team. They stand guard, and try to be ready to help me in hard times, and cheer me on in good ones. I hope you enjoyed the tour. ■

Come to Fort Able

There's a place called Fort Able. Fort Able is a very strong and safe place. It is a place in each brain where a person finds calm and good control. It's easiest for a person to make smart and friendly choices there.

This is Luke. He looks comfortable, calm, and in good control. He's in Fort Able. When Luke is in Fort Able, he's able to make smart or friendly choices.

Sometimes Luke may feel uncomfortable. Sometimes he may feel very anxious, angry, sad, or confused. He's outside of Fort Able. That's an *un*-comfortable place to be! It's harder for Luke to think smart or be friendly. Where did Fort Able go?

Fort Able is always there. Luke has been in Fort Able many times before, and he will be there many more times to come. So, it must be there now, somewhere.

Whenever Luke feels uncomfortable, he takes the first step back to Fort Able. He says to himself, *Come to Fort Able, Luke!* Wherever Luke is, there's a way to Fort Able. Taking the first step is more proof that his Fort is nearby.

My name is _____. Fort Able is a place in my brain. It is where I make smart and friendly choices. If I feel I am out of Fort Able, I will try to find it again. There are three steps that open door. The first step is to say to myself, _____, *Come to Fort Able!* Or *ComFortAble* for short. ■

The Steps to Fort Able

There's a place called Fort Able. Fort Able is a very strong and safe place. It is a place in each brain where a person finds calm and control. It's easiest for a person to do their best there.

My name is _____. Fort Able is a place in my brain. It is where I am smart and make friendly choices. If I feel uncomfortable, out of Fort Able, I will try to find it again. The first step is to say to myself, _____, *Come to Fort Able!* Or, _____, *ComFortAble* for short. If I can't find the first step, I will try to get help from My Team.

The second step is to try to think of one of the rooms inside. Sometimes, just thinking about that room, I may begin to feel a little better. I may be able to think smarter than I could a few moments before. If I can't seem to find the second step, I will try to get help from My Team.

The third step is to go inside. Once inside and comfortable again, I am able to do my best thinking. I may be able to solve the problem on my own. Or, My Team may be able to help me work things out, too. ▶

There are three steps to getting inside:

- Say—to myself, *Come to Fort Able!*

- Think—of a room there.

- Go—inside.

I have a place called Fort Able. I built it myself. It's a strong and safe place, with three steps to the door. ■

CHAPTER 5

Celebrations and Gifts

An Invitation to a Birthday Party

I have an invitation to Angela's birthday party. She is going to be six years old.

To guess what we will eat and do at Angela's party, I may try thinking of other birthday parties. Last year, I went to Tracey's party. There was a cake. We played games.

There is often a birthday cake at a birthday party. At Angela's party, there may be a _____.
There are often games at a birthday party. At Angela's party, there may be _____.

Angela is having a birthday. I'm invited to her party! ■

We're Going to a Big Family Party

Our whole, big family is having a holiday party. Last year we had a holiday party. There may be clues to what we will eat and do this year's party. My family is looking and listening for those clues, and making guesses about this year's party.

I will be going to the party with my mom, dad, my brother, Hunter, and our dog, Jasper. We're going to my Aunt Rhonda's house. Grandpa and Grandma Hill, Aunt Rhonda's boyfriend, Kevin, my Uncle Jess and his family, and my Aunt Rose and her family are invited to the party. *Invited* means they are welcome to come. Sometimes things happen, though, and people cannot come. We'll see for sure who is coming once we get to the party.

We had a big, holiday party last year. My dad has photos of last year's party in his computer. Dad says I may look at those whenever I want. Those photos help my family guess what we may do at this year's party. Some things may be the same. Some things may be different. Even if a party happens every year, it's never exactly the same as it was the year before. That would be impossible.

Last year, there was a lot of food. Some of it was adult food. I told my Grandma that the adult food looked pretty, but I did not want to eat it. There was good kid food, too. There were also a lot of desserts. Mom's guess is that there will be good kid food and desserts at this year's party. Last year, the people brought wrapped gifts. Hunter and I are hoping they will do that again! I told Grandpa Hill that I wish they wouldn't wrap the gifts. He says many people like to wrap gifts, so his guess is that they will wrap them this year, too.

Last year, I couldn't read. It was my job to give people gifts to open. Even though I couldn't read, it was easy. There was a small photo pasted to the corner of each gift. I would look at the photo, and take the gift to that person. I felt smart and important. ▶

This year, my younger brother, Hunter, gets to give people gifts to open. Last year it was my turn. This year, it's Hunter's turn. I can read now. My mom says that even though I can read the to-and-from cards, it's important to stay quiet. It's important to let Hunter look at the photos and feel smart and important, like I felt last year.

My mom has been talking a lot on the phone to my Aunt Rhonda and Grandma Hill. They are making the plans for the party this year. Plans are clues to what may happen. Sometimes, plans can change, though. That's important to try to remember. Mom writes down the plans for this year's party. She lets me look at the plans whenever I want to.

My family is going to a big holiday party. The whole family is invited. My family is looking and listening for clues to what we will eat and do at this year's party. We find clues in photos. We find other clues in party plans. This year's party will give us photos and clues for *next* year! ■

Why Are Gifts Important?

Most people like gifts. They like to give them, and they like to receive them. Here are three reasons why gifts are important to people.

First, a gift helps people celebrate and share their feelings. A gift may mean, *I hope you have a happy birthday!* Or, it may mean, *I love you*, *Thank you*, or *Good luck*. It may mean something else, too, but it usually means something nice. That's why giving a gift can be so much fun.

Second, the person who receives the gift did not have to make it, or use their money to buy it. It's free. Getting something for free is fun, especially when it's something that is useful or nice.

Third, gifts help people remember friends, or family, and the fun times they have together. That's why many people keep the gifts that they receive for a long, time—sometimes even forever.

Gifts help people share and remember good times and nice feelings. This makes gifts very important. ■

Why Do People Wrap Gifts?

Many people wrap gifts before they give them away. Why do they do this?

Wrapping hides a gift, and helps to keep it a secret. Later, when the gift is opened, it's a nice surprise. Many people think that nice surprises are fun.

A wrapped gift is pretty. Sometimes, there's colorful paper, a bow, or a card. Wrapping a gift is a beautiful way to hide a surprise.

Wrapped gifts are a part of celebrating special times and feelings. Because they are pretty and hide nice surprises, they make special times festive.

Wrapping a gift hides a nice surprise, and makes it pretty and festive at the same time. ■

The New Social Story™ Book, 10th Anniversary Edition
© by Carol Gray, Future Horizons, Inc.

How to Give Someone a Gift

It's important to learn how to give people gifts. Even though giving a gift is very nice, it may feel a little awkward the first few times. Knowing what to do helps to make gift giving easier.

When I give someone a gift, I only need to say a few words. For example, I may say, "Here's a gift for you," and maybe add to that, "I hope that you like it." If it's a birthday gift, I may say, "Happy Birthday." If it's a Christmas gift, I may say, "Merry Christmas!" If it's a gift for Hanukah, I may say, "Happy Hanukah!"

Often people will say "thank you" before opening a gift. They don't even know what is inside, and they are saying "thank you" already! Why? People know it takes time to find and wrap a gift. What they mean is, *Thank you for thinking of me and taking the time to get and wrap a gift for me.*

Sometimes, people open a gift right away. Other times, they wait until a later time.

At first, giving someone a gift may feel a little awkward. Learning what to do and say can help. It also helps to know what the other person may say or do. With practice, giving someone a gift becomes easier and more comfortable. ■

How to Open a Gift

Sometimes people give me gifts. I am learning what to think, say, and do when I get a gift.

It takes time and sometimes money to find and wrap a gift. For this reason, it's thoughtful to say "thank you" right when I get a gift (even before I open it). This means, *Thank you for thinking of me, and for getting this gift ready to give to me.*

It may be okay to open a gift right away. Or, it may be important to wait until later to open a gift.

After I open a gift, it's important to say "thank you."

I am learning what to think, say, and do when I get a gift. When I get a gift, I will try to practice! ■

The New Social Story™ Book, 10th Anniversary Edition
© by Carol Gray, Future Horizons, Inc.

Why Wait to Open My Gift?

A gift has a nice surprise inside. Waiting to open a gift may be a little frustrating, especially for children. How can adults be so calm? Why would they ask children to open a gift later, instead of right now?

It helps to know what adults are thinking. Adults have as much fun waiting to open gifts as they do opening them. They like the festive feeling of sitting and talking among pretty gifts.

Adults may think it's polite to wait a while before opening a gift. That's why, at many parties, people eat, talk, or play games before opening gifts.

Visiting with the people who bring gifts is sometimes more important than opening the gifts that they bring. So, visiting is first.

Usually, adults decide when to open gifts. It may be now, but often it is later. Sometimes, knowing what adults are thinking makes it easier to open gifts later. ■

Learning to Stay Calm around a Wrapped Gift

A wrapped gift is often exciting. There may be something fun inside! *Excited* is often a good feeling.

Sometimes, an excited person is asked to wait. When this happens, excitement may feel a little uncomfortable. Knowing what to think, do, and say may help.

It's important to remember that adults often decide when gifts are opened. Many times, children may want to open gifts right away. But right away may not be a good time to open a gift.

It's important to know what to do with a wrapped gift. Learning to wait until it is okay to open a gift helps me and everyone else. Finding something to do until it is time to unwrap a gift may make waiting easier.

When there's a wrapped gift around, knowing what to say may help. It's okay for children to ask, "Is it time to open the gift?" It's important, though, to only ask that question a few times. This is because some people begin to feel grumpy if they are asked the same question too often.

Adults often decide when gifts are opened. If I have questions about why I need to wait to open a gift, I may ask an adult. ■

The New Social Story™ Book, 10th Anniversary Edition
© by Carol Gray, Future Horizons, Inc.

Some Gifts Are Disappointing

Most of the time, a gift is a nice surprise. Once in a while, a gift may be disappointing. This can happen when people give gifts to one another.

Sometimes, disappointment is a surprising sadness. A person is happy and expecting something nice to happen. But it doesn't. That person is sad, and surprised to feel that way. When this happens, *disappointment* is sadness that arrives fast and without warning.

A gift may be disappointing when it is something that is not wanted. Here's an example. Charlie gives Angela a book about dinosaurs. But, Angela isn't interested in dinosaurs. She thinks dinosaurs are boring. For Angela, getting a book about dinosaurs is disappointing. ▶

A gift may be disappointing when it is something that is not needed. Here's an example. Parker likes rocks, and has a big collection of books about rocks. Parker gets a gift from his grandfather. It's a book about rocks. But Parker already has the book in his collection. He's disappointed because he doesn't need two books that are the same.

A gift may also be disappointing if the person opening it is hoping to receive one thing, and gets something else. Angela is hoping to receive a Barbie® doll for her birthday. She opens a gift from her grandmother. There are socks inside. Angela may be disappointed to see socks, because she was hoping to see a Barbie® doll.

Almost everyone is disappointed by a gift now and then. For this reason, parents teach their children about disappointing gifts. In this way, children learn what to think, say, and do when a gift is disappointing. ■

The New Social Story™ Book, 10th Anniversary Edition
© by Carol Gray, Future Horizons, Inc.

What to Think, Do, and Say If a Gift Is Disappointing

Someday, I may open a disappointing gift. It may be my birthday. It may be during the holidays. Most people are disappointed by a gift now and then.

When a gift is disappointing, knowing what to think may help. A disappointing gift is still a gift. Someone gave it to me. That person is hoping that I will like it. This is important to remember.

When a gift is disappointing, knowing what to do may help. Disappointment is a feeling that is best kept under my control. That way, I can be careful with the feelings of others. I will try to take control of my disappointment, and keep the feelings of others safe.

When a gift is disappointing, knowing what to say may help. I will try to say "thank you." Thanking someone for a gift—even if the gift is disappointing—is polite.

Some gifts are disappointing. Learning what to think, do, and say can help me get control of disappointment. With practice, I may be able to open a disappointing gift and keep the feelings of others safe at the same time. ■

CHAPTER 6

People Skills and Friendship

How to Greet Someone

There are many ways to greet someone.

When I see someone I know, especially if I am seeing that person for the first time that day, it's friendly to say "hello." They may say "hello," too. They may stop to talk with me.

Sometimes people shake hands to say "hello." People may try to shake my hand if they are meeting me for the first time. This will happen more and more as I get older.

Once in a while, I go to visit relatives or close friends. A short hug as I arrive means *hello*.

Sometimes, if I am just passing someone I know, I may smile, wave, or just nod my head. If I said hello to that person earlier in the day, smiling, waving, or nodding my head means, *Hello again*. This is a friendly thing to do. ■

Why Do People Shake Hands?

People shake hands for many reasons. They shake hands when they meet someone for the first time, or to greet someone that they have not seen for a while. Sometimes people shake hands as they leave a party or gathering. When people agree on a plan or a contract together, they may shake hands to "seal the deal." In each case, a handshake is used as a friendly gesture.

People who study history believe that people began using handshakes several hundred years ago in England. During that time, adults sometimes carried weapons. Men would sometimes hide weapons up their left sleeve. Extending the left arm, and shaking the hand of another person, was a gesture to show that neither person was hiding a weapon. Later, when carrying a weapon was not common anymore, handshakes switched to the right hand.

People shake hands for many reasons. It's likely that handshaking, with such a long history, will probably be a gesture that people will use for many years to come. ■

The New Social Story™ Book, 10th Anniversary Edition
© by Carol Gray, Future Horizons, Inc.

How to Shake Hands

As children grow, they learn about shaking hands. This is important, because adults often shake hands when they meet someone, or to say "hello." For this reason, I am learning to shake hands with adults.

Adults shake hands more often than children. Once in a while, though, children are expected to shake hands. This gives children practice with shaking hands, so they know how to do it before they become adults.

To shake someone's hand, I may try practicing these five steps:

- Reach forward with my right arm, right hand open.

- Grasp the other person's hand.

- Keeping the grasp, move my hand up and down.

- Open my right hand.

- Return my arm to my side. ▶

Not very often, but once in a while, one person reaches forward to shake hands and the other person keeps their arm at their side. This may feel a little awkward. If this happens, it's okay to lower my arm without shaking the other person's hand.

Knowing how to shake hands with other people is important. For me, shaking hands with another person is likely to become easier with practice. ■

The New Social Story™ Book, 10th Anniversary Edition
© by Carol Gray, Future Horizons, Inc.

Two-Person Hugs

Sometimes two people hug one another. It's a two-person hug when both people hug at the same time.

A two-person hug often means *hello* or *goodbye*.

Sometimes, people use two-person hugs to share their feelings. These hugs may mean, *I love you*, *We are both happy*, or *We are both sad*.

When two people hug each other at the same time, they often:

- Stand close, facing each other

- Wrap one or two arms around the other person

- Squeeze a little but not a lot

- End the hug when either person begins to relax their arms

Sometimes two people hug each other at the same time. A two-person hug is a way to share feelings. ■

One-Person Hugs

People use hugs to share their feelings. Sometimes, two people hug each other at the same time. This is a two-person hug. Other times, one person hugs another. This is a one-person hug. A one-person hug has many possible meanings.

In a one-person hug, one person hugs the other. One person wraps one or two arms around the other person.

Sometimes, a one-person hug means, *This is my friend*. Children often do this. One child places their arms around another child. If the other child doesn't want to be friends, these hugs may be a little confusing.

Sometimes, people may use a one-person hug to help another person feel better. Moms and dads use hugs this way when their children are really sad, hurt, uncomfortable, or frightened. Sometimes, it works. Other times, it doesn't.

A one-person hug may mean, *Way to go* or *I'm proud of you*. Moms and dads use these hugs with their children. Sometimes, a coach may use a one-person hug with a player. Proud hugs may begin or end with a pat on the back, or a "high five."

A one-person hug has many possible meanings. ■

The New Social Story™ Book, 10th Anniversary Edition
© by Carol Gray, Future Horizons, Inc.

When It Is My Turn to Listen

People talk with one another. They have conversations. As they grow, people learn that listening to others is important. Listening helps to keep a conversation fun and interesting for everyone. Listening also helps people make friends. I am learning what to do when it is my turn to listen in a conversation.

To have a conversation, people learn to take turns talking and listening. While one person talks, the other person listens. If both people talk at the same time, which does happen now and then, they can't hear what the other person said. Taking turns works much better.

Listening is hearing words and thinking about what they may mean. Sometimes people mean what they say, other times they mean something else. This can make listening difficult. In fact, for many people, talking is easier than listening. For this reason, many people have to work hard to become better listeners.

When it is my turn to listen, I will try to hear the words that people say. I will try to think about what their words mean. My mom, dad, and teachers are ready to help me, as I learn what to do when it is my turn to listen. ■

Thanking People for the Nice Things That They Say

Sometimes people say something helpful or kind. Saying "thank you" after someone says something nice means, *What you said to me is helpful* or *What you said to me is kind*. There are many times when saying "thank you" is a smart and friendly thing to do.

Sometimes people help me. Yesterday, I had a question about our math assignment. Sydney sits next to me in class. She remembered the assignment. She said, "We have to do all the problems on page 32." I said, "Thanks." That's a shorter way to say "thank you."

Sometimes people say kind things to me. Last week on my birthday I wore a new shirt to school. My teacher said, "Happy Birthday! Nice shirt, too!" It's easy for people to remember their own birthday, harder to remember someone else's birthday. I said, "Thanks," to my teacher.

Thank you is a friendly phrase that means, *It was nice of you to say that!*

I will try say "thank you" when people say nice things to me. That way, they will know that I like the nice things that they said to me. ■

The New Social Story™ Book, 10th Anniversary Edition
© by Carol Gray, Future Horizons, Inc.

Thanking People for the Nice Things That They Do

Sometimes people do nice things for me. Saying "thank you" after someone does something nice means, *What you did for me is helpful* or *What you did for me is kind*. There are many times when saying "thank you" is a smart and friendly thing to do.

Sometimes people help me. Yesterday, Mary let me borrow her pencil. If someone helps me, I will try to say "thank you."

Sometimes people share with me. When I play at Aiden's house, we play with his toys. Aiden shares his toys with me. When someone shares with me, I will try to say "thank you."

I will try to say "thank you." If I do, others will know that I like the nice things that they do for me.

Thank you is a friendly phrase that lets others know that I like the things that they do for me! ■

Learning to Help Others

Helping is doing something for another person. Being helpful is kind and thoughtful.

Sometimes people ask for help. My mom may ask me to carry a bag. She needs my help. Or, my dad may ask me a question about the computer. He needs help.

Other times, people may need help but do not ask for it. When this happens, it's very nice to offer to help.

There are many ways that I can be helpful. ■

The New Social Story™ Book, 10th Anniversary Edition
© by Carol Gray, Future Horizons, Inc.

Helping People Who Haven't Asked for Help

Many people need help. They may not ask for help, but they sure could use it. It's very nice when others see that help is needed.

People often need help when it's difficult to complete a task alone. It's difficult for a mom with a stroller to open a door. Holding the door open is helpful.

People often need help when they are doing something for the first time. There's a new boy in my class, and it's time for lunch. He's never been to lunch at my school before. He may need a little help to learn about how we get lunch at our school.

People often need help when they are in a hurry. When people are in a hurry, they try to do things faster. Offering to do one of those things makes their job easier.

If I look for people who need help, I may find them just about anywhere, doing just about anything. That's because people often need help. ■

It's Easiest to Help People Who Want Help

People often need help. They need help when a task is difficult to do alone. They may need help when doing something for the first time. Or, they may need help when they are in a hurry.

If I notice a person who needs help, I may offer to help. My sister just learned to tie her shoes. She is practicing, but it still takes her a while to make the bow. I have been tying shoes for many years. I can tie shoes quite fast. Once in a while I might offer to help my sister tie her shoes. I may start by saying, "Do you want help tying your shoes?"

It's important to listen carefully for her answer. This is because it is easiest to help people who want help.

When people want help, they cooperate with it. If my sister wants help with her shoes, she'll cooperate with me. She might hold her foot so that I can tie her shoe easily. Or, she may smile because that help is here. Cooperation is a clue that my sister is happy to have my help.

Most of the time, it's easiest to help the people who want my help. ■

The New Social Story™ Book, 10th Anniversary Edition
© by Carol Gray, Future Horizons, Inc.

It May Be Difficult to Help People Who Don't Want Help

People often need help. They need help when a task is difficult to do alone. They may need help when doing something for the first time. Or, they may need help when they are in a hurry.

If I notice a person who needs help, I may offer to help. My sister just learned to tie her shoes. She is practicing, but it still takes her a while to make the bow. Once in a while I might offer to help my sister tie her shoes. I may start by saying, "Do you want help tying your shoes?"

It's important to listen for her answer. This is because it is easiest to help people who want help.

My sister may not want help tying her shoes. She may say, "No," shake her head to mean no, or pull her foot away. All or any of these mean that my help is not wanted now. At another time, my sister may want help tying her shoes. But right now she doesn't.

There are many reasons why someone may not want help. My sister may want to tie her shoes by herself, to feel grown up. Or, my sister may want my mom or dad to help her.

When I offer to help and the answer is "no," this is okay. Unless the person is in real danger, it's okay to go and do something else. Sometimes, people feel a little sad when they offer to help and their help is refused. I may feel sad if my help is refused. Knowing that there are other people who want my help may make me feel better.

Sometimes people need help, but don't want help. When this happens, it may be a smart choice to do something else. There are many other people who need and want my help. ■

What Is Sharing?

I am learning about sharing. There are times when someone asks me to share. My mom may ask me to share. My dad may ask me to share. A classmate may ask me to share. Knowing what sharing is, and why people do it, may make it easier to share.

Sometimes, a share is a part of something. If someone has a great big chocolate cake, and there are twelve people who want chocolate cake, each person gets their share. Their piece of the cake is their share. And if each share is the same size, it's fair, too!

The New Social Story™ Book, 10th Anniversary Edition
© by Carol Gray, Future Horizons, Inc.

Other times, a share is a part of something—but each share is not the same thing or size. Sharing a lunch is like this. I may have a sandwich, an apple, and a bag of crackers in my lunch. If I decide to eat the sandwich and apple, and give the crackers to a classmate, that's sharing my lunch.

People can also share one thing that can't be broken apart. When four children sit on a sofa, they share the sofa.

People also share by taking turns. The people in my family share one computer. Each person uses the computer differently. Mom sometimes uses our computer to get recipes. My sister uses it for her homework. We can't all use it at the same time. So, each person has a turn using the computer.

As children grow, they learn to share. Many children discover that sharing is often a nice thing to do. Sharing helps make friends, too. My mom and dad were children once. As they grew, they learned how to share. They can answer my questions about sharing.

As I grow, I will try to learn more about sharing. ■

What Is Respect?

I am learning about respect. *Respect* is being careful and thoughtful with other people. People show respect with kind words and actions. Respect helps everyone feel welcome, comfortable, and safe.

At home, parents and children show respect when they use kind words and actions. Respect helps a family to feel comfortable and safe.

At school, teachers and students show respect when they use kind words and actions. Respect helps everyone in a classroom feel comfortable and safe.

I will try to be careful and thoughtful with other people. I will try to use kind words and actions. I will try to use respect to help everyone feel welcome, comfortable, and safe. ■

The New Social Story™ Book, 10th Anniversary Edition
© by Carol Gray, Future Horizons, Inc.

Saying What I Think with Respect

I am learning about respect and feelings. All children have feelings. Adults often teach children to talk about their feelings. Learning to tell others how I feel is an important skill. Learning how to talk about feelings with respect is the next step.

Usually, when children are happy and comfortable, it is easier for them to talk with respect. This may be true for me, too. When I am happy, it may be easy for me to talk with my calm voice and cooperative words. At the same time, I am talking with respect, too.

Sometimes, children feel frustrated or angry. When this happens, it is more difficult for them to talk with respect. It's important to share these feelings. It's also important, though, to try to use a calm tone of voice and cooperative words. This takes practice.

I have My Team. My mom, dad, and teacher are on My Team. If I am angry or frustrated, My Team will help me to talk about my feelings with respect.

As I grow, there will be times when I feel angry or frustrated. Practicing with My Team will help me to feel anger—and show respect to others at the same time. ■

Restating with Respect

I am learning about respect. Many children make mistakes with respect sometimes. This is called being disrespectful. They may use a disrespectful tone of voice or words. This can hurt others' feelings or cause them to feel insulted or angry.

Learning to talk with respect is a skill. That's why children sometimes make mistakes with respect. Children need to think, and practice, to talk with respect.

When children make mistakes with respect, adults can help. When adults hear a disrespectful tone of voice or words, they will try to stay calm and say, "Restate with respect." This gives children a chance to think and try again, using a calm tone of voice and cooperative words.

When an adult says to me, "Restate with respect, please," I will try to think and say it again using a calm voice and cooperative words. This will help to keep everyone's feelings safe as we work and learn together. ■

The New Social Story™ Book, 10th Anniversary Edition
© by Carol Gray, Future Horizons, Inc.

Using "Excuse Me" to Move through a Crowd

Once in a while, I will be one person in a crowd. A crowd is many people sharing a space together. Often a crowd of people have to stand close together to share the space that is available. This makes it difficult if one person has to get through the group to another place.

Here's an example. A popular movie opened last week at our movie theatre. My dad and I went to see it. We already had our tickets, and wanted to get some popcorn. There were many people waiting in the lobby for the theatre doors to open. The popcorn was on the other side of the lobby from my dad and me. This was a good time for me to practice what to say and do to move through a crowd.

I began by facing the line for popcorn. Then I said, "Excuse me." People began to move aside, so once in a while, I would say, "Thank you." I kept moving slowly. I had to keep repeating "excuse me" every few steps. That way, I could use a friendly voice that wasn't too loud for a movie theatre lobby. A little smile seemed to help, too.

With me in front and Dad behind me, we made it to the popcorn line a few slow steps at a time. Dad says he's proud that I practiced using "Excuse me" at the theatre. I felt proud, too, to see it work! ■

Learning to Chew Gum

I am learning about how people chew gum.

Sometimes gum comes in a wrapper. This keeps it clean. It's important to take the gum out of the wrapper before putting it in my mouth.

When gum is done, it is thrown away. When I am done chewing my gum, I may put it in a waste basket.

Many people, like my mom, dad, and grandparents, know how to chew gum. If I have questions as I learn about chewing gum, they can help. ■

The New Social Story™ Book, 10th Anniversary Edition
© by Carol Gray, Future Horizons, Inc.

Three Gum Manners That Matter

Gum can be fun until it's done. Knowing about gum manners makes gum fun for me and those who choose not to chew.

There are three gum manners that matter. They are important because they keep gum from looking gross while it is being chewed. Also, Gum Manners keep gum where it belongs. That way, it doesn't make a mess.

First, gum is made for chewing. It's a good idea to keep the gum in my mouth until I am ready to throw it away. Sometimes, a person may chew gum, take it out, and chew it again, over and over. This is a mistake. It's not a healthy idea. I will try to leave my gum in my mouth until I am finished chewing it. ▶

Second, chewing gum with the mouth closed helps others. Many people do not want to see gum being chewed. It's a little gross. That's why people who chew gum try to keep their mouths closed. When I chew gum, I will try to think of how it looks to others. I will try to keep my mouth closed.

The third gum manner matters long after the gum is chewed. It's about how gum is thrown away. Used gum belongs in a waste basket. It's sticky. If it is left anywhere else, it will stick to whatever comes along. Sometimes, that is somebody's shoe. Other times, it's somebody's clothing. To keep gum from sticking to other people, or to other things, it's important to throw it away correctly.

If everyone in the entire world followed the three gum manners that matter, no one would be grossed out by seeing gum being chewed or getting used gum stuck to them. I will try to remember and follow the three gum manners that matter. ■

The New Social Story™ Book, 10th Anniversary Edition
© by Carol Gray, Future Horizons, Inc.

What to Do When I'm Done with My Gum

When chewing gum is done, the best plan is to wrap it in a small piece of paper before throwing it away.

Sometimes, people save the gum wrapper in a pocket while they are chewing the gum. Then, when the gum is done, they use it to wrap the gum before throwing it away. This is a good plan.

If a person doesn't have a small piece of paper, its okay to throw gum into a waste basket without it.

When I am done with my gum, I will try to wrap it and throw it away in a waste basket. ◼

Games Based on Luck

Sometimes, children play board or card games. Many children like to play games. I am learning about games, and how to stay calm and in control when I play them. Some games are based on luck.

If a game is based on luck, it means that there's nothing a player can do to win or lose the game. Players win because of luck.

Candy Land® is a game based on luck. Children or adults win Candy Land® because they select the cards that get them to the finish line first. They do not have to think of a correct answer, or decide what to do, to win. They win because they were lucky to select those cards.

Many children learn to stay calm if they win or lose a game based on luck. That way, others may want to play the games with them again!

Sometimes I may play a game based on luck. Sometimes I may win. Sometimes I may lose. Winning or losing is not up to me or how I play. It is up to luck. I will try to stay calm and in control when I play a game based on luck. ■

The New Social Story™ Book, 10th Anniversary Edition
© by Carol Gray, Future Horizons, Inc.

Games Based on Skill

Many children like to play games. They may like to play board or card games, or team sports. I am learning about games, and how to stay calm and in control when I play them. Some games are based on skill.

When a game is based on skill, players try to use their best effort to win. Chess is a game based on skill. The Olympic games are based on skill. Players win these games by using their skills. Luck may also help, but skill is most important.

Many times, very smart and skilled players lose skill games. They try to stay intelligent and calm. They try to learn from their mistakes so they may win the next time.

Team sports are based on skill and teamwork. Players work together for a goal, like making baskets in basketball or a home run in baseball.

Sometimes I may play a game based on skill. I will try to win, whether playing on my own or as part of a team. Sometimes I may lose. Win or lose, I will try to stay calm and in control. ■

How to Lose a Game and Win Friends

Children often play games. Sometimes I play games with others. I may win a game. Other times, another person wins. This happens when people play games.

Winning is often a good feeling that is easy to control. Losing is harder to handle. Knowing how to lose can help me keep friends.

Children like to feel safe and comfortable when they play games. When they play with someone who suddenly becomes very upset, it can be a little frightening. It's not much fun. It feels uncomfortable. For this reason, staying in good control of feelings is one way to make and keep friends.

As children grow, friends become very important. So, they learn what to think, say, and do to stay in control when they lose.

First, here are some thoughts that help children stay in control when they lose:

- "I want the other children to play with me again sometime."

- "Oh well, I did have fun playing the game."

- "I may win the next time."

A child may think of something else to stay in good control, too. ▶

Second, when a child loses
he learns to say,

- "You won!"

- "Good game!"

- "Good job!"

- "Oh boy, and I thought I
  was going to win."

- "Let's play again."

There are many other friendly things to say, too.

Third, a child learns what to do to lose a game and win friends. He may:

- Take a slow, deep breath

- Ask to play the game again

- Tell the winner that she played well, or

- Choose to do something else.

The important thing to do is to try to stay in control.

I will try to practice what to think, say, and do to lose a game and win friends. ■

After a Game Ends

Many people enjoy playing games. Most of the time, a game ends when someone wins. "I won!" also means that the game is over.

Games are fun, but it's good that they end, too. That way, people can go and do other things.

Once in a while, it's *very* good that someone wins. Everyone is getting a little bored. They are very happy when the game ends. Finally, they can go and do something else. Sometimes, everyone is *so* happy when someone wins and the game ends, it's like everyone won!

Other times, though, a game is really fun. Suddenly there's a winner. The game is over. This is okay. Someone may say, "Let's play again!"

Most of the time, when someone wins the game ends. People are free to go and do other things, or to play the game again. ■

The New Social Story™ Book, 10th Anniversary Edition
© by Carol Gray, Future Horizons, Inc.

CHAPTER 7

Bullying:
What to Think, Say, and Do

Introduction to Bullying

WHAT TO THINK, SAY, AND DO

This is a very important chapter. Together, the Stories in this chapter describe how to *respond* to a child who bullies. They describe what to *think, say,* and *do* if someone tries to bully me. It is important to begin with some information.

Most students are *kind*. They *want* all students to feel *safe* and *comfortable* at school. *Almost* all of the time, kind students use friendly words. *Almost* all of the time, kind students *try* to follow the rules and help others. Sometimes, these students make *social mistakes* with one another. They may forget to share. Sometimes, kind students do not follow the rules. Soon, they want to make things right again. Adults help them learn from their social mistakes.

There are other students, not nearly as many in number, who attempt to bully others. They try to hurt another person's body, possessions, feelings, or friendships. These students are making a serious social mistake. They are out of control.

This chapter will help me to form a Team. My Team and I will learn about students who try to bully others. My Team will help me practice what to think, say, and do if someone tries to bully me. Together, we will learn and practice, working together to make each day at school safe and comfortable for me. ■

The New Social Story™ Book, 10th Anniversary Edition
© by Carol Gray, Future Horizons, Inc.

What Is Bullying?

Some students try to *bully* others by making them feel uncomfortable, frightened, or sad. They try to bully students who are *smaller or who have less power.* How can I know if someone is trying to bully me? It *may* be bullying if someone:

- Says something to me that is not kind, not true, or frightening

- Calls me by a name that is not mine, or that is unkind

- Writes messages that are not kind or that frighten me

- Hurts my body; for example, hits, trips, kicks, shoves, or pushes me

- Tells other students not to talk or play with me

- Asks me to do something that I know an adult would not ask, or want me to do

- Tells me to give them money, and not to tell an adult about it

- Makes the same or similar mistake many times, *over* and *over* ▶

There are many other ways that a student may bully, too. No one can predict exactly when someone may try to bully another person. No one can predict exactly what a student may do in a bullying attempt. What we do know is that students who bully are out of control.

It's important to know what to think, say, and do if someone tries to bully me. That way, I will be ready whatever the student who bullies tries to do. ■

The New Social Story™ Book, 10th Anniversary Edition
© by Carol Gray, Future Horizons, Inc.

Which Students Try to Bully Others?

Bullying can be very confusing. Getting more information can help. A student who bullies may be a boy or a girl. A student who bullies may be older or younger than me. A student who bullies may be alone or with others. A student who bullies may:

- Do something that makes other students laugh

- Do something that causes an adult to feel upset or angry

- Do something that I know is wrong, or that I guess may be wrong

- Use an unkind face and words

- Use a friendly face and confusing words

If I feel confused or have questions about bullying, it's a smart decision to get more information from adults. Adults were children many years ago. They remember students who bullied them. An adult can help me decide if someone is trying to bully me. ■

My Team

I know some adults who are concerned about bullying. They are on *My Team*. My Team will work with me to make sure my school and neighborhood are safe and comfortable. I am an important member of the team. We work together. My Team will help me finish this chapter. Below is a picture of me with My Team. The members of My Team will print their names below their picture. They may *sign* their names, too.

My Team is doing many things to make my school a comfortable and safe place for all students. They have been busy studying and learning new ways to respond to bullying. Even adults have to learn new skills. Later in this chapter, My Team will write a list of what they have learned. They will also write a list of what they are doing to keep our school and neighborhood safe and comfortable for all students. ■

The New Social Story™ Book, 10th Anniversary Edition
© by Carol Gray, Future Horizons, Inc.

Learning to Respond to Bullying

Sometimes, a student may try to bully me when My Team is not around. Sometimes, a student may try to bully me when a member of My Team is near, but does not see the bullying. I can learn how to *respond* to a student who bullies. I can learn what to *think, say,* and *do.*

When a student tries to bully someone, it is called a *bullying attempt.* Together with a member of My Team, we will review the picture of a bullying attempt on the next page. We will complete it step by step, following the directions and answering the questions together. ▶

DIRECTIONS AND QUESTIONS:

1. On the left is a student attempting to bully someone. Is this student using good self-control?

_____

_____

Sometimes if a student is not using good self-control, adults describe the student as being out of control. When a student makes a bullying attempt, he or she is out of control.

2. On the right is another student. This child is the target of a bullying attempt. The goal is for this student to use good control, to know what to think, say, and do. Is it better to have one student out of control, or two students out of control?

_____

_____

The student on the right is one of millions of students who are learning to use good self-control to respond to bullying. Learning to use good self-control in a bullying situation means:

1. Learning what to think.

2. Learning what to say.

3. Learning what to do.

With a member of My Team, I will try to complete the following pages in this chapter. We will return to complete this picture, writing in what to think, say, and do in response to a bullying attempt. ■

What To Say in Response to a Bullying Attempt and How To Say It

There are three steps to responding to a bullying attempt.

STEP 1 is:

_____

STEP 2 is: Say one sentence well.

Knowing what to say and how to say it helps a student use good self-control.

What to Say

There are three sentences in the list below. I may choose one of these sentences. I will try to choose the one sentence that is the most true for me and the easiest for me to say. This is to be written in the talk symbol. This one sentence is what I will try to say in response to a bullying attempt.

- "I hear you."

- "I need you to stop."

- "I don't like that; stop it." ▶

I have a choice. I may choose one sentence and write it in the talk symbol below.

When I say my one sentence, the student who bullies may keep talking. This can happen when a student is out of control. I have said my one sentence. I am finished. It's time to go. It is right to leave a bullying attempt, even if the student who bullies is still talking. This keeps me mistake-free and in good self-control. ▶

How To Say It

I have facts and a picture to think about to help me stay calm. I have one sentence to say. As I say the sentence, I will try to:

- Keep all parts of my body to myself

- Stand straight with my head up

- Use a steady in-control voice

- Keep a safe distance

- Walk away after one sentence

Knowing what to say and how to say it takes practice. A member of My Team can help me practice. STEP 2 is: *Say one sentence well*. ■

The New Social Story™ Book, 10th Anniversary Edition
© by Carol Gray, Future Horizons, Inc.

What To Do in Response to a Bullying Attempt

There are three steps to responding to a bullying attempt.

STEP 1 is:

_____

STEP 2 is:

_____

STEP 3 is: Report the bullying attempt to a member of My Team.

Knowing why a report is important, what to report, how to report it, and whom to give my report to helps me stay in good self-control.

I may write "Report the bullying attempt to a member of My Team" in the arrow-shaped action symbol on the next page. ▶

Why is it Important to Report Bullying Attempts?

Reporting is how people learn about important events that occur in other places. Often, an adult is not present when someone makes a bullying attempt. Sometimes, an adult may be present, but does not see the bullying attempt. My Team and I will make a plan for reporting bullying attempts. That plan will include deciding what to report, how I will make my report, and who will receive my report. ▶

The New Social Story™ Book, 10th Anniversary Edition
© by Carol Gray, Future Horizons, Inc.

What to Report

Like news reporters, it is important for all students to learn how to carefully report bullying information to adults. A good report will include:

- Where the bullying attempt occurred

- When the bullying attempt occurred

- Who made the bullying attempt

- What was said and done during the bullying attempt.

How to Report

My Team and I will make a plan for reporting that is immediate, factual, and that works well for everyone on the team.

The best reports of bullying attempts occur right after the attempt happens. That way, it is easiest to remember the facts to describe the bullying attempt. This is very important.

The best reports of bullying attempts are factual. A factual report uses true sentences to describe where the bullying attempt occurred, when the bullying attempt occurred, who made the bullying attempt, and what was said and/or done. A student leaves a bullying attempt and tries to immediately make a factual report to a team member. ▶

The first part of the plan is deciding how a student will report bullying attempts to the Team. Some students talk with a Team member to report a bullying attempt. Some students write to a Team member to report. Some students report bullying attempts by using a reporting form. Every Team has its own best plan. My Team and I will fill in #3 in the plan below. This completes the first part of our plan.

The second part of our plan is deciding who receives my report. Each adult member of My Team knows how to help when I have a report. Sometimes, one member of My Team may be sick or in another place. This is okay. There are other members of the Team. They are listed in order. I will try to give my report to the Team member at the top of the list. If that person is not nearby, then I will try to report to the Team member on the next line, and so on. It is important to report to a member of My Team. ■

My Team's Plan for Reporting Bullying Events

I will try to:

1. Report bullying attempts right away

2. Use facts to report bullying attempts.

3. Report bullying attempts by:

_____

_____

Adult Team Members will try to:

1. Listen to or read my report right away.

2. Clarify the facts if necessary.

3. Take helpful action.

I will give my report to:

1. _____. If not nearby, I will give my report to

2. _____. If not nearby, I will give my report to

3. _____.

The New Social Story™ Book, 10th Anniversary Edition
© by Carol Gray, Future Horizons, Inc.

What My Team Has Learned about Responding to a Bullying Attempt

A FACTUAL REPORT BY THE MEMBERS OF MY TEAM:

_____

_____

Team members sign on these lines.

This section completed by adult Team members.

My Team has learned a lot about how to respond to a bullying attempt. For example, the adult members of My Team have learned:

1. _____

2. _____

3. _____

My Team is working to keep our school and neighborhood safe and comfortable for all students. They are:

1. _____

2. _____

3. _____

This section completed by _____

My Team has learned a lot about how to respond to a bullying attempt. I have learned three steps to responding to a bullying attempt.

STEP 1 is: _____

STEP 2 is: _____

STEP 3 is: _____

My Team and I have learned the three steps to respond to a bullying attempt. Now, we can work together to fill in the thought, talk, and arrow symbols on page 118.

People are learning about bullying all over the world. Some people learn by completing workbooks and practicing. All people learn by working together. Look at what My Team has learned! Together, we will keep practicing. ■

Understanding Adults

Adults Are Children Who Kept Getting Older

Many children learn about adults as they grow. I am a child. I am learning about adults. Understanding adults can make it easier to work and play with them.

Adults are older people. They were children long ago. They would still be children if they hadn't been here for so long. They couldn't help it; they didn't *decide* to be adults. It wasn't a *choice* that they made. They just kept growing older.

Sometimes, it helps to think of adults as really, really, really old children. Children like to have fun. So do adults. Children like to eat their favorite foods (and snacks that may not quite be food). So do adults. Children like to play. So do adults. Children have feelings. So do adults. Thinking of adults as really, really, really old children may help me to remember that each adult was once a child, like me. Adults may be easier to understand if I try to remember that they were once children, too.

Someday, I will be an adult. My turn as an adult is on its way—it's closer each day. Until then, I will try to remember that adults were children once, too. This may make adults a little easier for me to understand. ■

The New Social Story™ Book, 10th Anniversary Edition
© by Carol Gray, Future Horizons, Inc.

Learning to Respect Adults

Adults were here before me. Their birth dates came before mine.

It's important for children to understand that adults *are adults*. Adults have been here a long time. Adults have read more, studied more, and learned more. For this reason, adults make most of the decisions. That's Life on Planet Earth.

Sometimes, children wish that they could make adult decisions. Adults were once children who wished that at times, too. Now that they *are* adults, they've learned how difficult it can be to make decisions. Understanding *this* may make it easier for children to respect adults and the decisions that they make.

I am a child. I am learning about adults. Adults have been here a long time. They have a lot of experience. They know a lot. I will try to respect adults, and the decisions that they make. ■

Do Adults Know Everything?

To children, it may seem like adults know everything. Adults know how to get ready in the morning. They know how to drive. Most adults know enough to get through each day without having to go to a book or the Internet for help.

To children, it may seem like adults always know what to do. The truth is, sometimes adults get confused. They may make a wrong turn while driving or say, "Hi Evelyn!" to Ellen. They may have a problem and not know how to solve it. Most of the time, this is okay. All people get confused at times.

Adults don't know everything. Most adults do know where to find the information that they need. They know where to get help. Knowing where to get information, or how to get help, takes practice. Some adults are better at it than others.

Sometimes it may seem like adults know everything. The truth is, adults don't know everything. This is okay. ■

The New Social Story™ Book, 10th Anniversary Edition
© by Carol Gray, Future Horizons, Inc.

There are tasks that may not be fun—but have to be done. Many people think taking out the garbage is not fun. It has to be done or our home would smell like garbage. **List B** has lines to write three tasks that are not fun and why they have to be done.

LIST B: MAY NOT BE FUN BUT HAVE TO BE DONE TASKS

1. _____

It has to be done because _____

2. _____

It has to be done because _____

3. _____

It has to be done because _____

Sometimes, parents decide that children need to complete tasks from List B, before choosing activities from List A. This is an adult decision to make. It's also called teaching children *responsibility*.

I am learning to be responsible. When an adult decides a task has to be done, I will try to complete it before my activities in List A. ■

The Up Escalator

In our community, people share the up escalators. An escalator is a moving set of stairs. An escalator is a good way to move people from one floor to another.

On a staircase, people move up from one step to the next. On an up escalator, people choose a step and ride it to the top!

To be safe, it's important to hold the handrail. The handrail moves at the same speed as the step. This makes an up escalator comfortable and safe for people to use.

Here's how to use an up escalator:

- Walk slowly to the bottom of the escalator.

- Pause just a little to decide which empty step to ride.

- Place a hand on the handrail next to that step.

- Look down, step with one foot, then the other, onto that step. This may be a big step.

- Ride up. To ride safely, stay on the same step.

- As the top gets closer, keep holding the handrail.

- At the top, the step begins to slowly flatten as it slides away under the landing. When this happens, let go of the handrail and walk off. ▶

It Was Fun but Now We're Done

There are times when adults start a fun activity with children. There are also times when children find a fun thing to do on their own.

All fun activities end. Adults are used to having fun activities end. So they often handle it better than children. Little by little, children learn to end fun activities, too.

It is helpful to know when a fun activity needs to end. So, an adult may say, "In a few minutes, we have to put the toys away." This means playtime will end soon, but not now.

A few minutes pass. Then, an adult may say, "It was fun, but now we're done." This is a special sentence. It means that the fun activity ends now. It's time to put things away. It's time to go to another activity or task.

Sometimes, children think, *There will be another time for fun*. This helps them to stay calm and cooperative. They are right, too. There will be another fun time.

When I hear the special sentence, "It was fun, but now we're done," I will try to think of fun times to come. When a fun activity ends, I will try to stay calm and cooperative. ■

The New Social Story™ Book, 10th Anniversary Edition
© by Carol Gray, Future Horizons, Inc.

Permission

Children have many ideas. They have ideas about things they would like to do. A child's idea may be an adult's decision to make. When this happens, children need to ask for permission.

Permission is something that adults give to children. It's not a *thing* like a toy or chocolate. Permission is an okay to go ahead with an idea. Sometimes children get the permission that they need, other times they don't.

Here are two examples:

Antoine has an idea. He wants to take Jasper, his hamster, outside. Antoine's idea is his mom's decision to make. So Antoine asks his mom, "May I take Jasper outside?" Antoine's mom says, "Not right now." *Not right now* means, *No, not at this time*. Jasper the hamster stays inside.

Brooklyn wants to pick flowers. She asks her dad, "May I pick a flower from our garden?" Her dad says, "Sure." *Sure* means, *It's okay for Brooklyn to pick one flower*. Picking more than one flower may be a problem, because Brooklyn got her dad's permission to pick only one flower.

Sometimes when children ask for permission, the answer means *no*. Other times when children ask for permission, the answer means *yes*.

Permission is needed when a child has an idea, and it's an adult's decision to make. Sometimes children get the permission that they need, other times they don't. Either way, that's Life on Planet Earth! ■

Many Adults Like to Say "Yes"

Children have many ideas. They have ideas about things they would like to do. A child's idea may be an adult's decision to make. When this happens, children need to ask for permission.

Children may be surprised to learn that most adults like to say "yes" whenever they can. For many adults, giving permission and saying "yes" is fun. It's definitely more fun than saying "no." Long ago, when adults were children, they had to ask for permission. They remember how fun it was when adults said "yes" to them. They want to be fun like that, now.

Still, adults may decide to say "no." It's their decision to make. They may wish they could say "yes." But, they are adults. They've learned a lot. It's an adult's job to think and make the best decision that they can. This is why they may say "no."

Children have many ideas. Some of them need permission. For many adults, saying "yes" is fun. As adults, though, it's their job to think and make the best decision. Once in a while, the best decision isn't "yes"; it's "no." ■

The New Social Story™ Book, 10th Anniversary Edition
© by Carol Gray, Future Horizons, Inc.

Three Ways to Say "Yes"

Children have many ideas. They have ideas about things they would like to do. A child's idea may be an adult's decision to make. When this happens, children need to ask for permission.

An adult may say *yes*, without saying "yes." This may be a little confusing for children.

Sometimes, an adult will say, "Sure!" *Sure* is a definite *yes*. The adult is *very sure* that it's okay to give permission. The adult feels confident giving permission. It may also mean that permission in this case was not needed. Here's an example:

Jake: "Dad, may I do my homework now?"

Dad: "Sure!" ▶

Other times, an adult will say, "Okay." *Okay* means *yes*. *Okay* may mean, *Yes this time, but not every time.* The adult feels comfortable giving permission. Here's an example:

Jake: "Dad, may Andrew and I do our homework together?"

Dad: "Okay."

Another way that adults often say yes is, "Okay, I guess," or, backwards, "I guess it's okay." This means, *Yes, but there is a good reason to say no.* The adult feels a little uncomfortable giving permission. This is why children often act fast when an adult says, "Okay, I guess."

Jake: "May I watch one television show before starting my homework?"

Dad, "Okay, I guess."

When children have ideas and ask for permission, adults may say *yes*. How they say yes can be a little confusing. Learning what adults mean when they say, "Sure," "Okay," or "Okay, I guess," can help. It's a clue to what adults may be thinking and feeling, too. ■

The New Social Story™ Book, 10th Anniversary Edition
© by Carol Gray, Future Horizons, Inc.

If the Answer Is "No": A Story of Hope for Children

I have many ideas. I have ideas about things I would like to do. My idea may be an adult's decision to make. When this happens, it's important for me to try to ask for permission. Sometimes the adult will say "no." If the answer is no, there may be hope.

Sometimes, when an adult says "no," it also means, *I'm too tired to do that now*. There's hope! Maybe tomorrow it will be okay.

Sometimes, when an adult says "no," it also means, *That isn't safe*. There's hope! Maybe it can be made safer for me.

Sometimes, when an adult says "no," it also means, *Later the answer will be yes*. There's hope! Later almost always comes.

Sometimes, when an adult says "no," it also means, *We don't have enough money to buy that*. There's hope! Maybe we can save some money to buy it someday.

Sometimes, when an adult says "no," it means, *No, I will never allow that*. There's hope! The world is full of other things to do. ▶

When adults have to say "no," they really love it when children try to stay calm. That way, the answer is "no" but everything else is still okay. And, they are more likely to say "yes" to another idea.

I have many ideas. Sometimes the answer will be "no." I will try to think, *There's hope!* and stay calm. ■

The New Social Story™ Book, 10th Anniversary Edition
© by Carol Gray, Future Horizons, Inc.

CHAPTER 9

Home and Community

Moving to a New Home

My family is moving to a new home. This is our moving plan, in three big steps:

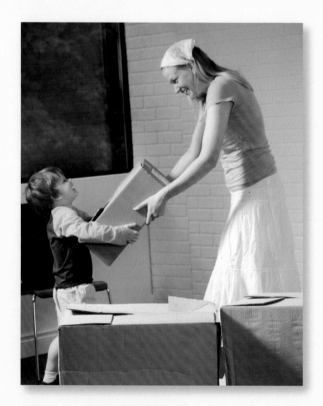

- Pack our furniture, and put other things in moving boxes.

- Take our furniture and boxes to the new home.

- Put our furniture and other things into the new home.

I am moving to a new home. I may pack some of my toys and things. This is my moving plan in three big steps:

- Pack. We'll put most of my toys and other things in moving boxes.

- Move. We'll take the boxes to the new home.

- Unpack. We'll put my toys and things in my home.

It's good to have a moving plan. My family and I have a plan for our move to a new home. ■

The New Social Story™ Book, 10th Anniversary Edition
© by Carol Gray, Future Horizons, Inc.

Moving to a New Community

My name is Mason. I live in Shelton, Connecticut. My dad got a job in Garretson, South Dakota. My family is moving to a new home in Garretson.

I have never been to Garretson, South Dakota. My mom and dad have been to Garretson twice. They went once to look for a new home. They went another time to buy our home. They took many photos. Those photos are in my *Moving to Garretson Book*.

In Garretson, we'll do many of the errands and activities that we do now. We'll do them in and around Garretson, South Dakota.

I go to Lafayette Elementary School. In Garretson, I will go to Garretson Elementary School. I have photos of both of these schools in my book.

I get my hair cut at Rich and Ben's Hair Styling. In Garretson, I will get my hair cut at Brandon Plaza Barbers. I have photos of both of these barber shops in my book.

My family gets groceries at the Beechwood Supermarket. In Garretson, we can get groceries at Garretson Food Center. I have photos of both of these grocery stores in my book.

My name is Mason. Soon I will be living in Garretson, South Dakota. I will be going to school and getting my hair cut there. My mom and dad will buy groceries there. Garretson will be my new community. ■

In Fletcher's Family, Who Knows What?

Fletcher knows a lot. He knows a LOT about dinosaurs. He knows a lot about his family, too. His father builds houses. His mother is a dentist. Fletcher's older sister, Emma, writes in her journal every day.

Someone in Fletcher's family knows how to build a garage. Guess who?

Someone in Fletcher's family knows a lot about cavities in teeth. Guess who?

Someone in Fletcher's family knows where to find the key to Emma's journal. Guess who?

Fletcher knows a lot about what the people in his family do. That gives him clues so he can guess *who* knows *what*! ■

The New Social Story™ Book, 10th Anniversary Edition
© by Carol Gray, Future Horizons, Inc.

Washing My Hands

Sometimes, my hands get dirty. My hands touch items with germs all day long. My hands touch doorknobs and pencils and many other things that have germs. I can't see or feel the germs on my hands. That's because germs are very, very tiny. Even though I can't see germs, I can wash them away. Washing with soap and water can help to kill germs.

This is a list of steps people follow when they wash their hands:

- Go to the sink.

- Turn the water on.

- Get hands wet.

- Put soap on hands.

- Rub hands together.

- Rinse hands with water.

- Turn the water off.

- Dry hands.

Washing my hands is a healthy habit. I will try to follow these steps to wash my hands. ■

Why People Take Baths or Showers

People take baths and showers. They have been taking baths since 3,300 B.C. During the Roman Empire, people began bathing as a daily ritual. Understanding why people take baths and showers may make it easier for me to take my bath/shower.

History is full of stories about bathtubs and bathing. The ancient Greek inventor, Archimedes, noticed that when he got into his tub, the level of the water would rise. He began using tubs to measure how big items were by the amount of water they displaced in his tub. This may be an interesting story, but it is also a unique reason to use a bathtub. Throughout history, people have taken baths or showers to get clean. But why do they do this?

People take baths to get clean, or to feel or smell better. Being clean, washing away dirt and germs, is a healthy habit. For many people, being dirty is a little uncomfortable, even a little itchy. Sometimes, dirty people smell bad. A bath or a shower makes their skin feel comfortable again, and makes them smell better, too.

People also take baths because of other people. They are concerned about what other people may think. Since so many people think being clean is comfortable, just being around someone who is dirty or smelly can make them uncomfortable. Many people don't want to be around a dirty person for long. And, they may not want to be friends with someone who is often dirty or smells bad. So, people sometimes take a bath or shower so that others will feel comfortable.

People have been taking baths throughout history. I am a part of history. By taking a bath or a shower, I may be more comfortable—and others will be more comfortable—as I make my mark on history. ■

The New Social Story™ Book, 10th Anniversary Edition
© by Carol Gray, Future Horizons, Inc.

Taking a Shower in Ten Steps

Many people use showers to get clean. Often, a person will say, "I'm going to take a shower." That means, *I am going to use the shower*. Soon, I will be learning to take a shower.

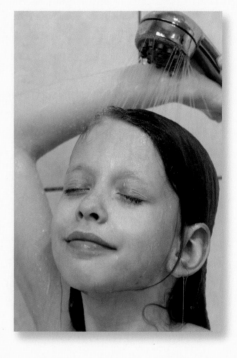

What follows is a list of steps that many people follow to take a shower at home. It is a list of what they do and why they do it.

TEN STEPS TO TAKE A SHOWER

- Go into the bathroom and close the door. Closing the door keeps a shower private.

- Take off clothes. This keeps clothes dry.

- Turn on the water and set a comfortable water temperature. If the water is too hot or too cold, a shower is uncomfortable. (Hint: Some people use the bathtub faucet to make sure the water temperature is comfortable, and then they send the water through the shower head.)

- Make sure the water is coming out through the shower head.

- Step carefully into the shower. Wet surfaces can be slippery. ▶

- Wash hair with shampoo, rinse, apply conditioner, rinse. Shampoo is soap made just for washing hair. Conditioner makes hair easier to comb and style. Rinsing well after the shampoo and conditioner is important for clean and comfortable hair and scalp.

- Wash skin with soap. This gets a body clean. Rinse. Rinsing well is important for clean and comfortable skin.

- When the shower is done, turn off the water. This saves water and energy.

- Use a towel to dry skin and hang up the towel. Dry skin makes clean clothes feel more comfortable. Hanging up the towel keeps the bathroom neat. It also prevents someone from saying, "Hey, come back and hang up your towel."

- Put on clean clothes. Carry dirty clothes out of the bathroom. This helps to keep a bath-room neat.

I may use this list as I am learning to take a shower. My mom and dad know how to take a shower. If I have questions about taking a shower, they will know the answer. With practice, I may not need the list—or help from my mom and dad. I will have learned how to take a shower on my own! ■

The New Social Story™ Book, 10th Anniversary Edition
© by Carol Gray, Future Horizons, Inc.

Sharing a Bathroom by Taking a Shorter Shower

In our home there are two bathrooms. One is for my mom and dad. The other is for me, my sister Emily, and my brother Austin, to share.

My sister Emily uses the toilet, shower, and sink in our bathroom.

My brother Austin uses the toilet, shower, and sink in our bathroom.

I use the toilet, shower, and sink in our bathroom.

Each of us needs to use the toilet, take a shower, and brush our teeth. To be fair, each of us needs time in the bathroom.

Shorter showers can help. When Emily takes a shorter shower, Austin or I can use the bathroom sooner. When Austin takes a shorter shower, Emily or I can use the bathroom sooner. When I take a shorter shower, Austin and Emily are able to use the bathroom sooner. Shorter showers help share a bathroom.

To share the bathroom with Emily and Austin, I will try to take a shorter shower. ■

How to Take a Shorter Shower

Sometimes it's important to take a shorter shower. Here's a list of ideas to make taking a shorter shower easier or more fun:

- Complete the steps to taking a shower, without playing in the bathroom.

- Set an alarm for ten minutes, and keep moving through the shower steps to finish before the alarm rings.

- Take a three-song shower. Record favorite songs on a shower radio. By the end of the first song, wash and rinse hair. By the end of the second song, wash and rinse skin. By the end of the third song, dry off and put on clean clothes.

At my house, it's often important to take a shorter shower. Having a plan can help. I may try using one of the ideas in this list. Or, my mom, dad, or I may have another idea. Whatever we decide, I will try to shorten my time in the shower to share the bathroom with others. ■

The New Social Story™ Book, 10th Anniversary Edition
© by Carol Gray, Future Horizons, Inc.

The Truth about Messes

My family lives in a home. We eat, take baths, sleep, get dressed, play, and work there. Sometimes, we make a mess.

When we eat, pots, pans, and plates get dirty. This can make a mess.

When we get ready for bed, we take off dirty clothes, put on pajamas, brush teeth, find bedtime stories, and find Slowmo, my turtle. This can make a mess.

When we sleep, the sheets get rumpled and our pajamas sometimes end up on the floor in the morning. It's starting to get messy already!

When we get dressed, things can get messy, too.

My family loves to play. That can really make a mess!

Sometimes Mom and Dad go outside to "clean up the yard." Uh oh—does that get messy, too?

There's one true thing about messes: A mess is a mess until someone cleans it up.

A person might sit there, and look at a mess, and hope it will go away. Without help from that person, the mess will stay.

The truth about messes is that only people can make them go away. ■

Restating with Respect at Home

I am learning about respect. Respect helps everyone in my family feel important, comfortable, and safe. Talking respectfully to parents is a skill. It takes practice.

Sometimes, children make mistakes with respect. A child may use a disrespectful tone of voice or words. Talking disrespectfully to a parent is a mistake.

Parents want their children to feel comfortable and happy, and to use respect with others. If my brothers, my sisters, or I make a mistake with respect, my parents say, "Restate with respect, please."

"Restate with respect" gives us an important second chance. It gives us a chance to think. Next, we try to say it again with a calm voice and cooperative words. We try to say the same thing, but with respect.

If my mom or dad says to me, "Restate with respect, please," that means that I have made a mistake with respect. I will try to think and say it again using a calm voice and cooperative words. I will try to say it again with respect.

Many children make mistakes with respect. With practice, they learn how to talk to their parents with respect. ■

What Is a Babysitter?

My name is Joseph. Sometimes I have a babysitter. A babysitter is a person who takes care of babies and children.

Moms and dads ask a babysitter to come. They try to choose a babysitter who will take good care of their children when they cannot be home.

The babysitter comes before the parents leave. When the parents get back, the babysitter leaves.

Sometimes, I may go to the babysitter's house to stay until Mom or Dad comes back for me. This is okay. My mom and dad go to do other things. Whatever they do, they know where I am, and how to get there from anywhere.

Sometimes I have a babysitter. A babysitter is a person who takes care of me when my parents are away. ■

My Babysitter Knows about Me

I have many babysitters. They read this story about me. They know about me.

My babysitter knows that I like Thomas the Tank Engine™.

My babysitter knows that I sleep with Herbie the Elephant.

My babysitter knows where Herbie the Elephant is.

My babysitter knows the food that I like, and how to make it.

My babysitter knows that my favorite bedtime stories are in the elephant bookcase that Dad made.

My babysitter knows that the light in the hallway stays on.

My babysitter knows to leave the vacuum in the closet.

My babysitter knows all of these things and more. She knows how to take care of me until Mom and Dad are home again. ■

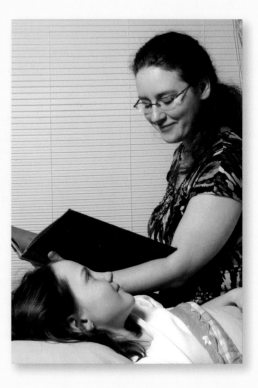

The New Social Story™ Book, 10th Anniversary Edition
© by Carol Gray, Future Horizons, Inc.

Most escalators are wide enough for two people to share a step. Sometimes I may have my own step. Other times, my mom, dad, brother, sister, or someone else that I know may ride with me.

Once in a while, an up escalator may be very, very busy. There are people waiting to use the escalator, and people on almost every step. When this happens, I may be told to share a step. At the top, it will be important to walk a few extra steps before stopping. This will leave enough room for other people to get off of the escalator.

The people in my community safely try to share the up escalators. I will try to safely share the up escalators, too. ■

The New Social Story™ Book, 10th Anniversary Edition
© by Carol Gray, Future Horizons, Inc.

Eating at the Food Court

My family is going to the mall. We may eat at the food court. The food court is a big area with many restaurants and one big area where people can sit and eat. People choose a restaurant, buy food, and then sit and eat at any open table.

There are many choices at a food court. Each person in my family *could* choose their favorite restaurant, and eat together at the same table. My family may use the food court that way. It's my parents' decision to make.

Food court restaurants are fast food restaurants. The people who work there work fast. They ask questions fast. They fill orders fast. They like it when customers make choices fast, too.

My mom or dad can help me buy my food. We may follow these steps:

- Choose a restaurant and walk to it.

- Get in line. We may be first. If there are other people in a line before us, they will be ordering their food before us. If the person in front of us glances at us quickly, it may mean that we are standing too close. It's hard to know for sure. Whether or not this is the case, taking a step back may help. ▶

- Order food. To know when to order food, it helps to watch the person taking the orders closely. When it is our turn to order, that person may glance at us. They may also say something, but they may say it very fast. For example, that person may say something like, "And for you?" or "Okay." This, that glance, and being next in line means that it is time for us to order.

- Place food on tray. Parents can help with this.

- Choose a place to sit. My mom or dad may already be at our table.

At the mall, my family may eat at the food court. ■

The New Social Story™ Book, 10th Anniversary Edition
© by Carol Gray, Future Horizons, Inc.

This Place Is Busy!

There are stores and restaurants in my community. Sometimes, they get busy. There are clues that a place is busy. A place may be busy if:

- There are a lot of people.

- People have to move slower than they would like to.

- To walk around, people have to stop to let others get where they are going.

- There are one or more long lines of people.

- There are many noises, and they are not just voices.

- My mom isn't smiling as much.

- Someone I am with says, "This place is busy!"

Some people enjoy busy places. Others do not. When parents enter a busy place, they may decide to stay. Or, they may decide to come back later or on another day. This is because it's hard for some parents to stay calm and happy in a busy place. ▶

If a place is busy, it may change our plans. This is okay. Finding another time, when a place is less busy, may make it more fun to visit there.

When we are in the community, we may go to a busy place. We may stay, or we may come back later or another day. ■

The New Social Story™ Book, 10th Anniversary Edition
© by Carol Gray, Future Horizons, Inc.

CHAPTER 10

School

Is Today a School Day?

I go to school on school days. Mondays, Tuesdays, Wednesdays, Thursdays, and Fridays are often school days. Sometimes, though, my school will close.

There are many vacation days during the year. Some vacations are long, and others are short. Vacation days are written on the school calendar.

There are other special days when my school may be open for teachers, and closed for students. These are called teacher training or work days. They are usually written on the school calendar.

In the winter, it may snow a lot, or there may be ice. If it's very unsafe or difficult for cars or buses to get around, my school will close. It's called a *snow day*. People expect a few snow days in the winter, but snow days are not listed on the school calendar. That's because no one knows for sure when snow will close my school. My parents watch the local news to learn about snow days.

Sometimes, it may be confusing if today or tomorrow is a school day. Parents can help. Parents are very interested in school days. They know how to use the school calendar and the local news.

I go to school on school days. Sometimes, my school will be closed. ■

Absent Today? This Is Okay.

I am absent from school today. My parents say it's okay.

There are many reasons why a child may be absent. A child may be absent from school if:

- He is sick and needs to be home.

- He needs to go to the doctor or the dentist.

- His family is on a trip.

- There are other reasons a child may be absent, too.

When a child is absent, it is okay. The teacher will help him get his assignments, so that he can finish his schoolwork.

Today, I am absent because _____.
This is okay. My teacher will tell me about my assignments. That way, I will be able to finish my schoolwork.

Tomorrow I may be back in school, or I may be absent again. Mom and Dad can answer my questions about when I will be going back to school. ■

The New Social Story™ Book, 10th Anniversary Edition
© by Carol Gray, Future Horizons, Inc.

When My Teacher Is Somewhere Else

My name is Andrea. My teacher's name is Mrs. Smith. Most school days, Mrs. Smith teaches the class. Sometimes, she has to be somewhere else.

Teachers get sick. Mrs. Smith may be sick. She may need to stay home.

Teachers go to teacher workshops. Mrs. Smith may go to a teacher workshop.

Many teachers have children, and their children get sick. Mrs. Smith has triplets. One of her triplets may be sick, so she needs to stay home.

We have a substitute teacher when Mrs. Smith needs to be somewhere else for the day. This is okay. Mrs. Smith will return to our class as soon as she can. ■

On a Substitute Teacher Day

Today my class has a substitute teacher. It's a substitute teacher day. This means that Mrs. Parker is not here. The substitute teacher is here. His name is Mr. McCuen. Some students may act differently.

On a substitute teacher day, many students work and play as they usually do. There are some students, though, who may talk more, get out of their seats more, break classroom rules more, and work less. They make mistakes that they don't usually make.

Many students want to help Mr. McCuen. If all the students in my class act like they do with Mrs. Parker, this will be most helpful. This probably won't happen today, though. There are some students who may not want to be most helpful to Mr. McCuen. There are other things that they want to do more.

Mr. McCuen knows about students who act differently when they have a substitute teacher. He expects some students to make that mistake. It's Mr. McCuen's job to make decisions about what to do. He's in charge of all students. He's in charge of students who may not be working as they usually do, too.

On a substitute teacher day, it's helpful if students work and play like they usually do. That's a good choice that helps the substitute teacher and other students, too. Some students may make another choice. The substitute teacher decides what to do about them. ■

The New Social Story™ Book, 10th Anniversary Edition
© by Carol Gray, Future Horizons, Inc.

Class Schedules

My name is Caitlyn. I am in Mrs. Jones class. Our class has a schedule.

Mrs. Jones made our class schedule. It is a plan for our class. It lists what we do on *most* school days.

Sometimes, Mrs. Jones will decide to follow another plan. The schedule will list an activity, and we will do another activity instead. This is okay. When this happens, Mrs. Jones will tell us about the new plan. We may follow the posted schedule tomorrow.

Most of the time, our class schedule matches what Mrs. Jones tells us to do. Sometimes, we'll have another plan. When this happens, I will try to do what Mrs. Jones tells us to do. ■

The Truth about Our Class Schedule

My name is Hailey. I am in Mrs. Carlson's class. Our class has two schedules.

A schedule is a planned list of times and activities. One lists our special classes each week, and the times that we plan to start and finish them. Art and gym are on that schedule. The other lists our subjects each day, and the times that we plan to start and finish them. Math, journal time, and science are on that schedule.

The truth about schedules is that they are not people. Schedules don't know anything. A schedule is paper with words on it. It's a plan that stays the same, posted high on the wall so that everyone can see it.

Mrs. Carlson knows a lot. Sometimes, she knows the planned schedule won't work for our class. So, she tells my class what we will do. Here's another truth about our class schedule: At any time, Mrs. Carlson can *overrule* the schedule.

In this case, this means that Mrs. Carlson has more power than the pieces of paper with our schedules. If she tells us to do something different from the schedule, we try to do it. ▶

The New Social Story™ Book, 10th Anniversary Edition
© by Carol Gray, Future Horizons, Inc.

Here's an example of how that works. Last week, the class schedule listed art next, at one o'clock (1:00). Mrs. Carlson told everyone to put their math books away. All of a sudden, the fire drill sounded. Mrs. Carlson said, "Okay, fire drill. Line up at the door. We're going outside." She overruled our weekly schedule, just like that. The fire drill took so long that art was cancelled.

A posted schedule is paper with a plan listed on it. At our school, most of the time, teachers have more power than schedules on paper. That's the truth about schedules. ■

Learning about Directions at School

Sometimes teachers, or other school staff, tell students what to do. They give students directions.

Directions help students work, learn, and play together. Directions help to keep students safe, too.

There are two parts to a direction. The first is giving the direction. Teachers often do that. Teachers give directions to me and everyone else in my class. The second is following the direction. That's the students' job.

I am learning about directions at school. Directions help a class work, learn, and play safely together. ■

The New Social Story™ Book, 10th Anniversary Edition
© by Carol Gray, Future Horizons, Inc.

The Big Yellow Everyone Look and Listen Sign

My name is Elijah. I go to school. Mr. Hunter is my teacher. He has a big, yellow sign.

This is The Big Yellow Everyone Look and Listen Sign. It's important. It means, *Everyone try to look at Mr. Carter. Everyone try to listen to Mr. Carter, too.* Most of the time, Mr. Carter just calls it the Look and Listen Sign. It's his sign, so he can do that.

There are times when Mr. Carter is talking to me and everyone else. Many times, he's at the front of the room when this happens. He puts his Look and Listen Sign where everyone can see it. It means that this is a time for everyone to pay attention to him.

Mr. Carter puts up his sign when he is teaching. It's up when he teaches us math, reading, writing, spelling, science, and other subjects. It's up when Mr. Carter tells us about a class assignment. It's up when he has directions for me and everyone else. It's up whenever he is talking to everyone in class at the same time. ▶

This is the back of Mr. Carter's sign. There are times when Mr. Carter does not need everyone to listen to him. In my class, we have times when everyone is working. Mr. Carter may talk to another teacher or the principal. Sometimes Mr. Carter is talking to a few students, like a reading group. Or, he may come and talk just to me, but not anyone else. During those times, this side of the sign is up.

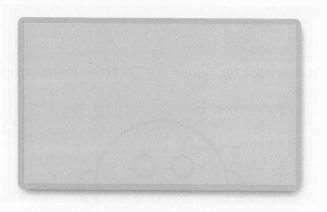

The Big Yellow Everyone Look and Listen Sign means, *Elijah and everyone else try to look at Mr. Carter, and listen to him, too*. It helps me to know when it is important for me to try to pay attention to Mr. Carter. ■

The New Social Story™ Book, 10th Anniversary Edition
© by Carol Gray, Future Horizons, Inc.

It's My Teacher's Decision

Teachers make many decisions for their class. A decision is a firm—and usually final—choice. Teachers make a lot of decisions, like who collects the lunch money and how to care for classroom pets. It's their job.

Teachers often make decisions about ideas from students. Asia has an idea. She wants to collect the lunch money today. Asia's teacher, Miss Capel, decides who collects the lunch money. Asia asks Miss Capel, "May I collect the lunch money today?"

"That would be fine," says Miss Capel. "That would be fine" is a *yes decision*. This *yes decision* means that Asia may collect the lunch money today.

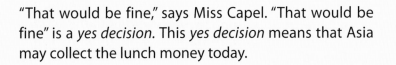

Christopher has an idea. He wants to let Angel, the hamster, out of her cage. Miss Capel decides when Angel is out of her cage. Christopher asks Miss Capel, "May I let Angel out of her cage?"

"Not right now, Christopher," says Miss Capel. "Not right now" is a *no decision*. This *no decision* means that Angel, the hamster, will be in her cage.

Teachers make many decisions each day. My teacher makes decisions, too. Sometimes, my teacher may make a *yes decision*. Other times my teacher may make a *no decision*. Making decisions is a part of my teacher's job. ■

My Place in Line

It's my teacher's job to give my class directions. It's our job to try to follow those directions.

Sometimes, many students move from one place to another. To walk safely, and to allow other groups to walk through the hall at the same time, it's important to try to walk in a line.

Many students like to be first in line. The teacher decides which student is first in the line. Sometimes, I will be the first student in line. Most of the time, another child will be first. When this happens, I will be at another place in the line. This helps the teacher give each student a chance to be first.

My teacher decides which student is first in the line. Once in a while, I will be first in line. Most of the time, another student will be first in line. That's how lines work at my school. That's Life on Planet Earth. ■

The New Social Story™ Book, 10th Anniversary Edition
© by Carol Gray, Future Horizons, Inc.

Learning about Respect at School

Respect is being careful and thoughtful with other people. People show respect with kind words and actions. Respect helps everyone feel welcome, comfortable, and safe.

Teachers and students try to show respect at school. Here are some examples:

- Respect is using kind words and actions.

- Respect is carefully helping another student.

- Respect is sharing.

Respect is being careful and thoughtful with other people. At school, respect helps everyone to feel welcome, comfortable, and safe. ■

Using Respect at School

Respect is being careful and thoughtful with other people. People show respect with kind words and actions. Respect helps everyone feel welcome, comfortable, and safe.

Teachers and students try to show respect at school. Here are some examples:

* Respect is using kind words and actions. When Miss Jacobs works with her fifth graders, she often uses a kind voice and a smile.

* Respect is carefully helping another student. Samantha dropped the envelope with her book-fair money in the hallway. Jose saw it fall. He picked up the envelope and said, "Here, Samantha. You dropped this."

* Respect is sharing. Aidan needed a blue marker. Jenna had one. "Here," Jenna said to Aidan, "You may use mine."

* "Thank you, Jenna," said Aidan. Saying "thank you" shows respect, too!

* Respect is working quietly when others are trying to think, or finish their assignments. Tristan finished his work first. He read a book silently until the test was over.

Respect is being careful and thoughtful with other people. At school, respect helps everyone feel welcome, comfortable, and safe. ■

Talking to a Teacher with Respect

Students learn to talk to teachers with respect. Respect is being careful and thoughtful with another person. When students talk with respect, they use a calm voice and kind words.

It's easiest for students to talk with respect when they're feeling happy, calm, or comfortable.

Sometimes, a student may have a problem, or feel frustrated or angry. *Frustration* and *anger* are two negative feelings. Negative feelings are uncomfortable. They make it more difficult to talk with respect. It's important to learn how to keep negative feelings under control. That way, a student can talk with respect even when feeling uncomfortable.

Many students work hard to learn how to keep their feelings under control. With practice, many students discover that keeping feelings under control makes it easier to talk with respect. ■

Restating with Respect at School

I am learning about respect. Respect helps everyone feel welcome, comfortable, and safe. Learning to talk with respect to a teacher is a skill. Students need to think about, and practice, talking with respect. Sometimes, a student may make mistakes with respect. A student may use a disrespectful tone of voice or words with a teacher.

Talking disrespectfully to a teacher is a mistake. Teachers want students to do well, and to use respect with others. Whenever a student talks to my teacher, Mr. Westra, with a disrespectful tone of voice or words, Mr. Westra says, "Restate with respect, please."

"Restate with respect," gives students an important second chance. This gives students a chance to think and say it again with a calm voice and cooperative words. This gives students a chance say the same thing, but with respect.

If Mr. Westra says to me, "Restate with respect, please," that means that I have made a mistake with respect. I will try to think and say it again using a calm voice and cooperative words. I will try to say it again with respect.

Many students make mistakes with respect. With practice, they learn the skill of talking to teachers with respect. ■

The New Social Story™ Book, 10th Anniversary Edition
© by Carol Gray, Future Horizons, Inc.

When I Talk with Respect at School

I am learning to talk with respect. Talking with respect is using a calm, controlled voice with cooperative words. When working and playing with adults, classmates, and friends, talking with respect is very important. That way, everyone feels comfortable.

Adults in charge of me at school notice when I talk with respect. For example, at the book fair, there was a book that I really wanted. I did not have enough money. An adult told me to put the book back on the shelf. I was very disappointed, but I used cooperative words, saying, "Okay," with a calm voice.

Here are other respectful things that I have said at school:

_____

_____

_____

People notice when I talk with respect! They feel calm and comfortable when I use cooperative words and a calm voice. ■

What Is Practice?

Students learn many important skills. Reading is a skill. Math, writing, and spelling are skills, too. Practice is one way that students learn.

Sometimes, teachers ask students to practice skills. *Practice* is carefully doing a skill over and over.

When students learn to add, they practice by solving many math problems.

When students learn to write, they practice making letters by writing each letter many times.

When students learn to spell a word, they practice spelling it correctly.

Practice helps students learn many important skills. ■

The New Social Story™ Book, 10th Anniversary Edition
© by Carol Gray, Future Horizons, Inc.

Mistakes Happen on the Way to Learning

Students often make mistakes. This is okay. Mistakes often happen on the way to learning.

Students often make mistakes when they learn to add or subtract. This is okay. Mistakes often happen on the way to learning math.

Students often make mistakes when they learn to write letters and words. This is okay. Mistakes often happen on the way to learning writing.

Students often make mistakes when they learn about plants, animals, rocks, or outer space. This is okay. Mistakes often happen on the way to learning science.

Students often make mistakes on the way to learning about other countries, their history, and their people. This is okay. Mistakes often happen on the way to learning geography, history, and social studies.

Mistakes often happen on the way to learning. I may make mistakes on the way to learning. This is okay. ■

That's Great!

WHAT TO DO WITH MISTAKES ON SCHOOLWORK

A mistake is an error. All students make mistakes. So, most students are not surprised to see them on their schoolwork. They may feel sad or disappointed, but not really surprised.

Expecting mistakes helps students prepare for the disappointment of seeing them on their corrected papers. Expecting mistakes helps many students stay calm, so they can think and handle any mistake well.

Sometimes, students are told to correct mistakes on schoolwork. That's one reason why most pencils have erasers. Students try to figure out what they did wrong. Then, they erase the mistake and make it right. That's one good way to handle a mistake.

Other times, it's difficult to figure out why an answer is wrong. Staying calm helps students do their best thinking. Sometimes, thinking a little longer helps a student correct the mistake. That's another great way to handle a mistake.

Often, there are times when students need help with a mistake. They try to figure out what they did wrong, and think a little longer, but still are confused by the mistake. So, they ask for help. Asking for help is another great way to handle a mistake.

I'm a student. I'm likely to make mistakes. I'm learning to expect them. That way, I may learn to be great at handling my mistakes! ■

The New Social Story™ Book, 10th Anniversary Edition
© by Carol Gray, Future Horizons, Inc.

Telling My Teacher about a Problem

Teachers and students talk about many things. They often talk about good news. They can also solve problems together.

Sometimes, a student may have a problem, or feel frustrated or angry. Telling the teacher can help. That way, the teacher will know there is a problem. Teachers want to help. They have a lot of ideas. Teachers can help to solve problems.

If I have a problem at school, telling the teacher may help. If I feel frustrated or angry, telling the teacher may help, too. My teacher has a lot of ideas. She can help to solve problems.

Teachers can help students solve problems and feel more comfortable again. ■

How to Make a Writing Box

Learning to write takes time and practice. Students have many wonderful ideas. A writing box keeps those ideas ready for writing!

A writing box begins as a shoebox, one shoebox for each student. Students may decorate their box, or leave it plain.

Each student's favorite items, like photos, toys, or other small objects, are placed in the box. These items transform a shoebox into a student's own Writing Box. The box is kept at school.

For many writing assignments, the items in the box may help students find a topic. Looking through the box, the student selects an item, an idea for a writing topic.

Sometimes, it helps to keep a selected item out while writing. A student may write what they remember about an item, or find interesting details in a photo. In this way, a writing box helps students develop their ideas.

Many students use writing boxes at school. It helps them to discover topics and develop their ideas. I may try to make a writing box for school, and maybe for home, too! ◼

The New Social Story™ Book, 10th Anniversary Edition
© by Carol Gray, Future Horizons, Inc.

How to Write a True Story

I am learning to use my writing box to write a true story. A true story describes something that really happened. Students often write true stories in journals. To learn to write a true story, I may try following these five steps.

STEP 1

A true story is about real people. They are the characters in a true story. The main character is the most important person in the story. I may be the main character in my true story. Or, I may write a true story about someone that I know. I will try to choose a main character for my story.

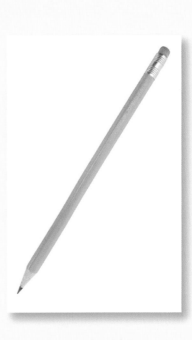

STEP 2

A true story often describes an experience. I have a writing box with photographs of real experiences. I may try choosing a photo to write about.

STEP 3

People who read my story want to know who is in the photo, and where the photo was taken. This makes a good beginning to my story. I will try to write a beginning to my story. ▶

STEP 4

People who read my story want to know about what the people or animals in the photo are doing. This makes a good middle to my story. I will try to write a middle to my story.

STEP 5

People who read my story want to know about how my story ends. They want to know what happened last. My story needs an ending. I will try to write an ending to my story.

A true story is a story about something that really happened. Following these five steps may make it easier to write my story. I will try to write a story with a main character, and a beginning, middle, and ending. ■

The New Social Story™ Book, 10th Anniversary Edition
© by Carol Gray, Future Horizons, Inc.

A-Okay Ways to Finish My Work

My name is Brandon. I am an awesome student at Lincoln School. Most of the time, it is important that students finish their work.

ONE WAY

One way to finish work is to finish it all at one time. This means that a student starts it, works on it, and finishes it. Then, that student begins another activity.

STUDENTS OFTEN HAVE TO DO THEIR WORK ANOTHER WAY

A school schedule is full of many activities. Sometimes, it's best if students finish their work Another Way. Adults decide if it's okay to use another way.

To finish work Another Way:

- Students begin working, then they

- Go do something else, and

- Come back to finish it later.

Begin working.   Go do something else.   Come back to finish it later.

Most of the time, it's important for students to finish their work. There are two ways to finish work: One Way and Another Way. Each school day, adults decide which way is okay. ■

Good Questions for Small Group Projects

Questions are an important part of learning. When students work together, what is a good question?

Mr. Hailey's class is dividing into small groups. Each group will choose a city to study. What are good questions for this project?

A good question may make a suggestion and ask others for their ideas at the same time. One example is this: "I'd like to do our report on Columbus, Ohio. What other cities could we study?"

A good question may invite others to join in. One example is this: "Zachary, you went to San Diego. Would that be a good city to add to our list?"

A good question may show interest in what others are doing. One example is this: "Jackson, I loved the map you drew of downtown. Could you make a city map for our project?" ▶

A good question may help add details to an idea. One example is this: "Jackson, what would you think about drawing a three-dimensional picture of one of the streets in our city, too?"

A good question may help students work things out. One example is this: "Jackson, Darla wants to draw the city map. What would you think if she does the map, and you do a three-dimensional drawing of one of the streets? That will save you time." Sometimes, help from an adult may be needed to find a solution.

A good question may seek help from others. One example is this: "I'd like to work on writing the report. But I'll need help. Who can help with that?"

When students work in small groups, a good question is one that helps students share ideas or solve problems. ■

An Emergency?

THE PEOPLE AT MY SCHOOL KNOW WHAT TO DO

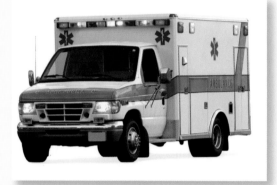

Once in a while, there may be an emergency at my school. An emergency is a dangerous, sometimes-unexpected situation. In an emergency, people need to act right away.

There are many kinds of school emergencies. Once, Kendra broke her arm when she fell on the playground. That was an emergency. Mr. Burns, our teacher, helped Kendra right away. He knew what to do. Kendra is okay now.

Another time, Nicholas in Miss Keyser's class was very sick. None of us expected that to happen. All morning Nicholas was fine. All of a sudden, he was sick. Miss Keyser got help right away. An ambulance took Nicholas to the hospital. Nicholas is okay now.

Fires and tornadoes are very big school emergencies. In these emergencies, *everybody* in the school needs to know what to do. Everyone has to act right away, at the same time. There has never been a fire at my school. There has never been a tornado, either. If there ever is a fire or tornado, though, everyone in my school knows what to do.

Once in a while there may be an emergency at my school. If there is, people in my school know what to do. ■

What Is a Drill?

In an emergency, it's important for people to act right away. It's important for them to know what to do. A drill can help people be ready for a big emergency. What is a drill?

A drill is *practice* that is done the same, best way each time. Drills help people make fewer mistakes.

In a big emergency, it is very, very, very important for everyone to know what to do. This helps to keep everyone safe. For this reason, many people use drills to practice for big emergencies. Firemen, policemen, doctors, nurses, and the people in my school use drills to practice for emergencies.

A drill is practice that is done the same, best way each time. That way, in a big emergency everyone knows the best thing to do. People use drills to help them practice. That way, they are ready for big emergencies. ■

Why Principals Schedule Drills

Most school buildings are safe places. Once in a very long while, there may be a big emergency at my school. School fires and tornadoes are big emergencies. A few times each school year, our principal schedules drills for us to practice what to do if there is a fire or tornado.

A drill is practice that is done the same, best way each time. In an emergency, it's important to act right away. Knowing exactly what to do helps to keep people calm and safe. During a drill, everything is really safe and okay. That's the very best time to practice for an emergency.

Our principal schedules the drills. She knows when they will happen. Most people in our school do not know when there will be a fire or tornado drill. Not knowing when it will happen is part of the drill. Since fires and tornadoes are often unexpected, it's important to practice for them that way.

On a school day, there are many people at school. Someday, there may be a tornado or a fire at my school. It's important for each person to know what to do. This takes practice. So, principals schedule drills. ■

The New Social Story™ Book, 10th Anniversary Edition
© by Carol Gray, Future Horizons, Inc.

Fire Drills at School

School buildings are safe places. Once in a very long while, a fire may start in a school. If this happens, it's very important for everyone to calmly, quickly, and safely leave the building at the same time. This takes practice. So, principals schedule fire drills.

During a fire drill, everything in a school is safe and okay. That's the very best time to for teachers and students to practice leaving a school.

A drill is practice that is done the same, best way each time. In a fire drill, each class has their own route to leave the building. This keeps people from bumping into one another. If there ever was a fire, a special route helps everyone get out of the building calmly, quickly, and safely.

Once outside, each class has a special safe area. This is where they stop and count to make sure everyone is out of the building. Then they wait for the "all clear" signal to return to class.

There is usually more than one fire drill each school year. Each time, every class leaves the school the same way. They go to the same area outside of the building.

Most school buildings are safe all of the time. Once in a very long while, a fire may start in a school. Fire drills help teachers and students practice so that everyone knows how to leave the school calmly, quickly, and safely. ■

The New Social Story™ Book, 10th Anniversary Edition
© by Carol Gray, Future Horizons, Inc.

Why Schools Have Fire Alarms

Every school has a fire alarm. A fire alarm is a safety device. My school has a fire alarm.

A fire alarm makes a very special, loud and uncomfortable sound. This is to get everyone's attention. It is used to start a fire drill. It is also used if there is a fire anywhere in a building.

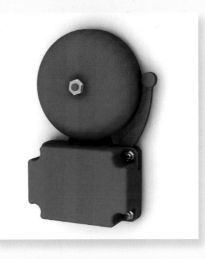

A fire alarm means leave the building now. Everyone in the school knows that when they hear it, it's time to leave the building and go to their safe area outside.

Fire alarms will always sound uncomfortable, like the one at my school. Knowing why they are made that way, and what they mean, doesn't make them any quieter. It does, though, help people understand why they are in every school. ■

The New Social Story™ Book, 10th Anniversary Edition
© by Carol Gray, Future Horizons, Inc.

About Tornado Drills

Most of the time, weather is safe for people. Once in a long while, there is severe weather. In severe weather, often people need to do special things to keep safe. A tornado is very severe weather.

There are many people in a school. If there is a tornado, it's important to get all of the people to safer places in the school. A tornado drill is how adults and children practice moving to safer places in the school.

A tornado drill starts with a loud and unique noise. It's a loud and unique noise so that no one confuses it with another bell, like the one that ends recess. When adults and children hear it, they know it is time to practice moving to a safer place in the school.

In a tornado drill, there is no tornado. It's a time to practice moving to a safer place calmly and quickly. If there is a tornado someday, the same loud and unique noise will sound. When a tornado drill is over, everyone finishes the school day.

My school will have tornado drills. We will practice what to do if there is a tornado. That way, if someday there is a tornado, we will all know what to do. ■

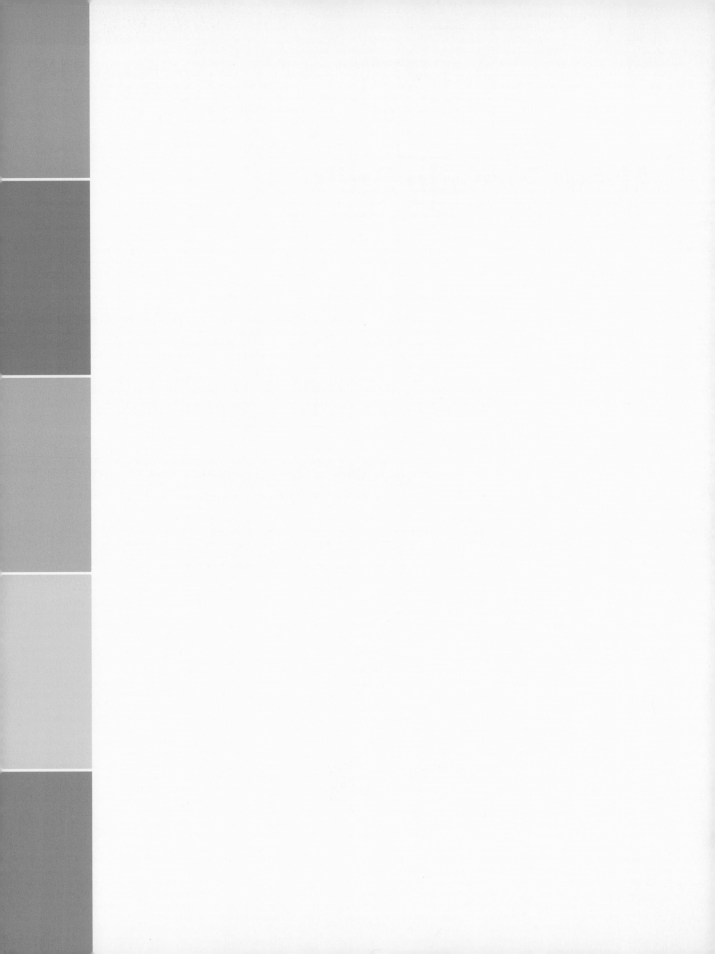

CHAPTER 11

Planet Earth

That's Life on Planet Earth

I live on Planet Earth. All people live on Planet Earth with me. It's our "home" planet. There are some experiences that almost all people have in common. These experiences are a part of life here, on Planet Earth.

People wake up. Sometimes they are happy to wake up. Other times they would like to be able to sleep longer. That's Life on Planet Earth.

People live in homes. Sometimes everything works, other times something needs to be fixed. That's Life on Planet Earth.

People often go places. Sometimes they arrive exactly on time. Sometimes they arrive late. Sometimes people arrive early. That's Life on Planet Earth.

People make mistakes. Sometimes they make big mistakes. Sometimes they make little mistakes. That's Life on Planet Earth. ▶

For all Planet Earth people, there are likely to be:

- Times when they are happy to wake up, and other times they'd rather sleep

- Days when everything works, and other days when something needs to be fixed

- Times when they are on time, late, or early

- They will make big mistakes and little ones, too. That's Life on Planet Earth.

Because I am a Planet Earth person, there are likely to be:

- Times when I am happy to wake up, and other times I'd rather sleep

- Days when everything works, and other days when something needs to be fixed

- Times when I'm on time, late, or early

It's likely that I may make big mistakes and little ones, too. That's Life on Planet Earth. ■

The New Social Story™ Book, 10th Anniversary Edition
© by Carol Gray, Future Horizons, Inc.

Sharing Planet Earth

People live on Planet Earth. They share it. Sometimes they share it well. Other times it's harder for people to share Planet Earth.

People on Planet Earth share some things easily. Day and night is one example. When one side of the planet has day, the other has night. There are times when some people on the planet get a lot of daylight, and others get a lot less. For some reason, even though daylight and night are unequal, people seem to be okay with that. The seasons are another example. When one part of the planet has summer, somewhere else it is fall. Many people love summer, and there are parts of Planet Earth that get a lot more of it than others. People seem to be okay with that, too.

Even though the sun and seasons are really big and important, people share them easily, without having to think much about it. Sometimes, parents may tell their children that they "need to learn how to share." This isn't completely true.

Children share sun and seasons as easily as their parents. Here's a theory: It's easier for people to share what they can't possibly own, or to share when it is just a part of their routine. ▶

People on Planet Earth have to think and work together to share other things. This includes adults. The list of things that are harder to share is a lot longer than this whole book. Here are six of them: money, malted milk balls, oil, televisions, macaroni and cheese, and neighborhoods. The things on this list are smaller than the sun, and may be less important than a season, but they are harder for many people to share.

Here's another theory: It's more difficult for people to share something that has a limited supply. Sometimes, even adults have to think about how to share things like that. They try to teach their children to share, too.

People live on Planet Earth. They need to share it. Sometimes they share it easily. Other times they have to think about it. Sharing is a part of life for the adults and children of Planet Earth. ■

I'm Taking a Flight

My name is Jordan. Mom and Dad told me that I will be taking a flight with them soon. That means that I will be riding in an airplane.

There's a lot to know about flying in an airplane. I have a set of stories to help.

I am riding on a plane soon. People will probably be saying to me, "Have a good flight!" ■

Who Are the Crew?

Every flight has a crew. Most crews have a pilot, co-pilot, and one or more flight attendants. They wear uniforms. That way, passengers know which people are members of the crew.

The pilot and co-pilot fly the plane. They have studied and practiced to learn how to fly a plane. The pilot and copilot work near the front of the plane in the cockpit. It's their job to fly the plane and to lead the crew.

Flight attendants work in the cabin of the airplane. They studied and practiced to learn how to keep passengers comfortable and safe. The cabin has a small kitchen, one or more bathrooms, and many seats for passengers.

The crew works to keep passengers comfortable and safe. ■

The New Social Story™ Book, 10th Anniversary Edition
© by Carol Gray, Future Horizons, Inc.

Who Are the Passengers on an Airplane?

Many airplanes carry passengers. A passenger is a person with a ticket to ride on the plane. A passenger may be a child, like me. Or, a passenger may be an older adult, like my grandparents. Sometimes, a baby or toddler is a passenger.

Passengers do not need to know how to fly a plane, or how to keep everyone safe. It's important, though, for passengers to listen to directions from the pilots and flight attendants. It's so important that there are laws about following directions on an airplane. This helps the pilot and flight attendants keep everyone safe.

I may be a passenger on a plane, too. If I am, I may see babies, toddlers, children, and adults who are passengers with me. We will all have a ticket to ride the plane! ■

What Does "Going through Security" Mean?

Keeping passengers and crew safe on an airplane is very important. Going through security helps to find passengers or items that could be a problem on a flight. That's why all passengers and crew have to "go through security" before they get on an airplane.

There are airport officers that help everyone go through security. These airport officers are friendly with people who cooperate and suddenly serious with people who don't. That's because they are helping people and looking for problem people and items, all at the same time.

Catching problems early is better than discovering them after the crew and passengers get on the plane. Going through security is one way to discover problems. Airport officers have a very important job. Cooperative passengers help everyone "go through security," so that they can get on their plane. ■

The New Social Story™ Book, 10th Anniversary Edition
© by Carol Gray, Future Horizons, Inc.

Directions for Going through Security

Following directions when going through security is very important. Most people do not like to go through security. It's just something they have to do if they want to ride on a plane.

These are the directions for going through security:

- If there's a line of people at any point in security, wait for a turn.

- If airport officers tell you to do something that is not on this list, do it.

- Show your boarding pass and identification to the first officer.

- Put shoes and cases on the conveyer belt to go through the scanning machine.

- Place other things in the bins as directed.

- Walk through the short security tunnel.

- Put items back in their cases, put on shoes.

Following the directions for going through security helps the airport officers find problem passengers or items. This helps to keep everyone safe. ■

Moms, Dads, and Airport Security

Sometimes, moms and dads are serious or stressed when they go through security at an airport. It helps children to know why this happens, and what their parents may be thinking or feeling as they go through security.

First, it's a little harder for a family with children to go through security. Families have more stuff that they carry with them onto a plane. This stuff makes traveling with children easier and fun. It makes going through security a little stressful, though. Some items have to be unpacked and placed on the scanner. Moms and dads worry about getting everything through the scanner. They also worry about forgetting something when they repack everything afterwards. And, most important, they are keeping track of their children, too. They've a lot to do in a short time.

Second, especially if there's a long line, parents are hoping their children really cooperate and follow the rules. When moms and dads start thinking about the people who are waiting in line behind them, it adds to their stress. This is because they know others want to get through security quickly. Sometimes, moms and dads may try to get their children to move faster. Their children, though, may be distracted by interesting things, like the conveyer belt and the security scanner.

Families going through security are a little slower than others. Sometimes moms and dads may seem serious or stressed. Knowing why they feel this way is helpful information for their children. ■

The New Social Story™ Book, 10th Anniversary Edition
© by Carol Gray, Future Horizons, Inc.

What Airport Officers Say and Mean

Airport officers ask questions—or tell people what to do—as they go through security. Once in a while or maybe more than that, an airport officer may ask a question to tell someone what to do. This may be a little confusing. Airport officers do this because they want to be polite as they watch for problem items and people. This results in friendly questions without choices; questions that give a direction. Knowing about questions that are really directions helps passengers to do the right thing, at the right time.

Here are some examples:

- An airport officer may say, "May I see your boarding pass?" This means, *You must show me your boarding pass now.*

- An airport officer may say, "May I look in your bag?" This means, *I need to look in your bag. If you say "no," you may not be getting on the plane.*

- An airport officer may say, "Would you please remove your belt and walk through the scanner again?" This means, *Remove your belt and walk through the scanner.*

Airport officers try to be friendly while doing a very, very serious job. Knowing that this may cause them to use friendly questions to give no-choice directions helps everyone get through security more easily. ■

Jet Way Lines May Be Slow at Times

Planes fly in and out of airports. Many times a jet way is used to connect an airplane to an airport. People walk in the jet way to get onto a plane. Sometimes, passengers need to stop and wait in the jet way. Knowing why this happens helps people stay calm.

Passenger airplanes have many seats. This gives each person a place to sit on the plane. It doesn't leave a lot of room for people to walk. When fifty, one hundred, or more people get on a plane, the aisle fills up very quickly. A line forms out into the jet way.

Meanwhile, other passengers are already in the airplane, getting settled into their seats. Sometimes they have to take off their coats, put their luggage away, or help another passenger. All of this takes time, especially when there are a lot of passengers.

Jet way lines can be slow at times. Jet way lines often stop, then move, then stop, then move. Even so, it is the fastest way to get many people with bags and luggage down one aisle and into their seats.

Most passengers would rather be in their seats than standing in a slow jet way line. They may feel a little uncomfortable or frustrated. It's important to try to stay calm. Sometimes thinking can help. Passengers may think, *This is what happens when two hundred people get on an airplane*, or, *The line will move again soon*, or, *Others will wait for me when I am getting settled into my seat*. Thinking to stay calm in a jet way is smart.

I may use a jet way to get onto a plane. If there are many people, the line may move slowly. The line of people, with me in it, may need to stop and wait now and then. This is okay. I will try to think to stay calm. This is smart for me, and helpful for the passengers around me. ■

The New Social Story™ Book, 10th Anniversary Edition
© by Carol Gray, Future Horizons, Inc.

Parents Are Important Passengers

Parents are important passengers. They help the pilot and flight attendants.

Parents are important adult passengers. They listen for directions, and help their children follow those directions.

That's why my mom or dad may tell me to wait to use the bathroom on the airplane, or tell me to stay in my seat. It's their job to follow directions from the pilots and flight attendants.

Parents are important. They follow directions from the crew. This helps the pilot and flight attendants make sure that everyone has a safe and comfortable flight. ■

Children Are Important Passengers

Children often help everyone on a plane have a safe and pleasant flight. Listening to parents and trying to follow directions is one way that children can help.

I will try to help mom and dad when we fly. They can tell me about the rules for flying. I will try to listen and follow those rules. My mom, dad, and everyone around us in the airplane will be pleased if I follow the airplane rules.

Pilots first—and moms and dads second—decide when it's okay for people to take off their seatbelt or move around.

Pilots decide when people can leave their seats. In every airplane there's a little picture of a seatbelt. It's also a light. When I am in the airplane, my mom or dad can show me where it is. There's a little seatbelt sign in each row.

The pilot turns the seatbelt sign on and off. If the seatbelt picture is on, that means everyone must keep their seatbelts on. It's the law.

I will try to listen to my parents and follow directions. This will help everyone to have a safe and comfortable flight. ∎

The New Social Story™ Book, 10th Anniversary Edition
© by Carol Gray, Future Horizons, Inc.

Is This Flight on Time?

Most flights are on time. Some flights are delayed. Other flights are cancelled. This happens with air travel.

Most flights are *on time. On time* means that everything is safe for the plane to fly at the scheduled time.

Sometimes, a flight is *delayed*. This means that there's a new, later time to take off, and a new, later time to land. This is okay. Sometimes it takes longer to make sure a plane is ready to fly.

Other times, a flight is *cancelled*. This means that the plane will not be taking off as planned. When this happens, passengers often fly on another plane.

Most planes fly on time. Some flights are delayed. Other flights are cancelled. This happens with air travel. That's Life on Planet Earth. ■

Why Are Some Flights Delayed?

A plane may be delayed at any time during a flight. A plane may be delayed before the passengers get on it. A plane may be delayed after the passengers are on it. Sometimes, a plane is delayed while it is in the air. Other times, a plane is delayed after it has landed. There are times when a plane is delayed more than once during a flight.

There are many reasons why a flight may be delayed. Something may need to be fixed. There may be a storm. The crew may need to rest. There may be a line of planes on the ground waiting to take off, or a line of planes in the sky waiting to land. There are other reasons a plane may be delayed, too.

At first, many passengers feel a little disappointed or frustrated when a flight is delayed. These negative feelings don't last for long, though. Passengers know that a delayed flight almost always means that care is being taken to keep everyone on the plane safe. Knowing that helps passengers feel patient, calm, and comfortable once again.

A flight may be delayed. There are many reasons why. Delaying a flight often helps to keep it safe. ■

The New Social Story™ Book, 10th Anniversary Edition
© by Carol Gray, Future Horizons, Inc.

A Wildfire Is near Our Home

There is a wildfire getting closer to our home. This makes this story very important.

Fire is the flame, heat, and light that is caused by burning. Fire can be helpful. Fire can also be a very serious problem. Fire is always dangerous. Knowing about fire helps people stay safe.

Fire can be helpful. People often use fire for heat and energy to keep their homes warm and comfortable, or to cook food. When camping, adults may build a campfire, or use fire to light a lantern. There are many ways that fire is helpful.

Adults know about the dangers of fire, and how to use fire safely. They know and follow all of the rules for using fire intelligently. They know, too, that it is very, very, very important to be careful with fire. That way fire stays safe, helpful, and under control.

Sometimes fire becomes a very big and serious problem. The fire spreads and gets larger. The people try to keep it under their control but the fire spreads too quickly. The fire becomes too big for them to put out. When this happens, people call the fire department. ▶

When a fire is outside and spreading very quickly it is called a wildfire. Wildfires are a very, very, very, big and serious problem. They get bigger very fast. A wildfire is very, very, very, very difficult for people to control. Many times firefighters ask other firefighters to help get a wildfire back under control.

There is a wildfire about ____ miles away. It's difficult for the firemen to get it under control. To keep my family safe and healthy, we may be asked to leave our house. The firemen are watching the fire very closely. They will tell my mom or dad if it's important for us to leave our house. ■

The New Social Story™ Book, 10th Anniversary Edition
© by Carol Gray, Future Horizons, Inc.

What Does *Evacuate* Mean?

Sometimes people are told to *evacuate* their house. *Evacuate* means *to empty and leave.* Sometimes, though, *evacuate* means *to take what is most important and leave the rest.*

Usually, a family is asked to evacuate because their house may be in danger. Fire is dangerous to a house. The house may burn. It's very important to keep the family safe and away from the fire. For this reason families are asked to evacuate their house. They are asked to go to a safer place.

Most families never have to evacuate their house. Once in a very long while, though, some families do have to evacuate. When people are told to evacuate a house, it is very, very, very important to follow that direction.

Evacuation is one way that parents keep their children safe. I may be able to help if my family has to evacuate our house. I may be able to help to keep the people in my family safe. Mom or Dad will have ideas about how I may help. ■

Why Do We Have to Go?

Many children have questions about evacuation. Often they want to know why their family has to evacuate the house. Sometimes children will ask their mom or dad, "Why do we have to go?"

When firefighters tell a family to evacuate, it's very, very, very important for people to leave their house. Firefighters have studied fires for a long time. They are fire experts. Firefighters decide when a fire is too close and people have to evacuate their houses. It's intelligent to listen and follow their directions.

Sometimes, it may seem that a fire is not that close. It may seem like it would be okay to stay. The problem is, when a fire is out of control it spreads quickly. That is why firefighters ask families to evacuate when it is still safe to go, before the fire is very close.

Firefighters decide when a fire is too close. They tell people when it is time to evacuate. If a firefighter says, "It's time to evacuate," it's time to evacuate. Following the directions of firefighters helps people stay safe. ■

The New Social Story™ Book, 10th Anniversary Edition
© by Carol Gray, Future Horizons, Inc.

People Would Rather Stay in their Houses

People evacuate a house because they have to leave. If they had a choice, they would choose to stay and do what they usually do. They wish the fire was out. They wish their home was farther away from the fire. They wish the fire was under control. Wishing doesn't put a fire out, though. If it did, the fire would be out by now.

By the time people grow to become adults, they have learned to do things they don't want to do without whining or having a tantrum. They may feel sad, nervous, or uncomfortable, but they know it's important to keep thinking and working to keep their family safe.

Sometimes adults help themselves feel better by remembering that life isn't always like this. They know that fires end and someday it will be possible to do the things that they usually do. That's when adults say things like, "It will be nice when life gets back to normal." That helps them to remember life without wildfires, and they feel better.

If my mom and dad say, "It's time to evacuate," it's important to follow their direction. ■

The Evening News

HOW WE CHANGED TODAY

At the same time, every day, the evening news is aired on television. It starts at the same time each day, usually with the same person, called the *anchor,* who reports the news. The news, though, is all about change.

Some anchors have a phrase that they use somewhere in the opening of the evening news, like "Nightly news begins now." They use it with each newscast. They often have another same-phrase-each-day to end the news, like, "And that's the way it is." ▶

The New Social Story™ Book, 10th Anniversary Edition
© by Carol Gray, Future Horizons, Inc.

To watch the evening news, many people sit in the same chair, at about the same time each day, to watch the news. They watch the same station. Same time. Same channel. Same anchor. Same phrases. Same chair.

The news itself, though, is never, ever the same as the day before. The news reports change.

Expected changes are usually not newsworthy. They are not big news. What would those reports sound like? "It's fall here in Vermont. I'm standing in front of a tree. It was here yesterday. It dropped a few leaves today, though."

The most newsworthy changes are often those that are unwelcome and unexpected. The very biggest, most important changes make the evening news everywhere.

Here's a theory: The evening news reports change. How news is reported, though, stays pretty much the same. For people on Planet Earth, learning about change seems to work best if it is done the same way each day. ■

The New Social Story™ Book, 10th Anniversary Edition
© by Carol Gray, Future Horizons, Inc.

At the End of Each Day

A LITTLE BIT CHANGED AND MOSTLY THE SAME

Here's a theory: At the end of each day, Planet Earth is a little bit changed and mostly the same.

A lot changes in a day. Each day:

- 216,000 babies are born. They are Planet Earth's newest people, until tomorrow.

- Every person is a day older.

- Every building, car, sofa, television, and many, many other things are a day older.

- Many people have changed their *location*. Some people drive their car, take a bus, ride a train, or a boat to another place. They may fly to another place, too. There are about 49,000 airline flights each day.

- Some plants are bigger, all plants are older, some trees have fallen.

- There have been about 2,600 earthquakes, most of them very small and unnoticed.

At the end of each day, it is likely that there have been more changes on Planet Earth than anyone could count before tomorrow. ▶

The New Social Story™ Book, 10th Anniversary Edition
© by Carol Gray, Future Horizons, Inc.

For all the changes that happen each day, from space Planet Earth always looks pretty much the same. The really, really big things don't change a lot. The Earth travels around the sun the same. The Earth turns the same. Oceans, mountains, rivers, and valleys are in about the same place that they have been in for many, many years. People don't need to make a new topographical map of Earth each day!

People depend on Planet Earth to stay mostly the same. It helps them to plan their year, month, and day. It helps them to know, pretty much, what life will be like tomorrow. It helps them to feel comfortable here, and focus on what is important to them.

At the end of each day, with all of the changes on Planet Earth, it's still pretty much the same. It's a theory that helps many people fall asleep each night. ■

Maybe I Could Do That

Someday, I will be an adult. What will I do? It may be fun to think about that.

There are people who work to save Planet Earth's resources. Maybe I could do that.

There are people who sell tickets at the movie theatre. Maybe I could do that.

There are people who write poems and sonnets. Maybe I could do that.

There are people who work at the radio station. Maybe I could do that.

There are people who teach. Maybe I could do that.

There are people who stock the shelves at the grocery store. Maybe I could do that. ▶

The New Social Story™ Book, 10th Anniversary Edition
© by Carol Gray, Future Horizons, Inc.

There are people who find cures for diseases. Maybe I could do that.

There are people who design and draw. Maybe I could do that.

There are people who work in big cities. Maybe I could do that.

There are people who work outdoors. Maybe I could do that.

Someday, I will be an adult. What will I do? Just watch as I answer that. ■

Glossary

Cooperative words (adjective+noun)

Cooperative words are single words, phrases, or sentences that help people work and play together for the same goal. Cooperative words are stated in a calm and friendly tone of voice (*see* Calm voice).

> Sample sentence: *Talking with respect is using a calm, controlled voice with cooperative words.*

Expect (verb)

When *expect* is used in this book, it has one of two meanings.

Expect may mean to think ahead, to guess that something will probably happen.

> Sample sentence: *As an inventor, he expected to make mistakes.*

2. *Expect* may mean to believe that something should happen.

> Sample sentence: *Once in a while, though, children are expected to shake hands.*

Experience (noun)

When *experience* is used in this book, it has one of two meanings.

Experience may mean an event or activity, something that a person sees, hears, or does.

> Sample sentence: *A true story often describes an experience.*

Experience may mean knowledge that is gained by doing something, or by practicing a skill.

> Sample sentence: *They have a lot of experience.*

Frustrate/Frustrating (verb)

Frustrate means to be stopped or kept from reaching a goal, or unable to do what a person wants to do.

> Sample sentence: *Waiting to open a gift may be a little frustrating, especially for children.*

Guess (verb or noun)

When *guess* is used in this book, it has one of two meanings.

Guess may mean to believe something *may* be true, correct, or the right thing to do, without enough information to know for sure if it is true, correct, or the right thing to do. (verb)

> Sample sentence: *Another way that adults often say yes is, "Okay, I guess," or backwards, "I guess it's okay."*

Guess may mean a belief without enough information to know for sure if it is correct or true. (noun)

> Sample sentence: *Grandpa says that many people like to wrap gifts, so his guess is that they will wrap them this year, too.*

Predict (verb)

To *predict* is to know something will happen ahead of time; often it is a guess that is based on information. Weather forecasters try to predict the weather.

> Sample sentences: *No one can predict exactly when someone may try to bully another person. No one can predict exactly what a student may do in a bullying attempt.*

Step (noun)

When *step* is used in this book, it has one of three meanings.

Step may mean putting one foot forward, backward, or sideways.

> Sample sentence: *I had to keep repeating "excuse me" every few steps.*

Step may mean a place to put one's foot to move up or down. One step is one part of a set of stairs or staircase.

> Sample sentence: *For example, they may forget their lunch, trip going up steps, or dial a phone number incorrectly.*

Step may also mean one of a series of actions that complete a task, or reach a goal.

Sample sentence: *We will complete it step by step, following the directions and answering the questions together.*

Social Story (noun)

A *Social Story* is a true story that describes a situation, skill, or idea. It is researched, written, and illustrated according to ten criteria or characteristics.

Sample sentence: The New Social Story™ Book *by Carol Gray contains many Social Stories.*

Surprise (verb or noun)

When *surprise* is used in this book, it has one of two meanings.

Surprise may mean something that happens unexpectedly. (verb)

Sample sentence: *Children may be surprised to learn that most adults like to say "yes" whenever they can.*

Surprise may mean something that is not expected, for example, a statement, gift, action, or event. (noun)

Sample sentence: *Many people think that nice surprises are fun.*

Theory (noun)

A *theory* is a guess or opinion that explains how or why something happens. A theory is often based on some facts, or experience, but not proven.

Sample sentence: *Here's a theory: It's easier for people to share what they can't possibly own, or to share when it is just a part of their routine.*

Thing (noun)

In this book, *thing* has one of seven meanings.

Thing(s) may mean any real object(s) or item(s).

> Sample sentence: *He invented many other things, too.*

Thing(s) may mean almost any topic(s) or idea.

> Sample sentence: *When I look at these photos, it reminds me of one thing that I have learned about parties.*

Thing(s) may mean almost any activity (activities).

> Sample sentence: *There are things that I like to do.*

Thing(s) may mean one person's clothing, toys, or personal items.

> Sample sentence: *We'll put most of my toys and other things in moving boxes.*

Thing(s) may mean almost any statement(s) that is said, or written.

> Sample sentence: *We try to say the same thing, but with respect.*

Thing(s) may mean almost any event(s).

> Sample sentence: *Sometimes things happen, though, and people cannot come.*

Thing(s) may mean the condition of a friendship, relationship, event, or activity.

> Sample sentence: *Soon, they want to make things right again.*

There are more meanings for the word *thing* in the dictionary. In this book, when *thing* is used in a sentence, it has one of these listed meanings.

That's Life on Planet Earth (phrase)

That's Life of Planet Earth is a phrase that usually follows a description of an experience that almost all people have in common. These may be comfortable, good, experiences. Or, they may be uncomfortable or unwanted experiences. Either way, they are a part of life for almost all people on Planet Earth.

Sample uses of the phrase, *That's Life on Planet Earth:*

Sad is an uncomfortable feeling. It's okay for people to feel sad. When people feel sad they try to find a way to be happy again. That's Life on Planet Earth.

Mistakes are a part of Life on Planet Earth. That is correct.

Permission is needed when a child has an idea, and it's an adult's decision to make. Sometimes children get the permission that they need, other times they don't. Either way, that's Life on Planet Earth!

This is Okay (phrase)
This is okay is a phrase that usually follows a description of a surprising, unwanted or uncomfortable situation. *This is okay* means that even though a situation may not be what someone would like, it needs to happen—or will happen—in the way just described. *This is okay* also means that while a situation may be surprising, unwanted, or uncomfortable, it is safe.

Sample uses of the phrase, *This is okay:*

The truth is, adults don't know everything. This is okay.

The line of people, with me in it, may need to stop and wait now and then. This is okay.

Sometimes, I may go to the babysitter's house to stay until Mom or Dad come back for me. This is okay.

Transform (verb)
Transform means to completely change how a living being or thing looks or functions (how it works).

Sample sentence: *Just watch me transform as I grow!*

The New Social Story™ Book, 10th Anniversary Edition
© by Carol Gray, Future Horizons, Inc.

Transformation (noun)
A *transformation* is a big change in how a living being or thing looks or functions (how it works).

> Sample sentence: *This is the transformation stage.*

Transformer (noun)
In the dictionary, a *transformer* is a device that changes electrical voltage. In this book, *transformer* is a living being that makes big changes in appearance or function (how it works).

> Sample sentence: *A butterfly is a real transformer.*

Welcome (verb, noun, or adjective)
When *welcome* is used in this book, it has one of two meanings.

Welcome may mean to give someone a friendly greeting as they arrive (verb).

> Sample sentence: *Welcome to Fort Able!*

Welcome may mean to receive in a friendly way (adjective).

> Sample sentence: *Here's a theory: Expected and welcome changes are the easiest.*

Unexpected (adjective)
Unexpected means happening as a surprise, without any warning.

> Sample sentence: *Since fires and tornadoes are often unexpected, it's important to practice for them that way.*

Unwelcome (adjective)
Unwelcome means not wanted, accepted, or welcome.

> Sample sentence: *A flat tire on a car is an unexpected and unwelcome surprise.*

WORDS AND PHRASES ABOUT FREQUENCY

Many words and phrases describe how often something happens, or its *frequency*. For example, the word "always" means continuously, every time, or on every occasion. The word "never" means at no time, not on any occasion. "Always" and "never" have opposite meanings: "always" is every time, "never" is not ever.

In the drawing below, "always" and "never" are placed at opposite ends of the line to show the opposite meanings. Several people were asked to arrange words and phrases from this book, according to their frequency. The results are placed on the line between "never" and "always." The closer the word or phrase is to "always," the greater its frequency. Words with similar meanings are the same color. To figure out the meaning of a word or phrase, look at its color and placement on the line. There are many other words and phrases used to describe how often something happens, but these are the words and phrases used in this book. ■

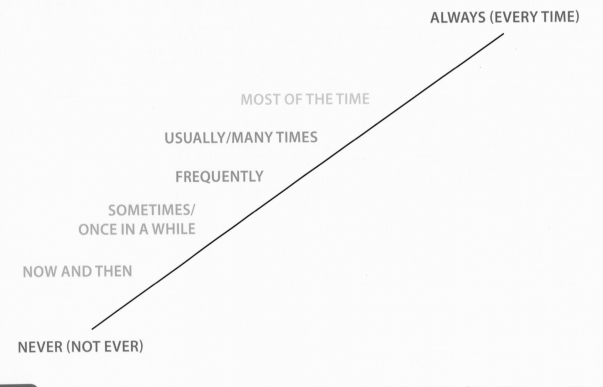

ALWAYS (EVERY TIME)

MOST OF THE TIME

USUALLY/MANY TIMES

FREQUENTLY

SOMETIMES/
ONCE IN A WHILE

NOW AND THEN

NEVER (NOT EVER)

References

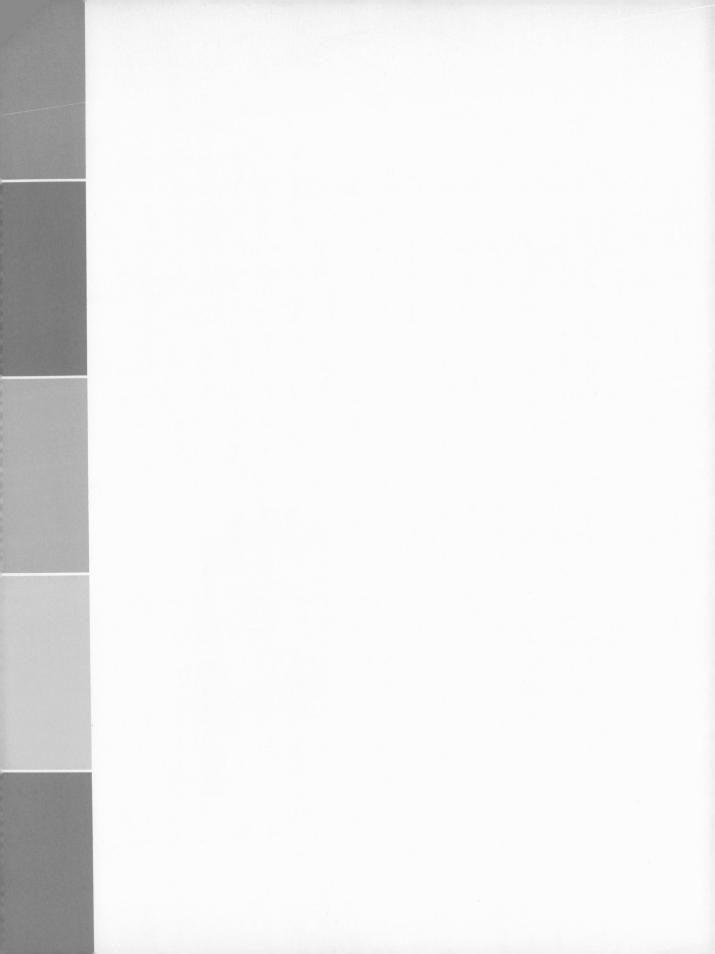

References for Stories in The New Social Story™ Book

(listed by title in sequential order)

The Transformers Around Us: Butterflies

Montana State University. Butterflies: The children's butterfly site. Life cycle of butterflies and moths. Retrieved October 4, 2009 from *www.kidsbutterfly.org/life-cycle*

The Transformers Around Us: Frogs.

All About Frogs.org. Life cycle of a frog. Retrieved October 4, 2009 from *http://allaboutfrogs.org/weird/general/cycle.html*

The Transformers Around Us: Ladybugs

Mrs. Seagraves QUEST class homepage. The life cycle of the ladybug. Retrieved October 4, 2009 from *www.geocities.com/sseagraves/ladybuglifecycle.htm*

Thomas Edison and Mistakes

Google. Cynthia-ga. Did Thomas Edison really say this? Retrieved on October 1, 2009 from *http://answers.google.com/answers/threadview/id/747226.html*

Why Do People Shake Hands?

Ramsey, L. Shaking Hands Throughout History and Around the World. Retrieved August 8, 2009 at *www.mannersthatsell.com/articles/shakinghands.html*

Bullying: What to Think, Say, and Do (Chapter 7)

Gray, C. (2004). Gray's guide to bullying: The original series of articles parts I-III. Enclosed student workbook: How to respond to a bullying attempt: What to think, say, and do (1-8). Jenison Autism Journal, 16:1.

Moving To a New Community

All listed online resources retrieved on September 12, 2009.

City of Shelton, Connecticut. *www.cityofshelton.org/*

LaFayette Public School. *www.trulia.com/schools/CT-Shelton/Lafayette_Elementary_School/*

Rich and Ben's Hair Styling.
http://yellowpages.lycos.com/search?C=Barbers&L=Shelton%2C+Connecticut&diktfc=5D914DF65
29AF950D797FDEF3EF5F419B795CAEE7864

Beechwood Supermarket. *www.beechwoodmarket.com*

City of Garretson, South Dakota.
www.garretsonsd.com/index.php?option=com_content&view=article&id=42&Itemid=17

Garretson Elementary School. *http://garretson.k12.sd.us/*

Brandon Plaza Barbers.
http://yp.yahoo.com/yp/Garretson_SD/Personal_Care_Barbers/8109930.html

Garretson Food Center. *www.garretsonsd.com* .

Washing My Hands

Mayo Clinic. Hand washing: Do's and don'ts. Retrieved September 19, 2009 from *www.mayoclinic.com/health/hand-washing/HQ00407*

Why People Take Baths or Showers

All listed online resources retrieved on August 15, 2009. Radmore, C. The evolution of bathing and showers. *www.talewins.com/family/historyofshowers.htm* Wikipedia. Archimedes. *http://en.wikipedia.org/wiki/Archimedes*

It's My Teacher's Decision

Gray, C. (Author) & Shelley, M. (Director/Producer). (2006). It's the teacher's decision (motion picture). In Storymovies™: Social concepts and skills at school. United States: The Specialminds Foundation.

Talking to a Teacher with Respect

Gray, C. (Author) & Shelley, M. (Director/Producer). (2006). Talking to a teacher with respect. (motion picture). In Storymovies™: Social concepts and skills at school. United States: The Specialminds Foundation.

What Is Practice?

Gray, C. (Author) & Shelley, M. (Director/Producer). (2006). What is practice? (motion picture). In Storymovies™: Social concepts and skills at school. United States: The Specialminds Foundation.

Mistakes Happen on the Way to Learning.

Gray, C. (Author) & Shelley, M. (Director/Producer). (2006). Mistakes may happen on the way to learning (motion picture). In Storymovies™: Social concepts and skills at school. United States: The Specialminds Foundation.

Good Questions for a Small Group Project.

Gray, C. (Author) & Shelley, M. (Director/Producer). (2006). What is a good question? (motion picture). In Storymovies™: Social concepts and skills at school. United States: The Specialminds Foundation.

At the End of Each Day: A Little Bit Changed and Mostly the Same.

All listed online resources retrieved on October 1, 2009. Answers.com: WikiAnswers. How many babies are born each day in the world? *http://wiki.answers.com/Q/How_many_babies_are_born_every_day_in_the_world* Answerbag.com. How many commercial airline flights are there per day in the world? *www.answerbag.com/q_view/93860* Answerbag.com. How many earthquakes happen each day? *www.answerbag.com/q_view/93860*

References for The New Social Story™ Book Glossary

Agnes, M. (Ed.). (1999). Webster's new world children's dictionary (2nd Edition). Cleveland, Ohio: Wiley Publishing, Inc.

Agnes, M. (Ed) (2003). Webster's new world dictionary (4th Edition). New York, N.Y: Pocket Books, Simon & Schuster, Inc.

Delahunty, A. (2002). Barron's first thesaurus. Hauppauge, N.Y: Barron's Educational Series, Inc.

Houghton Mifflin Harcourt. (2007). The American heritage student dictionary. Boston, MA: Houghton Mifflin Harcourt Publishing Company.

Leany, C. (2008). Junior dictionary & thesaurus. New York, N.Y: Barnes & Noble.

Levey, J.S. (Ed.). (1990). Macmillan first dictionary. New York, N.Y: Simon & Schuster Books for Young Readers.

Levey, J.S. (Ed.). (2006). First dictionary. New York, N.Y: Scholastic.

Morris, C.G. (Ed) (2007). Macmillan fully illustrated dictionary for children. New York, N.Y: Simon & Schuster Books for Young Readers.

Scholastic, Inc. (2005). Scholastic pocket dictionary. U.S.A.: Scholastic, Inc.

Social Story™ Research and Related References

Agosta, E., Graetz, J. E., Mastropieri, M. A. & Scruggs, T. E. (2004). "Teacher-researcher partnerships to improve social behaviour though social stories." *Intervention in Schools and Clinic* 39 (5) 276 – 287.

Barry, L. M. & Burlew, S. B. (2004). "Using social stories to teach choice and play skills to children with autism." *Focus on Autism and Other Developmental Disabilities* 19 (1) 45-51.

Bledsoe, R., Smith, B. and Simpson, R. L. (2003). "Use of a social story intervention to improve mealtime skills of an adolescent with Asperger syndrome." *Autism* 7 (3) 289-295.

Brownell, M. (2002). "Musically adapted social stories to modify behaviors in students with autism: Four case studies." *Journal of Music Therapy* 39, 117-144.

Chalk M. (2003). Social stories for adults with autism and learning difficulties. *Good Autism Practice* 4(2), pp. 3-7.

Committee on Educational Interventions for Children with Autism. (2001). "Family roles." In C. Lord & J.P. McGee (Eds.), *Educating children with autism*. Washington, DC: National Academies Press.

Del Valle, P. R., McEachern, A. G. & Chambers, H. D. (2001). "Using social stories with autistic children." *Journal of Poetry Therapy* 14 (4) 187-197.

Erangey, K. (2001). "Using social stories as a parent of a child with an ASD." *Good Autism Practice* 2 (1) 309-323.

Gastgeb, H.Z., Strauss, M.S., & Minshew, N.J. (2006). "Do individuals with autism process categories differently? The effect of typicality and development." *Child Development* 77, 1717–1729.

Gray, C. (1998). "The advanced social story workbook." *The Morning News* 10(2), 1–21.

Gray, C. (2004). "Social stories 10.0: The new defining criteria and guidelines." *Jenison Autism Journal* 15, 2–21.

Gray, C.A. & Garand, J.D. (1993). "Social stories: Improving responses of students with autism with accurate social information." *Focus on Autistic Behavior* 8, 1–10.

Gray, C. (1998a). "Social stories and comic strip conversations with students with Asperger syndrome and high functioning autism." In: E. Schopler, G. Mesibov & L. Kunce (Eds.). *Asperger syndrome or high functioning autism?* (pp. 167-198). New York: Plenum Press.

Hagiwara, T., & Myles, B. S. (1999). "A multimedia social story intervention: Teaching skills to children with autism." *Focus on Autism and Other Developmental Disabilities* 14, 82-95.

Howley, M. (2001). "An investigation into the impact of social stories on the behaviour and social understanding of four pupils with autistic spectrum disorder." In R. Rose and Grosvenor (Eds) (2001). *Doing research in special education*. London: David Fulton.

Howley, M.,& Arnold,E. (2005). *Revealing the hidden social code*. London: Jessica Kingsley.

Ivey, M.L., Heflin, L.J., & Alberto, P. (2004). "The use of social stories to promote independent behaviors in novel events for children with PDD-NOS (autism spectrum disorder)." *Focus on Autism and Other Developmental Disabilities* 19, 164–176.

Jones, D., Swift, D., & Johnson, M. (1988). "Nondeliberate memory for a novel event among preschoolers." *Developmental Psychology* 24, 641-645.

Klinger, L.G., & Dawson, G. (2001). "Prototype formation in autism." *Development and Psychology* 13, 111–124.

Kluth, P., & Schwarz, P. (2008). *Just give him the whale! 20 ways to use fascinations, areas of expertise, and strengths to support students with autism*. Baltimore: Paul H. Brookes Publishing Co.

Kuoch, H., & Mirenda, P. (2003). "Social story interventions for young children with autism spectrum disorders." *Focus on Autism and Other Developmental Disorders* 18, 219–227.

Kuttler, S., Myles, B. S., & Carlson, J. K. (1998). "The use of social stories to reduce precursors to tantrum behaviour in a student with autism." *Focus on Autism and Other Developmental Disabilities* 12, 176-182.

Lorimer, P. A., Simpson, R., Myles, B. S. & Ganz, J. (2002). "The use of social stories as a preventative behavioral intervention in a home setting with a child with autism." *Journal of Positive Behavioral Interventions* 4 (1) 53-60.

Miller, D. (2002). *Reading with meaning: Teaching comprehension in the primary grades.* Portland, ME: Stenhouse Publishers.

Moffat, E. (2001). "Writing social stories to improve students' social understanding." *Good Autism Practice* 2 (1) 12-16.

Norris, C., & Dattilo, J. (1999). "Evaluating the effects of social story intervention on a young girl with autism." *Focus on Autism and Other Developmental Disabilities* 14, 180-186.

Rowe, C. (1999). "Do social stories benefit children with autism in mainstream primary school?" *British Journal of Special Education* 26 (1), 12-14.

Rust, J., & Smith, A. (2006). "How should the effectiveness of social stories to modify the behavior of children on the autism spectrum be tested? Lessons from the literature." *Autism: The International Journal of Research and Practice* 10, 125–138.

Sansosti, F.J., Powell-Smith, K.A., & Kincaid, D. (2004). "A research synthesis of social story interventions for children with autism spectrum disorders." *Focus on Autism and Other Developmental Disabilities* 19(4), 194–204.

Scattone, D., Wilczynski, S., Edwards, R. & Rabian, B. (2002). "Decreasing disruptive behaviors of children with autism using social stories." *Journal of Autism and Developmental Disorders* 32 (6) 535-543.

Smith, C. (2001a). "Using social stories to enhance behaviour in children with autistic spectrum difficulties." *Educational Psychology in Practice* 17, (4) 337-345.

Smith, C. (2001b). "Using social stories with children with autistic spectrum disorders: An evaluation." *Good Autism Practice* 2 (1) 16-25.

Swaggart, B. L., Gagnon, E., Bock, S.J., Earles, T.L., Quinn, C., Myles, B. S., & Simpson, R. L. (1995). "Using social stories to teach social and behavioural skills to children with autism." *Focus on Autistic Behaviour* 10, 1-16.

Wright, L.A. (2007). *Utilizing social stories to reduce problem behavior and increase pro-social behavior in young children with autism*. Unpublished doctoral dissertation, University of Missouri, Columbia.

Index

A

Absence from school, 170
Accuracy, xxx, xxxi, xlvii, xlviii, xlix, lv–lvi, 127
Activities, 13, 14, 15, 39, 68–69, 136, 138, 140, 149, 159, 237, 241
Adam, xxxi–xxxii
Adults, 4, 7, 16, 18, 25, 26, 29, 34, 36, 68, 75, 76, 84, 85, 99, 100, 106, 112, 113, 115, 116, 119, 126, 127, 128, 129, 132–146, 185, 193, 195, 201, 208, 211, 217, 221, 225, 230, 231, 239, 240, 242
Affirmation, xxxv, lxxi
Affirmative sentences, lviii–lix, lxii
Aidan, 182
Aiden, 91
Air, 11
Airplanes, 209, 211, 212, 213, 216, 218, 219, 220, 220f, 228
Airport officers, 212, 212f, 213, 213f, 215, 215f
Airports, 212, 213, 214, 215, 216, 219f, 220
Airport security, 215
Alarms, 156, 200
"Almost always," 145, 220
Alphabetization, 235
Alternative vocabulary, xlix
"Always," 5, 11, 23, 62, 200, 221, 229, 244
Ambulances, 196, 196f
Analogies, xlviii
Anchors, 226–227
Andrea, 171

Angel, 179
Angela, xxxvi, 67, 77, 78
Anger, 43, 62, 99, 100, 183, 189
Animals, 16, 16f, 17, 17f, 18, 18f
Anniversaries, 4
Antoine, 141
Anxiety, 37, 43f, 44, 62, 225
Apples, 97
Appointments, 13, 14, 15
Archimedes, 152
Art, 174, 175
ASD, xxv, xxvi, xxvii, xxxiii–xxxiv, xlvii, xlviii
Asia, 179
Asking questions, 76, 94, 95, 102, 188, 194–195
Assignments, 90, 170, 177, 188
Assumptions, xxxiv
Audience
    ability of, xli–xlii, xliii
    age of, xli–xlii, xlvii
    comfort of, xlix, lxx, 37, 38–39, 40
    correction of, xlvii–xlviii, lix, lxix
    definition of, xix, xxvi
    emotional reactions in, xlix
    frustration in, xxxiv, xliii, 75, 99, 183
    insulting, xlii, xlvii
    interest of, xxxii, xliii, lxv–lxvi
    learning profile of, xliii
    responses, xxxi, xliii, 74, 76, 79, 85–86, 90, 91, 106, 107, 108–109, 112–130
    sequencing difficulty of, xl
Audience-coaching sentences, lvii
Aunt Jeannie, 3, 3f
Aunt Rhonda, 68, 69

Aunt Rose, 68
Austin, 155
Author
    challenges of, lii
    definition of, xxvi
    interaction with Team, xxxiv, lxviii–lxix
    mistakes of, xxxii
    primary concern of, xxxi
    writing strategy for, liv
Autism spectrum disorder, xxv, xxvi, xxvii, xxxiii–xxxiv, xlvii, xlviii
Autumn, 207
Awkwardness, 73, 86

B

Babies, 135, 137, 159, 211, 228
"Babyish" language, xlii, xlvii
Babysitters, 159, 160, 160f
Bad feelings. See Discomfort
Baggage, 213, 214, 215, 216
Bags, 92, 215
Balloons, 67f
Barber shops, 149
Barbie doll, 78
Baseball, 11, 107
Basketball, 107, 107f
Bathing, xxxi, 45, 135, 152, 153, 157
Bathrooms, 153, 154, 155, 155f, 210, 217
Beaches, liii, 207f
Bed, 11, 12, 13, 135
Bedrooms, 4
Bee stings, 37, 43, 44
Beginning of a story, 192

Context, xxxi, lv–lvi
Contractors, 150
Contracts, 84
Control of a Social Story by the
    Audience, lviii
Conversation. *See* Talking
Cooking, 221
Cooperation, xxxi–xxxii, 94, 99,
    100, 140, 158, 184, 185, 212,
    214, 237–238
Co-pilots, 210
Copyright, xix
Correcting mistakes, 188
Crackers, 97
Crayons, 48*f*
Crew, 210, 210*f*, 211, 212, 220
Criteria of a Social Story, xxvi,
    xxx–lxxi
        criterion 1: goal, xxx–xxxii
        criterion 2: discovery,
            xxxiii–xxxviii
        criterion 3: parts, xxxix–xl
        criterion 4: format, xli–xlv
        criterion 5: voice and
            vocabulary, xlvi–li
        criterion 6: "wh" questions,
            lii–liv
        criterion 7: sentence types,
            lv–lxi
        criterion 8: formula for
            sentence use, lxii–lxiv
        criterion 9: personalization,
            lxv–lxvii
        criterion 10: editing and
            implementation, lxviii–lxxi
Crowded places, 43, 101, 101*f*,
    162, 165, 165*f*
Crying, 45, 46

D

Dads, 29, 36, 36*f*, 41, 52*f*, 70, 87*f*,
    88, 89, 95, 96, 97, 99, 100*f*, 101,
102, 116*f*, 135, 137, 141,
    143–144, 149, 150, 154, 155,
    156, 157, 158*f*, 159, 160, 162,
    163, 164, 170, 209, 214, 217,
    218, 223, 224, 225
Danger, 95, 112, 196, 221, 223
Darla, 195
Day, 228
Daylight, 11, 207
Days, 229
Daytime, 12, 207
Decisions, 133, 136, 137, 139, 141,
    142, 143, 145, 163, 165, 172,
    174, 179, 180, 193, 218, 242
Delays, 205, 219, 220
Dentists, 150, 170
Descriptive sentences, lv–lvi, lxii
Desserts, 68
Detail, xliii
Diapers, 135
Dice, 106*f*
Dictionaries, 235
Dinosaurs, 77, 150
Directions, 176, 180, 211, 217
Dirt, 46, 152
Disappointment, 77–78, 77*f*, 79,
    141, 185, 188, 220
Discomfort, 43, 43*f*, 44, 45, 62, 73,
    88, 113, 144, 152, 153, 183, 200,
    216, 225
Diseases, 37, 43, 44, 170, 170*f*,
    196, 231
Disrespect, 100, 158, 184
Doctors, 36*f*, 170, 197
Dogs, 34, 68
Doorknobs, 151
Doors, 48, 51, 62, 64, 93, 93*f*, 101,
    153, 175
Drawing, 40, 51, 53, 55, 57, 59, 61,
    121, 231
Dressing, 157
Drills, 175, 197, 198, 199, 200, 201
Driving, 134
Drying, 151

E

Earliness, 205
Earth, 11, 203*f*, 229, 229*f*
Earthquakes, 11, 228
Eating, 38, 43, 68, 69*f*, 75, 96*f*,
    132, 135, 157, 160, 163–164,
    163*f*, 221
Edison, Thomas, 24
Editing and implementation,
    lxviii–lxxi
Eggs, 16, 16*f*, 17, 17*f*, 18, 18*f*
Elaine, 3
Electricity, 24
Electronic games, 49, 55
Elephants, 160
Elijah, 177
Ellen, 134
Emergencies, 196, 197, 198
Emily, 155
Emma, 150
Emotional safety, xxxii, xlvii–xlviii,
    79, 98, 100
End of a story, 192
England, 84
Escalators, 161–162, 162*f*
Evacuation, 222, 223, 223*f*,
    224, 225
Evaporation, 11
Evening news, 169, 226–227, 226*f*
Excitement, 76
"Excuse me," 101, 239
Expectations, xxxi, 11, 13–14, 15,
    24, 77, 85, 169, 172, 188, 196,
    198, 227, 235, 238, 240, 243
Experience, xix, xx, xxix, xxxii,
    xxxiv, xxxv, xxxvi, xl, xlvii, xlviii,
    xlix, lx, lxi, lxv, 6, 23, 133, 191,
    205, 238, 240, 241

F

Facts, 120, 127
Fairness, 89, 96, 97, 155
Fall, 207
Family, 3f, 36f, 46, 68–69, 97, 98, 100f, 116f, 132f, 135f, 148, 150, 158, 163, 170, 214, 223, 224, 225, 225f
Fathers, 29, 36, 36f, 41, 52f, 70, 87f, 88, 89, 95, 96, 97, 99, 100f, 101, 102, 116f, 135, 137, 141, 143–144, 149, 150, 154, 155, 156, 157, 158f, 159, 160, 162, 163, 164, 170, 209, 214, 217, 218, 223, 224, 225
Fear, 37, 43, 88, 108, 113
Feelings, 33–64, 73, 75, 88, 99, 132
Fill-in-the-blank, lix, lxix
Finishing work, 193
Fire alarms, 200, 200f
Fire departments, 221
Fire drills, 175, 198, 199, 200
Firefighters, 197, 221–222, 221f, 224
Fires, 196, 198, 199, 200, 221–222, 221f, 223, 224, 243
First-person voice, xxviii, xlvii
Flames, 196, 198, 199, 200, 221–222, 221f, 223, 224, 243
Flat tires, 14, 243
Fletcher, 150
Flight attendants, 210, 210f, 211, 217
Flowers, 141
Flu, 43
Flying, 209, 210, 211, 217, 217f, 218, 218f, 219, 228
Following directions, 176, 180, 211, 213, 214, 217, 218, 223, 224, 225, 240
Food, 38, 43, 68, 69f, 75, 96f, 132, 135, 157, 160, 163–164, 163f, 221

Food court, 163–164, 163f
Fort Able, xix, 48–49, 50, 50f, 51–64, 243
Frequency, 235, 244
 "almost always," 145, 220
 "always," 5, 11, 23, 62, 200, 221, 229, 244
 "frequently," 235, 244
 "many times," 62, 76, 90, 91, 107, 113, 177, 186, 216, 222, 244
 "most of the time," 42, 77, 94, 110, 134, 173, 175, 177, 180, 193, 201, 244
 "never," 68, 93, 145, 149, 196, 223, 227, 244
 "no," 135, 141, 142, 145, 179
 "now and then," 78, 79, 89, 216, 242, 244
 "once in a while," 23, 77, 83, 85, 86, 94, 95, 101, 110, 137, 142, 162, 180, 196, 215, 235, 238, 244
 "sometimes," 17, 23, 34, 35, 37, 39, 41, 43, 44, 45, 46, 47, 62, 63, 68, 69, 71, 72, 73, 74, 75, 76, 77, 83, 84, 87, 88, 89, 90, 91, 92, 95, 96, 97, 99, 100, 102, 103, 104, 105, 106, 107, 108, 110, 112, 117, 119, 126, 128, 132, 133, 134, 136, 137, 139, 140, 141, 143, 145, 146, 151, 152, 156, 157, 158, 159, 162, 165, 169, 171, 173, 174, 176, 178, 179, 180, 183, 184, 186, 188, 189, 190, 193, 195, 196, 205, 207, 208, 211, 214, 216, 219, 220, 221, 223, 224, 225, 241, 242, 244
 "usually," 29, 71, 75, 99, 169, 172, 179, 199, 223, 225, 226, 227, 241, 242, 244

"Frequently," 235, 244
Friendliness, 83, 84, 88, 90, 91, 101, 109, 112, 212, 237, 243
Friends, 31f, 41f, 46, 52f, 70, 88, 88f, 96f, 108, 152, 163f
Friendship and people skills, 83–110
Frogs, 17, 17f, 242f
Frustration, xxxiv, xliii, 75, 99, 183, 188, 189, 216, 220, 238
Furniture, 148

G

Games, 49, 55, 67, 75, 106, 106f, 107, 108, 110, 110f
Garbage, 102, 139
Geography, 187
Germs, 151, 152
Getting bigger, 4, 19, 19f, 34, 34f, 35, 35f, 83, 89, 95, 132, 228, 242
Gifts, 65f, 68–69, 70, 70f, 71, 72f, 73f, 74f, 75f, 76f, 77f, 238, 240f
Gifts and celebrations, 67–79
Girls, 115
Glossary, 235–236
Go, 63, 64
Goal of Social Story, xxx–xxxii
Going down a slide, 1f, 6, 6f
Good feelings. See Comfort
Gossip, 113
Grandma and Grandpa Schuldt, 4, 4f
Grandma Hill, 68, 69
Grandpa Hill, 68
Grandparents, 4, 4f, 68, 69, 78, 81f, 92f, 102, 135f, 136, 211, 239
Graphics
 avoiding use of, xx
 copyrighted, xix
 use of custom, xix–xx
Graphs, xliii
Gratitude, 73

R

S

The New Social Story™ Book, 10th Anniversary Edition
© by Carol Gray, Future Horizons, Inc.

180, 180*f*, 186*f*, 188, 189*f*, 190, 193, 199, 238*f*
Substitute teachers, 171, 172
Summer, 207
Sun, 11, 207, 229
Surprises, 12, 240
    bad, 14, 15, 77, 196, 227, 243
    good, 13, 15, 72, 75, 77, 240
Surveys, 25–26, 27
Swimming, xxxi
Sydney, 91
Synonyms, 141, 143–144

T

Tables, 163, 164
Tadpoles, 17, 17*f*
Taking turns, 89, 97, 132, 180, 213
Talking, 40, 75, 83, 89, 98, 99, 100, 101, 112, 113, 122–123, 124, 177, 181, 182, 183, 185, 189, 237, 238
Tastes, 37
Teachers, xxiii*f*, 6, 25–26, 29, 36*f*, 58, 89, 90, 98, 98*f*, 99, 99*f*, 116*f*, 133*f*, 137, 137*f*, 169, 170, 171, 172, 173, 174–175, 176, 176*f*, 177–178, 179, 179*f*, 180, 180*f*, 181, 181*f*, 182, 183, 183*f*, 184, 184*f*, 186, 186*f*, 189, 189*f*, 194*f*, 196, 199, 238*f*
Teaching, 230
Team, xxvii, lvii, lxviii–lxix, 36, 49, 60, 60*f*, 61, 63, 99, 112, 116, 116*f*, 117, 126–130
Team-coaching sentences, lvii
Team sports, 107
Teenagers, 137
Telephones, 69
Television channels, 227
Television programming, 226
Televisions, 208, 228
Telling stories, 6

Temperature, 153
Temptation, 113
Thanks, 73, 74, 79, 90, 91, 182
"That is okay," 23, 29, 76, 95, 110, 128, 134, 159, 166, 170, 171, 173, 187, 193, 196, 216, 219, 242
Theatres, 101
Theories, 240
    about change, 13, 15, 227, 229, 243
    about sharing, 207–208, 240
Things, 4, 7, 14, 15, 23, 24, 25, 27, 33, 37, 39, 40, 42, 43, 44, 45, 49, 57, 63, 68, 70, 71, 76, 77, 78, 83, 89, 90, 91, 92, 93, 94, 95, 96, 97, 105, 106, 108, 109, 110, 112, 113, 115, 116, 134, 140, 141, 142, 143, 145, 146, 148, 151, 157, 158, 159, 160, 164, 172, 174, 184, 185, 189, 191, 192, 193, 195, 197, 198, 199, 201, 205, 206, 207, 208, 213, 214, 215, 219, 220, 225, 228, 229, 235, 238, 239, 240, 241, 242, 243, 244
Think, 63, 64
Thinking, 40, 63, 79, 89, 100, 108, 120, 137, 140, 146, 184, 188, 216, 225
Third-person voice, xxviii, xlvii
"This is okay," 23, 29, 76, 95, 110, 128, 134, 159, 166, 170, 171, 173, 187, 193, 196, 216, 219, 242
Thomas the Tank Engine, 160
Thoughts, 49, 59
Threats, 113
Thunderstorms, 11
Tickets, 101, 211, 230
Tight places, 43
Time, 29, 74, 174*f*, 227
    required to read a Social Story, xli
    saving, xxxiv, 155, 156, 195

Timeliness, 205, 206, 218
Toddlers, 137, 211
Toilets, xliii, 135, 155, 155*f*
Tomorrow, 145, 169, 170, 173, 228, 229
Tone of a Social Story, xxxii, xlvii–xlviii, xlix
Topic of a Social Story, xxxiv, xxxv
Topics, 40, 190
Tornado drills, 198, 201
Tornadoes, 196, 198, 201, 243
Towels, 154
Toys, 33, 40, 91, 140, 141, 148, 190, 241
Trains, 228
Transformation, 16, 17, 18, 19, 242, 243
Trash, 102, 139
Travel, 170, 205, 219, 228
Trees, 11*f*
Trevor, 36
Trust, xxxiii
Truth, 30, 99, 113, 120, 122, 127, 134, 157, 174, 175, 191, 192, 207, 238, 239, 240, 242
Tub. *See* Bathing
Turtles, 157
Tutorials for writing Social Stories, xxi, xxv–lxxi
Tying shoes, 6, 94, 94*f*

U

Uncle Jess, 68
Understanding, xxx, xxxi
Unexpectedness, 243.
    See also Expectations
Uniforms, 210
Unpacking, 148
Unsafeness, 43, 44, 45, 95, 112, 145, 169, 196, 221, 223
Unwelcomeness, 13, 14, 15, 227, 243

Here are some other helpful resources by Carol Gray!

This DVD and accompanying workbook provide step-by-step training for writing effective Social Stories™.

ISBN 9781932565607 $99.95

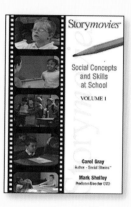

A Storymovie™ is a Social Story™ illustrated with a short movie. (Stories in this book that have corresponding Storymovies™ available have a "scene slate" icon near the Story number.)

Standard Edition: $89.95

Use simple drawings to illustrate interactions and explore social events, concepts, and skills with students.

ISBN 9781885477224 $9.95

Through the use of the Teacher Manual, Student Workbook, and an instructional DVD for teachers, this peer violence prevention program addresses bullying behaviors.

ISBN 9781932565447 $79.95

Extend teaching and learning with these great resources!

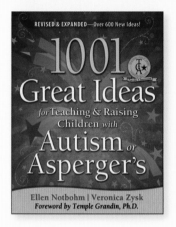

Winner of Learning Magazine's Teachers' Choice Award, this book presents parents and educators with try-it-now tips, eye-opening advice, and grassroots strategies.

ISBN 9781935274063 $24.95

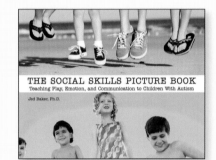

Winner of an iParenting Media Award, this book shows photos of students in real-life social situations, along with guidance on the right and wrong ways to react.

ISBN 9781885477910 $39.95

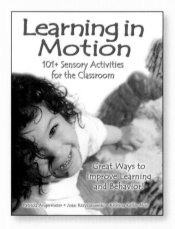

Ideal for preschool, kindergarten, and primary classes, each activity has been developed to attract and keep children's interest by using a multi-sensory approach.

ISBN 9781932565904 $39.95

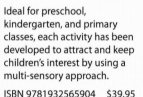

This picture book picks up where the first book left off, with social situations that teens and tweens will relate to. Winner of an iParenting Media Award!

ISBN 9781932565355 $39.95

Available at fine retailers everywhere!

These highly acclaimed books are great for parents!

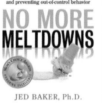
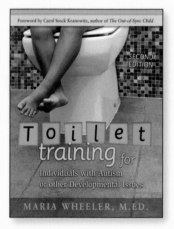
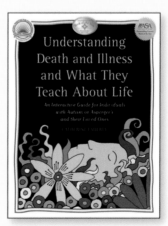